Personalising Learning in Open-Plan Schools

Personalising Learning in Open-Plan Schools

Edited by

Vaughan Prain, Peter Cox, Craig Deed, Debra Edwards, Cathleen Farrelly, Mary Keeffe, Valerie Lovejoy, Lucy Mow
La Trobe University, Australia

Peter Sellings
Federation University, Australia

and

Bruce Waldrip
University of Tasmania, Australia

SENSE PUBLISHERS
ROTTERDAM/BOSTON/TAIPEI

A C.I.P. record for this book is available from the Library of Congress.

ISBN: 978-94-6300-191-5 (paperback)
ISBN: 978-94-6300-192-2 (hardback)
ISBN: 978-94-6300-193-9 (e-book)

Published by: Sense Publishers,
P.O. Box 21858,
3001 AW Rotterdam,
The Netherlands
https://www.sensepublishers.com/

All chapters in this book have undergone peer review.

Printed on acid-free paper

All Rights Reserved © 2015 Sense Publishers

No part of this work may be reproduced, stored in a retrieval system, or transmitted in any form or by any means, electronic, mechanical, photocopying, microfilming, recording or otherwise, without written permission from the Publisher, with the exception of any material supplied specifically for the purpose of being entered and executed on a computer system, for exclusive use by the purchaser of the work.

TABLE OF CONTENTS

Acknowledgments		vii
Acronyms		ix

Section 1: Key Orientations

1. Characterising Personalising Learning   3
   Vaughan Prain, Peter Cox, Craig Deed, Debra Edwards, Cathleen Farrelly, Mary Keeffe, Valerie Lovejoy, Lucy Mow, Peter Sellings and Bruce Waldrip

2. A Model of Teacher Adaptation to Open-Plan Settings   27
   Craig Deed

3. Using a Game-Design Project to Afford Teacher and Student Agency   43
   Craig Deed

4. A Whole-School Approach to Adolescent Wellbeing in Open-Plan Schools   57
   Cathleen Farrelly and Valerie Lovejoy

5. "It's Not a Plug-In Product": Making Digital Technologies Serve Learning in a School with an Open-Plan Setting   77
   Vaughan Prain, Valerie Lovejoy and Debra Edwards

Section 2: Curriculum Case Studies

6. Creating and Analysing Multi-Modal Texts in English Classes in Open-Plan Settings   97
   Valerie Lovejoy, Lucy Mow, Stephanie Di Palma, Vaughan Prain and Debra Edwards

7. Personalising Mathematics for Low SES Students in Schools with Open-Plan Settings   121
   Peter Cox, Bruce Waldrip and Vaughan Prain

8. "They Can't Just Google the Correct Answer": Personalising Science Learning in an Open-Plan Secondary School   143
   Vaughan Prain, Bruce Waldrip and Valerie Lovejoy

TABLE OF CONTENTS

9.	Personalised Learning and Differentiation in Studio Arts: Juggling Prescriptive Curriculum and Artistic Nurture *Mary Keeffe and Valerie Lovejoy*	163
10.	Using Student Voice in Social Studies/Humanities to Personalise Learning *Peter Sellings, Bruce Waldrip, Vaughan Prain and Valerie Lovejoy*	181
11.	Developing Student Agency in a Teacher Advisor Program *Mary Keeffe*	205
12.	Remaking Schooling through Open-Plan Settings: Some Conclusions and the Future *Vaughan Prain, Peter Cox, Craig Deed, Debra Edwards, Cathleen Farrelly, Mary Keeffe, Valerie Lovejoy, Lucy Mow, Peter Sellings and Bruce Waldrip*	221
13.	Some Reflections *Anthony Edwards*	231
Index		237

ACKNOWLEDGMENTS

This research was supported under the Australian Research Council's Linkage Projects funding scheme (Grant LP100200179). We would also like to thank participant schools, staff and students.

ACRONYMS

ACARA	Australian Curriculum Assessment and Reporting Authority
AusVELS	Australian Curriculum/Victorian Essential Learning Standards
BEP	Bendigo Education Plan
BLPCP	Bendigo Loddon Primary Care Partnership
DEECD	Department of Education and Early Childhood Development (Victoria)
ICSEA	Index of Community Socio-Educational Advantage
NAPLAN	National Assessment Program-Literacy and Numeracy
PLEQ	Personalised Learning Experience Questionnaire
SAR	Students as Researchers
SES	Socio-economic Status
SRC	Students' Representative Council
SSC	Student Support Centre
TA	Teacher Advisor

SECTION 1
KEY ORIENTATIONS

VAUGHAN PRAIN, PETER COX, CRAIG DEED, DEBRA EDWARDS, CATHLEEN FARRELLY, MARY KEEFFE, VALERIE LOVEJOY, LUCY MOW, PETER SELLINGS AND BRUCE WALDRIP

1. CHARACTERISING PERSONALISING LEARNING

PERSONALISING LEARNING

Can removing classroom walls enable more personalised learning and enhance student wellbeing? In this book we claim these outcomes are possible in an open-plan school for low SES students, if appropriate conditions are met. A major condition is the development of these spaces as supportive communities where teams of teachers address learners' individual and collective needs. In making this case, we draw on a three-year Australian Research Council study (Improving Secondary Students' Learning and Wellbeing, 2011–2013) where we analysed an attempt to improve educational and wellbeing outcomes for 4000 Years 7–10 predominantly low SES secondary students in regional Australia. This approach, the Bendigo Education Plan (BEP, 2005), entailed three major strategies. These were: (1) rebuilding four schools to include open-plan layouts, (2) developing teachers' professional knowledge to enable effective teaching, learning, and student wellbeing in the new settings, and (3) curricular reform leading to a more explicit, differentiated curriculum, replacing a traditional age-based curriculum with a stage-based one. We argue that these three strategies in combination were crucial to positive outcomes for the BEP (see Prain, et al., 2014). We also report on attempts to personalise learning in two other regional schools with similar SES profiles.

The BEP strategies operated partly as intended by the designers, but also in unexpected ways, and provide insights into effective curricula for like-student cohorts. In researching challenges and gains we have developed new understandings of influences on students' engagement with schooling, and how personalising learning, student wellbeing, and a quality curriculum interact. In arguing that quality learning and wellbeing require personalised learning experiences, our book deals with larger questions of effective schooling for low SES students and curricular renewal in general.

In developing our case, we focus on both generic conditions to promote academic success and wellbeing for low SES students in open-plan settings, and conditions that personalise subject-area learning across four years of secondary schooling (Years 7–10). By generic conditions, we refer to influences such as broad teacher professional learning and adaptation to the possibilities of these new settings, whole-school approaches to curricula and student wellbeing, and effective, coherent use of virtual technologies (ICTs). The first section of our book outlines these generic conditions, while in the second section we report on case studies of quality learning in English, mathematics, science, art, social studies/humanities, and a teacher advisor program. We recognise that differentiation poses distinctive challenges in different subjects, and makes increased demands on teacher professional expertise. Our book concludes with a summary of findings and an invited response from an independent expert, Anthony Edwards.

In this chapter, we (1) provide an overview of the context of our study including the open-plan design of the schools, and a brief vignette of the four participant BEP schools; (2) outline our multi-theoretical perspective for the study, including our research aims and methods; (3) present our account of quality learning as personalised in these settings; (4) provide a snapshot of student learning gains (2008–2014); and (5) identify key generic principles we consider enabled success in addressing BEP goals.

Changing Education in Bendigo

The BEP (2005) was devised to address concerns about the quality of education and wellbeing in this predominantly low SES student cohort. These concerns included low rates of student school attendance, modest student academic performance when compared with metropolitan counterparts, and persistent signs of poor student wellbeing, evident in high rates of teenage pregnancy, bullying, high levels of psychological distress, and disengagement (Prain et al., 2014). The Plan also entailed the demolition of five Years 7–10 schools, and rebuilding four schools, with each school structured into four open-plan communities. The four Years 7–10 schools have a significant number of students in the lowest socio-economic status group, as judged by Youth Allowance payments (ranging from 32 to 52% per school) (Bendigo Loddon Primary Care Partnership, 2012).

Aims and Strategies of the BEP

The BEP aimed to improve student educational outcomes by ensuring:

- Substantial improvement in student attendance in Years 7–10 and retention from Years 7–12;
- Significant increase in the range of subjects available to students in Years 9–10;
- All students, particularly high-achieving students were extended in their studies;
- Improved student engagement and interest in subjects, particularly for average and low-achieving students, and those from lower socio-economic backgrounds;
- Improved teaching methods, classroom management, discipline and wellbeing of students.

Three main strategies were enacted to achieve these aims: redesigning school settings, developing teachers' professional learning, and personalising learning through a differentiated, stage-based curriculum. These strategies are consistent with extensive research on improving schools with high concentrations of low SES students through focusing on student learning, high expectations of students, and instructional leadership (Muijs, Harris, Chapman, Stoll, & Russ, 2004).

Strategy One: Redesigning School Settings

Drawing on Nair (2005), the new schools included large flexible spaces to allow teams of teachers to work with up to 125 students at a time, where each school consisted of four self-contained learning communities, each with two learning neighbourhoods. This up-scaling of the traditional classroom community of 30 students to groups of 150–250 was based on a belief that a radical change was needed to improve students' experience of schooling. The BEP designers drew on Dunbar's (1993) anthropological claim that an optimal community size of 250 people could build meaningful personal relationships. Therefore the proposed design of learning communities aimed to maximise student access to a supportive learning context where students established meaningful relationships with other community members. Every student was expected to learn how to be an active, integrated member of that community. Students would be free to interact with a larger group of teachers and students than in traditional classrooms, facilitating more informal learning. Spaces were designed to accommodate multiple users and multiple purposes concurrently and consecutively, with use of formal and informal furniture pointing to possible varied usage. In the smaller learning neighbourhoods, ICT access was intended to be ubiquitous, movable furniture would further enhance usage and support flexibility. The buildings were also designed to integrate previously discrete functions, so that eating areas and formal/informal areas supported sharing/learning throughout the school day. Design features and functions aimed to optimise staff/student relationships, with open staff rooms, visual links between all areas, and minimal exclusion zones. These changes were intended to personalise student learning and wellbeing because of increased informality in staff/student interactions, and increased scope for teams of teachers to identify and address diverse student needs and capabilities.

In 2013 the four schools varied in size from 500 to 1200 students, and in design details of their four communities (Prain et al., 2014). The following diagram (Figure 1.1) represents an initial blueprint of how these principles were translated into one learning community's design in a school with a total student population of 600. The design aimed to accommodate 150 students and seven community-based teachers as well as visiting teachers for specialist subjects, such as language learning. The design included a welcoming open foyer area (the Einstein area), and the total space of the community was expected to provide flexible settings and opportunities for formal and informal learning. These included not only the large open-space areas for learning neighbourhoods, but also smaller spaces, such as a Socratic studio with its traditional closed classroom space, the Da Vinci science/art studio for specific subject studies, and smaller interview rooms for groupwork and meetings. Staffrooms are open areas attached to Learning Neighbourhoods. Each school site also had new technology and performing arts buildings as separate complementary learning areas, but we focus in this book on student learning in the learning communities.

The listed activities in the open areas point to vague, aspirational design aspects, and do not specify precisely the relationship between the types of seating layout and intended activities. The regimentation of seating layout in some areas points to traditional models of the classroom as a mini-auditorium where learning is focused through a teacher using a whiteboard, while other areas are presented as informal learning opportunities. The conceptual or practical justification for this division of space usage, and transitions between kinds of usage, were left tacit, or for teacher experimentation. The prescription that art and science classes share the same space represented a significant break with traditional practices, and implied capacity for professional collaboration and learning by teachers in each subject. Communities were also designed to promote potential sharing of facilities with local communities and to create environments that prompted more learner freedom and creativity. However, these early templates assumed that questions of syllabus structure, student transitions between activities, protocols for student behaviour, and expectations of student roles could be easily established through a combination of 'open' and 'closed' spaces, and shared perspectives by all participants.

Our research (Prain et al., 2014) indicated that these new up-scaled learning communities posed many challenges for teachers and students. Principals and teachers experimented with various options around organising time and space. Some

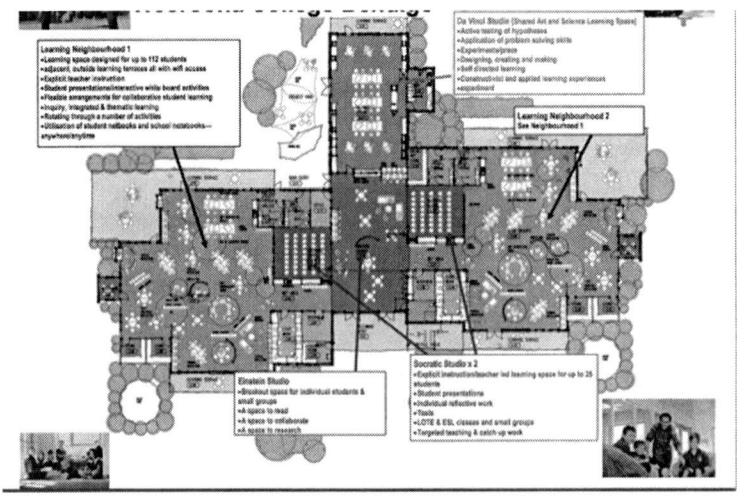

Figure 1.1. Proposed design of a learning community

communities were structured into multi-age groupings of Years 7 to 10 students where teachers and students belong to the community over four years, while others were structured into year-level communities. Lesson lengths in communities were a focus of experimentation, with lessons lasting from 35 to 120 minutes. Most schools decided eventually that 70-minute lessons were the most practicable in terms of lesson goals and effective transitions between lessons. Initial challenges included: addressing raised noise levels and student distraction; time-wasting during lesson transitions and changes to seating arrangements; developing effective community and distributed leadership; developing teacher teamwork; productive synchronised decision-making about space use; establishing student behaviour protocols; and actual and desirable teacher and student spheres of influence (Prain et al., 2014).

Strategy Two: Developing Teachers' Professional Learning

In addressing improved teacher effectiveness, the BEP designers drew on a range of prescriptions including those by Bransford et al. (2000), Elmore (1996), Brandt (1998), Danielson (1996), Schlechty (1997), and Wiggins and McTighe (1998). For Bransford et al. (2000), teachers needed to draw out and work with students' prior and current understandings, teach some subject matter in depth, using many examples to show multiple applications of the same concept, and integrate the teaching of metacognitive skills into the curriculum. Following Elmore (1996), teachers needed to work in teams where they observed, discussed and provided feedback on their own practices to lead to peer-coaching and problem-solving. Drawing on Brandt (1998), Danielson (1996), Schlechty (1997), and Wiggins and McTighe (1998), the BEP designers claimed expert teaching focused on disciplinary understanding, where students wrestle with profound ideas, use what they learn in meaningful ways, and where teachers guide students to organise and make sense of what they are learning and its connection to the wider world. Following Harpaz (2005), the BEP proposed that effective teaching and learning is characterised by fertile questions, intrinsic motivation, an environment that promotes active dialogue and communication, authentic problem-solving, informed feedback to teachers and learners, and rich, positive unconditional relationships.

Many strategies to support teacher growth in expertise were implemented during the three years of the study, including regular monthly professional support for teachers from consultants on curriculum design, effective pedagogy, and informed review of teaching processes. Subject teachers across schools worked to devise a shared curriculum in literacy and mathematics (Prain et al., 2014). Many teachers reported high levels of informal and incidental learning from working together with colleagues in team-teaching in the new settings (Prain et al., 2014). Challenges included initial staff turnover as some staff reacted negatively to the new roles and a sense of exposure in the new settings. These settings also revealed varying degrees of teacher professional capacity to adapt to the challenges of these settings (Prain et al., 2014).

Strategy Three: Personalising Learning through a Differentiated, Stage-Based Curriculum

Drawing on Tomlinson (2005), Seaton (2002) and others, the BEP designers claimed that personalising student learning entailed teachers designing and enacting a stage-based curriculum with appropriate task differentiation. For Tomlinson (2005), teachers differentiated a curriculum by varying student task demands, the pace and type of learning experiences, and/or the forms of assessment. This cast personalising learning as a predominantly teacher-directed approach to academic learning. The BEP designers also noted the need for strong positive relationships between teachers and students. Students needed to feel closely connected to teachers. The BEP proposed teacher advisor groups, where an individual teacher was responsible for the academic progress and personal welfare of 16–20 students. In this view, quality learning was possible when academic, social, cultural and personal developmental needs and capabilities were addressed, as suggested by Fielding (2004), Rogers (2013) and others. The BEP also claimed that an effective curriculum addresses student perspectives and learning styles, where students participate in negotiating aspects of content, modes of learning and assessment, and where a variety of progression pathways were available to all students. Following Seaton (2002), the BEP claimed that an effective middle years curriculum entailed focused learning, trans-disciplinary investigations, community development activities, and personal learning projects.

In characterising how such curricula might be achieved, the BEP (2005, p. 18) argued that students should participate in planning and evaluating instruction, and where "experimentation and experience…become the basis for learning experiences." Following Kubow and Kinney (2004), the BEP writers noted that this required a more democratic approach to learning. Students should participate actively, self-assess their efforts, set goals and reflect on learning outcomes, leading to strategic gains in new learning tasks. In place of the traditional structuring of the curriculum (fixed syllabi, age-based education, annual student progressions, and one teacher a class), the BEP proposed that the new learning communities entailed teaching teams that customised learning experiences to promote individual student progress and wellbeing. Challenges included: some teacher lack of confidence and/or willingness to take on teacher advisor roles; and perceived lack of time and expertise for teachers to develop a robust vertical curriculum that catered for all students' academic capabilities and wellbeing needs (Prain et al., 2014). In subsequent chapters we focus on strategies that enabled these challenges to be addressed successfully.

Overview of Participant Schools

The four BEP Years 7–10 colleges Whirrakee, Ironbark, Melaleuca, and Grevillea that form the basis for our study have varying populations and cultures. While they are broadly similar in physical design in that they incorporate flexible open spaces and break-out areas, they vary in learning community organisation. These differences are briefly outlined here and summarised in Table 1.1 (see Prain et al., 2014).

Whirrakee College, the largest of the four schools (over 1000 students in 2013), is the least disadvantaged, being classified as of average socio-economic status (SES) with a proportion of 24% of students coming from the lowest SES quartile, approximately half of the other three schools, while the proportion of students coming from the highest SES quartile is higher than the other three schools combined. Whirrakee College's focus is on student personal growth for social responsibility where students are developed into ethical citizens capable of contributing to the broader society. This focus is consistent with the school culture of emphasising academic excellence and a strong belief in the need for students to develop as independent and resilient learners in their four years at the school. Independence is encouraged from Year 7 as all students are responsible for keeping track of their attendance, learning tasks, and progress via a virtual dashboard on their personal computers. The learning communities are horizontally organised into year levels with a triadic system of student grouping. Three teachers teach 75 students in the open space, in three groups based on ability, for the core subjects of English, mathematics, science and humanities.

Ironbark College is the smallest of the four schools with fewer than 600 students in 2013. It is also the most disadvantaged school being classified as below average SES with a proportion of 57% of its students in the lowest SES quartile and only 3% in the highest SES quartile. The school is very closely connected to its broader community and has a culture of supporting its student cohort through an emphasis on respect for self, others and the school. Recognising the great need for student social and emotional learning that underpins academic success, the school takes a whole-school approach to student wellbeing that begins with a strong and well-conceived teacher advisor program. Communities are organised vertically into Years 7–10 groups and each community has two learning neighbourhoods, one comprising the Years 7 and 8 students, and the other comprising the Years 9 and 10 students. Students remain in one community with largely the same group of teachers throughout the four years of secondary schooling. This connectedness to a small community is seen by teachers as vital for introducing stage-based learning as envisaged by the BEP, and allows cross-fertilisation of culture and ideas among older and younger students.

Grevillea College is also a small school with a cohort of just over 600 students in 2013. Its priority, to foster students' personal attributes as a basis for academic success, is regarded as particularly important for its low SES cohort. Only 6% come from the highest SES quartile, and 48% of Grevillea's students come from the lowest SES quartile. Learning communities are vertically organised and each learning community has two neighbourhoods, each with a cohort of Years 7–10 students. The neighbourhoods form the basis for teacher advisor groups, and special subjects designed to develop student resilience, wellbeing, leadership and connections with same-age peers and the wider community. Students remain in one community

Table 1.1. Organisational differences among schools

	Whirrakee	Ironbark	Melaleuca	Grevillea
Students (2013)	Over 1000	About 600	Over 800	About 600
Staff/Student Ratio (2013)	16.0	10.0	13.0	13.0
SE Level (ICSEA value for 2013)	Average	Below average	Below average	Below average
SE Distribution in lowest half	55%	86%	76%	78%
Community Organisation	Each community houses one year level (Years 7, 8, 9 and 10 buildings). Students progress through the buildings as they move through their school years. Each year level has distinct teaching teams	Four community buildings, each of which houses a cohort of Years 7, 8, 9 and 10 students who remain in this community for their four years at the school.	Two learning community buildings house Years 7 and 8 students with separate communities for Years 9 and 10. Students progress through the buildings as they move through their school years. From 2014, change to Years 7 to 10 in each community	Four community buildings, each of which houses a cohort of Years 7, 8, 9 and 10 students who remain in this community for their four years at the school.
Domains where team-teaching and flexible groupings predominate	Maths, Science, Humanities, English	Maths, Science, Humanities, English	Maths, Science/Humanities (Transdisciplinary Inquiry), English, LOTE	Maths, Science, Humanities, English

through their four years at the school but may move between neighbourhoods. It is believed that this form of organisation allows modelling of behaviour and peer support from older to younger students. As teachers also remain in their communities from year to year, it is felt that the long-term relationships built among staff and students promote wellbeing and connectedness. Learning sessions are divided into four 70-minute classes per day and core subjects are blocked in each learning neighbourhood to enable stage-based learning. The College has a specialised trade-training centre which allows increased pathways for Years 9 and 10 students. Its outdoor area includes a centrally situated grass-covered hill, unique among the BEP colleges, which is a most popular social area where students gather out of class time.

Melaleuca College is the second largest of the BEP colleges with over 800 students in 2013. It has a strong focus on meeting each student's individual learning and wellbeing needs, moving from building a strong knowledge and skill base in Years 7 and 8 to increasing choice, independence and inquiry-based learning at Years 9 and 10. Like Ironbark and Grevillea it is classified as a school of below average SES, with 45% of its students in the lowest SES quartile and only 6% in the highest SES quartile. Like Grevillea, the school has a well-equipped trade-training centre to cater for student needs. The school has experienced much change in the period of our study. As well as high staff turnover and leadership changes, the organisation of communities has also gone through several iterations, moving from combined Year 7 and 8 communities and separate Year 9 and 10 communities, to horizontally organised year-level communities, to the current organisation of vertical Years 7–10 communities. At Melaleuca, personalisation of learning has been built into the assessment design as well as community and timetable structures. In core subjects, three classes of the same subject are scheduled at the same time in the same space, affording opportunities for teacher collaboration and planning in a range of subjects.

Our Analyses and Research Methods

In analysing the BEP's goals, strategies and outcomes, we drew on multi-theoretic perspectives to interpret teacher and student adaptation. Guided by Cultural Historical Activity Theory (CHAT) perspectives (Edwards, 2005, 2011) we understood continuity and change in cultural practices including schooling/teaching/learning in terms of the values, goals and material/symbolic tools participants used in these practices. We also drew on pragmatist perspectives on the situated and contextual nature of teacher problem-solving, reasoning, knowledge generation, values clarification and meaning-making (Dewey, 1916; Haack, 2004; Peirce, 1931–58; Wittgenstein, 1972). From these viewpoints, what personalising learning means depends on analysing the goals, values, strategies and outcomes that occur in its name in this context. We understand a pragmatist orientation to be a systematic method of inquiry that avoids a priori judgements and incorporates a reasoned collective analysis of attempted personalising practices to identify justifiable beliefs about their effects. Rather than naming decontextualised essential truths about personalising processes, we sought to identify justifiable rules for successful action in this particular setting. The new physical school settings were catalysts for change, unsettling teachers' habitual behaviour and perspectives on effective teaching and learning, causing them to reflect and experiment with a range of new options judged by their practicability in enabling meaningful student learning. We also drew on Gibson's (1979) ecological psychological perspective to explain teacher and student adaptive actions and rationales.

In defining these adaptive practices we analysed (a) accounts in the relevant literature by advocates and critics of the rationale, goals, methods, and outcomes for personalising learning, (b) the perspectives and practices of participant teachers and students in our study, and (c) learning outcomes for both students and teachers. As already reported (Prain et al., 2014), we developed a new instrument to assess student perceptions of a personalised learning environment, and conducted an annual survey over three years with the student cohort. We report the findings of this survey in subsequent chapters to corroborate themes. Through case studies in various subjects across different schools, entailing qualitative and quantitative data analyses, and drawing on relevant literature, we aimed to identify and explain key conditions and practices that enabled quality student personalised learning and wellbeing in these contexts.

Our understanding of these adaptive practices has been influenced not only by teacher/teacher and teacher/student collaboration and partnerships in these settings, but also by applying Gibson's account of affordances to explain these changes. In this sense our pragmatist approach aims to take into account how the values, intentions, beliefs and practices of participants interacted with the symbolic and material structures/tools in the setting. We saw this interaction as critical to understanding and assessing adaptive processes and outcomes. According to Gibson (1979, p. 128), affordances are "action possibilities" latent in the environment, objectively measurable, and independent of the ability to recognise them, but always available in relation to the actors' intentions and therefore dependent on their capabilities. For us, these environments offer new possibilities for how curricula can be imagined and enacted. Whether teachers feel empowered or constrained by increased visibility in up-scaled learning communities, with larger spaces and reduced formal spatial structures, depends on how they interpret and respond to these aspects. Whether they view this as a chance to extend their sphere of influence, to participate in productive informal teamwork with colleagues, and to learn from others' practices, or as an intrusion and/or distraction, depends on their perceptions of how these affordances enable or constrain their aims and practices as teachers. As we have noted elsewhere (Prain et al., 2014), adaptive change can be prompted by dissatisfaction with past ineffective practices, whole-school support for change, innovative initiatives from individual teachers, and cross-school teacher collaboration.

Conceptualising Personalising Learning

Researchers generally agree that personalising learning is understood as a practical way to increase students' sense of learning as individually engaging and meaningful (see Prain et al., 2014 for extended review). Personalised learning thus entails processes around quality learning, raising larger questions about the ultimate purposes of school-based education in terms of learner knowledge, attributes and values. Personalising learning is based on the principle that students have rights and capacities as learners for self-realisation/self-actualisation that can be addressed by flexible approaches to curricular structure and developmental sequences, thus reducing constraints/hindrances/blockers implied by assuming student abilities and needs are best addressed through standardised age-based curricula. The grounds for enacting personalised learning are based on the assumption that teachers and students are able to co- and self-regulate learning through shared decisions around roles, practices, values, and mutual responsibilities. Our view of personalising learning is therefore not based on a principle of unfettered student freedom and unconstrained deliberative choice, but rather one of productive constraint on student focus and activity.

As pragmatists, our inquiry focuses on the particular features of the regional and school priorities and contexts to address the issue of what personalising learning means under these conditions. We recognise that engagement and meaningfulness as curricular effects pose heightened challenges for teaching low SES students, who are often alienated from schooling. What learners find meaningful can be prompted by learner and teacher intentions and strategies, and vary over time. Our inquiry therefore entailed resolving practical questions assumed to have identifiable causes in these contexts, and where knowledge about personalising learning is generated through dialogue with participants, and in logical proof. Our accounts of successful personalising of learning across the curriculum, as reported in subsequent chapters in this book, are therefore highly context-dependent. However, our research also provides leads for enacting personalising learning in other settings.

We claim that learning is personalised when learners are motivated to learn because they view the learning task or experience as engaging and meaningful, and as directly addressing immediate and/or longer-term learning needs. Motivation may be intrinsic, extrinsic or both (see Dweck, 2000). Both kinds of motivation occur concurrently or sequentially and contribute to personalising learning. Learners are best placed to judge the extent to which they perceive their learning as personalised, but this process also leaves scope for teachers to make informed judgements. For their part, teachers contribute to learner perceptions and experiences through designing curricular tasks and activities, motivating students, providing targeted teaching and timely feedback, and, where appropriate, negotiating with students their goals, tasks, and performance evaluation. Students over time are expected to develop self-reliance and initiative as learners. The teaching experience is personalised for teachers when their energy and flair provide meaningful learning experiences for their students.

This account raises further questions about what enables learner perceptions of meaningfulness, what exactly counts as meaningful and why, what responsibilities are, or should be, distributed between teachers and students, and who should shape curricular content and methods. Our case studies in subsequent chapters flesh out detailed answers to these questions, but here we summarise key aspects of our reasoning.

On the question of what contributes to student perceptions of meaningful learning, we recognise crucial complementary insights from pedagogical, cognitive, socio-cultural, and psychological perspectives. From pedagogical perspectives (Moje, 2007), a robust mainstream curriculum includes opportunities to differentiate what, how, when, why, with whom, and at what pace students learn, and is likely to be perceived as more engaging and meaningful than a standardised curriculum. This is especially the case where there is a wide student ability range. Learning is likely to be meaningful when there is a good fit between individual learner needs, interests, capacities, and the demands or level of the learning activities. This implies that a well-designed and differentiated curriculum increases the likelihood of student motivation.

From cognitive perspectives, learning is meaningful when learners self-regulate their learning (Pintrich & de Groot, 1990). This entails constructive and intentional use of personal strategies to achieve academic and wellbeing goals (Boekaerts & Corno, 2005; Butler & Winne, 1995). Pintrich's (2004) widely adopted model of self-regulated learning (SRL) involves: (a) forethought, planning and activation (planning and enacting behaviour such as effort and persistence); (b) monitoring (such as tracking task requirements); (c) control (such as adapting behavioural strategies to ensure task completion); and (d) reflection (such as use of self-assessing strategies achieve task requirements). For Zimmerman (2008), independent learning or self-regulated learning refers to the degree to which students are metacognitively, motivationally and behaviourally active participants in their own learning processes. Learning is likely to be personalised and meaningful when students know and use a repertoire of such strategies. We acknowledge that self-regulation is developmental, and that teacher co-regulation of learning experiences enables this development. We also agree that learning can be personally meaningful when students with limited self-regulatory capacities are supported by this co-regulation. The crucial element is reflection-guided action leading to a sense of student learning achievement.

We also wish to clarify how we see the relationship between students' individual and collective experiences. For us, learning is personalised when it promotes in learners a sense of their individual capabilities and interests. However, we regard isolationist views of personalising learning, where programs are highly individuated, as misguided. Learners are likely to view their learning as personalised and meaningful through relational connections with peers, teachers and parents. From socio-cultural perspectives, meaningful learning for students depends on successful participation in culturally valued activities (Moje, 2007). The development of an individual identity as a person, a student of a particular subject, a class member, a group participant, or a learning community member depends on productive relationships with others that enable individual and group goals and wellbeing to be integrated and enabled. This is evident when learners contribute to activities such as large- and small-group discussion, debates, academic and sporting teams, group projects, musical ensembles, school community decision-making, and teamwork around small or large school-based or broader community projects.

From psychological perspectives, learners perceive their learning as personalised if teachers demonstrate concern for and knowledge of students as individuals, and provide strategies to address particular academic and wellbeing needs (Hattie, 2009; Sugarman & Martin, 2011). An individual learner's sense of self and personhood depends on being valued individually and achieving recognition through personal achievement and through connection with others (Fielding, 2004; Sugarman & Martin, 2011). We argue that with low SES students, this achievement and sense of connection is enhanced by a focus on an explicit developmental curriculum around social and emotional learning to support students becoming active functional members of their learning community (see Chapter 10).

On the question of who should decide the curriculum, we argue that in the context of highly prescriptive national and state curricula and testing regimes in high-stakes subjects, teachers need to have a significant role in shaping how curricular content and goals are addressed. We argue, following Moje (2007), that a socially just curriculum provides access for all students to a quality mainstream curriculum, implying necessary productive constraint on both the content and appropriate teaching and learning methods. We reject the view that personalising learning is inevitably a misguided return to student-centred education from the 1960s (Hartley, 2009), although we claim there is scope in some subjects for more student initiative on curricular content and methods (Prain et al., 2014). Learning mathematics is more likely to depend on successful progression through topics/levels than learning in interest-based humanities and technical subjects. More contentiously, we argue that personalising learning is compatible with testing regimes in that such regimes provide an evidential starting point for curricular design, incorporating future curricular differentiation to address learner needs (see Chapter 7). At the same time, we recognise that student academic success is not the sole indicator that learning is personalised, and that students may succeed without attaching much personal meaning to their success. We think it preferable that students find their subject content deeply engaging, where teachers adapt the curriculum to meet student needs and interests.

On the ideological underpinnings of personalising learning, we disagree that this form of learning necessarily equates with neoliberal consumerism (Beach & Dovemark, 2009), or inevitably increases disadvantage for low SES students (Campbell et al., 2007; Cutler, Waine, & Brehony, 2007; Pykett, 2010). The ideological character of this approach emerges from its enactment rather than any inherent traits, and it can equally serve a social justice agenda, as well as contribute to a more democratic trusting school culture (Rogers, 2013). We confirm that low SES students benefit academically and socially from the approaches to personalising learning enacted in this regional setting, and that inherently this approach does not exacerbate privilege or disadvantage.

Quality learning necessarily integrates psychological, epistemological, epistemic and cultural dimensions that align with personalising learning. When students are motivated to learn, engage with appropriate cognitive and material tools for knowing in the topic or subject (the epistemological dimension), learn how knowledge is developed in the topic or subject (the epistemic dimension), and participate in culturally-valued learning experiences that are made meaningful to them, then these processes and outcomes entail quality learning over time (Prain et al., 2014). We appreciate that these experiences are often deeply contested, as in claims made for particular values/content in high-stakes subjects such as literacy and numeracy (Edwards, 2010; Green, 2008). We also recognise that there are contested views about how goals around citizenship, ethnicity, class, gender, and the predicted needs, capabilities, and values of future citizens are addressed. We clarify answers to these questions and elaborate our view of how personalising learning processes enables quality learning through case study instantiation across different curricular areas in subsequent chapters in this book.

Enacting Personalised Learning

We claim that a personalised learning approach entails differences as well as similarities in the responsibilities, goals, constraints, learning needs, and roles of teachers and students. We view personalising learning as necessarily developmental, and therefore requiring multiple teacher and learner strategies, experiences, and understandings over extended time. This leads to increased student capacity to contribute to and co-design curricular content and methods with teachers (see Chapter 9). Many factors contribute to a personalised approach to learners and learning, including school leadership, teacher skill sets and practices, and learner capacities and goals. Teachers need the expertise, time, resources and teamwork to develop a flexible robust curriculum that is adequately structured in content, learning tasks, and adaptable classroom practices to engage all learners and address contrasting learner needs. This need not imply fixed labelling of learner capacities and long-term streaming, but rather ongoing responsive flexible programming to address each student's needs.

Relational and Nested Agency

We view "relational agency" (Edwards, 2005, 2007, p. 4, 2011) among teachers, and between teachers and students, to achieve teaching and learning goals as critical in supporting personalised learning. For Edwards (2005, 2007, p. 4) "relational

CHARACTERISING PERSONALISING LEARNING

agency" refers to a capacity for professionals to work with other professionals to develop a "network of expertise" to serve shared goals, where agency of individuals is built around distributed intelligence and diverse expertise across the group. Rather than emphasise individual action, Edwards (2007, p. 6) foregrounds "responsibility to and for others", where a shift to the relational is "an important move in the development of meshes of mutual responsibility." These meshes generate "common knowledge" (in this case of teacher professional needs and student curricular needs) that "mediates responsive professional action" (Edwards, 2011, p. 35). In enacting this mutual responsibility, Edwards (2011, p. 35) notes the need for participants to (a) demarcate power in decision-making to both clarify and ensure spheres of influence, (b) focus on "the whole child in the wider context", (c) create and develop better tools for collaboration, (d) refine processes for sharing knowledge, and (e) continuously review socially-constructed boundaries to ensure that they serve shared long-term goals effectively.

We argue this relational agency operates within a "nested agency" in the development of differentiated curricula and learners' self-regulatory capacities (see Figure 1.2 and Prain et al., 2013). The construct of "nested agency" recognises that teacher and student agency is constrained by structural, cultural and pedagogical assumptions, regulations, and practices, including prescriptive curricula, actual and potential roles and responsibilities of teachers and students in school settings, and expectations about norms for teaching and learning processes. Low SES students are also typically constrained by low aspirations, histories of modest academic

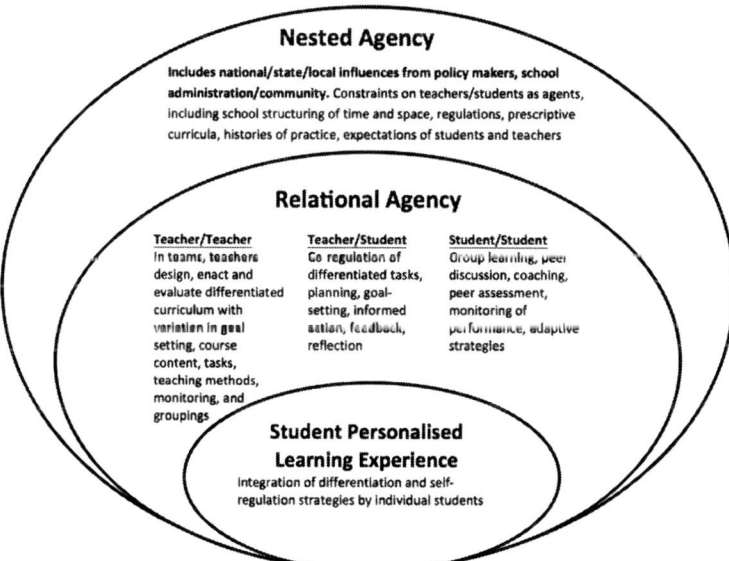

Figure 1.2. Framework for conceptualising and enacting personalised learning

17

achievement, and low self-efficacy that may hinder their willingness and capacity to participate in co-regulated learning (Domina & Saldana, 2011). Whether these constraints function productively or otherwise depends on practices developed within this nested agency. We argue that well-designed curriculum differentiation, coupled with a developmental approach to learner self-regulation and growing independence, support relational agency within these constraints.

We recognise our framework focuses only on student learning but claim that learning can also be personalised for teachers. This entails more than a technicist view of how teachers acquire a repertoire of effective pedagogical strategies, parallel to student acquisition of curricular skills and gains. Our research confirms multiple pathways and choices whereby teachers personalise the ways in which they learn about pedagogical effectiveness from their own actions and reflections, and those of others. Personalising learning also means scope for creative self-actualising, for developing a sense of self as both individual teacher and as team contributor within broader goals and practices. We revisit these multiple interlocking aspects of personalising learning throughout our book.

A Snapshot of Student Learning Gains

Over the duration of this study, student performance in BEP schools in national testing of reading and numeracy made significant gains in their ranking against their own 'similar schools' nationally (see Figures 1.3 and 1.4). These 'similar schools' were based on the educational disadvantage based on their ICSEA scores (see Prain et al., 2014 and Chapter 4). A ranking of 1 in Figure 1.3 indicates that the school is the top performing school among similar schools, while a ranking of 0 indicates

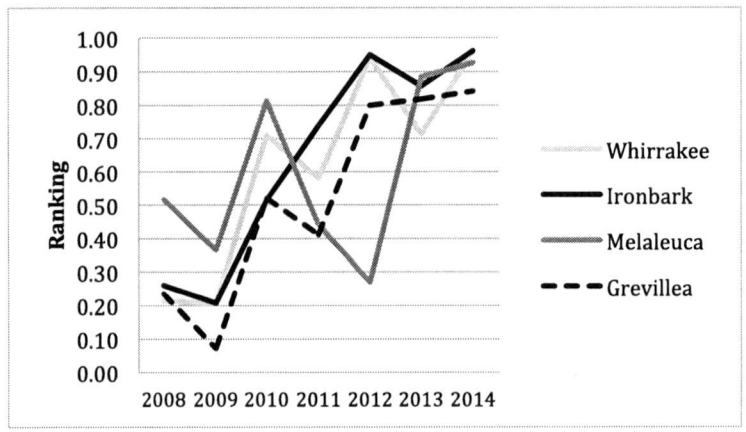

Figure 1.3. School ranking among 'similar schools' for year 9 reading, 2008–2014

CHARACTERISING PERSONALISING LEARNING

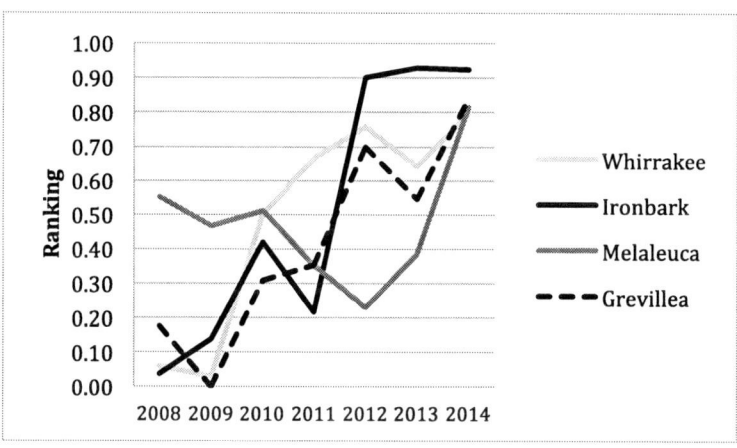

Figure 1.4. School ranking among 'similar schools' for year 9 numeracy, 2008–2014

that the school is the lowest performing school among similar schools. While these graphs provide only a snapshot of learning, they point to some of the effects of attempts to adapt teaching and learning approaches to the opportunities of new open-plan settings in ways that personalised students' learning experiences. In subsequent chapters we explore in detail what we consider were major contributors to the trends in these graphs, as well as identifying other influences on student learning and wellbeing. We conclude this chapter by summarising generic principles that underpinned attempts to personalise student learning in these settings.

PRINCIPLES THAT SUPPORT PERSONALISING LEARNING IN
OPEN-PLAN SETTINGS

Two key principles have guided traditional schooling's goals and methods. These are: (1) a unified, collective, caring approach to students' personal and intellectual development; and (2) enactment of a high quality diverse curriculum that nourishes all students' engagement with learning and schooling (Muijs, Harris, Chapman, Stoll, & Russ, 2004). While narratives around traditional approaches to schooling stress the need for a shared collective vision and ethos (Fullen, 2007), in practice this goal is enacted traditionally through high levels of segmentation of teachers and students in separate classrooms and an age-based curriculum. While curricular planning and review may entail collective, cooperative staff input, the curriculum is not enacted in this way. Our research over the past three years indicates that these two principles remain crucial today, but require new practices, skills, new openness to change and adaptation, and new supporting narratives to imagine, enact and sustain successful personalised learning in open-plan settings.

Schooling as Collective Participation in a Community of Learners

Open-plan settings facilitate a collective enactment of a shared vision and ethos through providing diverse opportunities for team-teaching and participant contributions and interactions. Principals, teachers and students can develop a school culture, within and across learning communities, that values and addresses individual needs through productive ongoing participation in these communities. This orientation aligns with broader claims by Putnam (2001, 2004) and Grissmer and colleagues (2004) about the crucial roles of trust and the quality of communication within cohesive communities to support student educational achievement. While these researchers referred to the social capital in effective communities beyond schools, the open-plan settings can function as sites to develop this social capital within schools. As further noted by Schreiner and Sjoberg (2007), contemporary adolescent student work on self-realisation and identity formation is shaped and influenced by opportunities to participate collaboratively in meaningful communities. To develop this productive culture, teachers and students need a common shared knowledge about learning goals, strategies, and participant contributions as the bases for personalising learning and wellbeing.

Strategies to support the development of a participatory culture include staff buy-in to a shared vision of the broad goals and methods of the school through extensive consultation with participants, and the development of distributed leadership within and across learning communities through professional learning support (Prain et al., 2014). These processes facilitate the development of a "common knowledge" (Edwards, 2014) for all participants about whole-school approaches and the bases for priorities and decision-making in these settings. A multi-layered whole-school approach to wellbeing builds a positive school culture that fosters the connectedness and relationships that are foundational to improved learning outcomes (see Chapter 4). This approach is achieved through three complementary areas: school organisation, ethos and environment; curriculum, teaching and learning; and partnerships with parents and community services (WHO Health Promoting Framework, 1996). Strategies include: a welfare structure that supports staff and students; a school ethos of respectful, trusting relationships; strong procedures for student management; an explicit curriculum that teaches core community values in teacher advisor classes; outreach to access community based programs; and visits from family and professional services that connect the school to its local community (see Chapter 4).

Organisational changes support new teaching and learning practices. Leadership is distributed into communities with community leaders taking responsibility for leading teaching and learning practices in their communities. Time and space is organised to take advantage of the flexible open-plan settings and to support large groups of students working with teams of teachers. Timetables reflect the need to program like subjects simultaneously, to minimise the necessity for frequent movement of students and staff, and to allow time for teacher teams to plan and review lessons (see Prain et al., 2014, Chapters 2, 7, 8 and 9).

A Multi-Year-Level High-Quality Developmental Curriculum is Designed, Enacted and Reviewed by the School Community

This kind of curriculum is implied in expected student learning trajectories in national curricula statements about student achievement over multiple years (Australian Curriculum and Assessment Reporting Authority (ACARA), 2014), but is often constrained by age-based student progressions and teacher focus on individual year-level learning outcomes. A multi-year curriculum, if effectively enacted, enables all students to be successful participants. Strategies that support its design, implementation and review include:

Teachers share responsibility for the design of multi-year curricula. In mainstream compulsory subjects, such as English and mathematics, teachers identify the current performance range of the whole student cohort in the relevant subject as a basis for designing learning opportunities to meet all students' needs. This means that teachers use existing standardised tests or create new ones as the basis for this diagnostic testing and analysis. This process leads to teachers having a shared understanding of the developmental curriculum of these subjects across Years 7–10, not just standards or expectations for the expected range of performance at individual year levels. (see Chapters 6, 7 and 8). In subjects with more open-ended content, teachers can use their professional expertise and initial learning tasks to ascertain the range of student initial understandings and interests (see Chapters 9 and 10). Teachers motivate students by assessing their current levels of attainment and negotiating goals to reach improved performance, with diagnostic, formative, and summative assessment contributing to informed assessment of student progress.

Teacher teams enact and review curriculum. Working in teams, rather than in isolation, enables teachers to vary students' learning experiences to cater for individual and group needs. Teachers differentiate the curriculum by varying: (a) content (what students should know and be able to do, and the materials that will support them in their learning), such as key concepts, procedural and analytical skills and dispositions in subject areas (see especially Chapters 3, 4, 5, 6 and 7); (b) learning processes (the activities that help students make sense of their learning) such as workshops, peer tutoring, small-group projects, whole group activities; and (c) products (range of evidence that students provide of their learning). Students can demonstrate explicit understandings or process skills in multiple ways such as verbal, written, multi-modal text, team performance, and peer assessment (see Chapters 5 and 6). Evaluative and review strategies include diagnostic, formative and summative assessment by teachers, individual students, and their peers. Test results can be used to reset goals, temporarily regroup students, and as a basis for teacher analyses of their effectiveness across taught topics, and improvements to curricular content and/or implementation.

ICTs are used strategically to enhance students' learning. These technologies in these contexts can serve a range of current educational purposes identified by many researchers in this field. These include:

- providing a resource for planning, tracking and evaluating learning progress for teachers, students and their parents;
- providing resources and tools to support student learning activities and tasks;
- providing a platform for dissemination and discussion of learning outcomes and artefacts within and beyond the school; and
- providing a repository for curricular and other documents to support student learning.

By meeting these purposes, ICTs can support learning being personalised for individual students in the open-plan settings, but also contribute to a culture of a community of learners. Teachers who facilitate the use of ICTs as learning tools can change their own and students' roles. As facilitators they can encourage active and independent learning by enabling students to control the scope, pace, and depth of their inquiries and projects, by allowing students to access a broad range of expertise beyond the classroom and by fostering peer learning conversations.

NEW PRACTICES AND NEW NARRATIVES TO SUPPORT PERSONALISED LEARNING IN OPEN-PLAN SETTINGS

Our research indicates that the strategies outlined above create new challenges and opportunities around teacher work and how it is understood and supported (see Chapter 2). Teacher experimentation with various patterns of space use has led to flexible practices, and new understandings of openness to learning opportunities (see Chapter 2). The large foyer in each learning community building was variously used for specialist subject teaching, independent student work, and more informal discussions within and outside official subject timetabling (see Chapter 2). Interview rooms functioned as multi-purpose areas, including teacher planning meetings and small-group student project work. Learning communities become defined by the ways in which teachers 'practicalise' their emerging knowledge, where the integration of practical affordances and subsequent questions and tensions inform this new knowledge. We recognise the unpredictability in outcomes, acknowledging that increased participant interconnectivity is both a major potential strength and challenge in these settings. Continuous participant review is critical to maintaining the health of these learning communities. The open-plan settings enable teachers and students to change routine ways of teaching and learning to enhance learning and wellbeing. This is evident through: an altered sphere of influence for teachers working with a larger group of students, and for students an increased expectation of self-reliance and self-organisation skills; more incidental and informal learning opportunities for both staff and students; and use of web-based interactive technologies. In the longer term, students can develop more autonomy as learners who participate in designing what, how, why, and where they learn in these new settings, and with whom.

Following Gibson (1979), the major properties of the settings (increased visibility for all participants, reduced spatial structures, and more scope for staff and student movement) act as primary affordances for changes to teacher and student intentions and actions. Consequential secondary affordances around participant goals and behavior include opportunities for more interaction, more informality, and extended staff and student spheres of influence. There is scope for more collaboration to develop and enact curricula, increased opportunities for team-teaching, more flexible student groupings, closer relationships with students, and more diverse daily contacts between a larger group of teachers and students. Teachers can use the affordances of the different spaces in the learning communities to synchronise their roles and support learning (see Chapter 2). Teachers can frame tasks in terms of personalising learning through different approaches, flexible use of space, varying task structures, use learning resources as scaffolding, and support student agency (see Chapter 3).

These new arrangements in up-scaled learning communities that are detailed in the following chapters offer workable ways to overcome past student disenchantment with schooling, engage with technological realities of unpredictable accelerated change and connectedness, and support teams of teachers to identify all learners' needs, and nurture individual and collective capabilities. Removing the walls enlarges the zones and horizons for participant learning.

REFERENCES

Australian Curriculum and Assessment Reporting Authority (ACARA). (2014). *My school.* Retrieved from http://www.acara.edu.au/reporting/my_school_website_page.html

Beach, D., & Dovemark, M. (2009) Making right choices? An ethnographic account of creativity, performativity and personalised learning policy, concepts and practices. *Oxford Review of Education, 35*(6), 689–704. doi:10.1080/03054980903122267

Bendigo Education Plan Steering Committee (BEP). (2005). *Bendigo education plan.* Bendigo, Victoria, Australia: Loddon Mallee Region, DEECD. Retrieved from http://www.weeroona.vic.edu.au/site-content/strategic-plans/BEP.pdf

Bendigo Loddon Primary Care Partnership (BLPCP). (2012, June). *Community health and wellbeing Profile – June 2012.* Bendigo, Victoria. Bendigo Loddon Primary Care Partnership. Retrieved from http://www.blpcp.com.au/BLPCP%20Community%20Profile%2022%20November_2012.pdf

Boekaerts, M., & Corno, L. (2005). Self-regulation in the classroom: A perspective on assessment and intervention. *Applied Psychology: An International Review, 54*(2), 199–231. doi:10.1111/j.1464-0597.2005.00205.x

Brandt, R. (1998). *Powerful learning.* Alexandria, VA: Association for Supervision and Curriculum Development.

Bransford, J., Brown, A., & Cocking, R. (Eds.). (2000). *How people learn.* Washington, DC: National Academy Press.

Butler, D., & Winne, P. H. (1995). Feedback and self-regulated learning: A theoretical synthesis. *Review of Educational Research, 65*(3), 245–281. doi:10.3102/00346543065003245

Campbell, R., Robinson, W., Neelands, J., Hewston, R., & Mazzoli, L. (2007). Personalised learning: Ambiguities in theory and practice. *British Journal of Educational Studies, 55*(2), 135–154. doi:10.1111/j.1467-8527.2007.00370.x

Cutler, T., Waine, B., & Brehony, K. (2007). A new epoch of individualization? Problems with the personalization of public sector services. *Public Administration, 85*(3), 847–855. doi:10.1111/j.1467-9299.2007.00672.x

Danielson, C. (1996). *Enhancing professional practice: A framework for teaching.* Alexandria, VA: Association for Supervision and Curriculum Development.

Domina, T., & Saldana, J. (2011). Does raising the bar level the playing field? Mathematics curricular intensification and inequality in American high schools, 1982–2004. *American Educational Research Journal. 49*(4), 685–708. Retrieved from http://aer.sagepub.com/content/early/2011/11/12/0002831211426347

Dunbar, R. (1993). Coevolution of neocortical size, group size and language in humans. *Behavioural and Brain Sciences, 16*(4), 681–694. doi:10.1017/S0140525X00032325

Dweck, C. S. (2000). *Self-theories: Their role in motivation, personality, and development.* Philadelphia, PA: Psychology Press.

Edwards, A. (2005). Relational agency: Learning to be a resourceful practitioner. *International Journal of Educational Research, 43*, 168–182. doi:10.1016/j.ijer.2006.06.010

Edwards, A. (2007). Relational agency in professional practice: A CHAT analysis. *Actio: An International Journal of Human Activity Theory, 1*, 1–17.

Edwards, A. (2010). *Being an expert professional practitioner.* Dordrecht, The Netherlands: Springer.

Edwards, A. (2011). Building common knowledge at the boundaries between professional practices: Relational agency and relational expertise in systems of distributed expertise. *International Journal of Educational Research, 50*(1), 33–39. doi:10.1016/j.ijer.2011.04.007

Edwards, A. (2014). Epilogue: The end of the beginning. In V. Prain, P. Cox, C. Deed, D. Edwards, C. Farrelly, M. Keeffe, ... Z. Yager (Eds.), *Adapting to teaching and learning in open-plan schools* (pp. 205–210). Rotterdam, The Netherlands: Sense Publishers.

Elmore, R. (1996). Getting to scale with good educational practice. *Harvard Educational Review, 66*(1), 1–27.

Fielding, M. (2004). Transformative approaches to student voice: Theoretical underpinnings, recalcitrant realities. *British Educational Research Journal, 30*(2) 295–311. doi:10.1080/0141192042000195236

Fullan, M. (2007). *The new meaning of educational change* (4th ed.). New York, NY: Teachers College Press.

Gibson, J. J. (1986). *The ecological approach to visual perception.* Hillsdale, NJ: Erlbaum. (First published 1979)

Green, B. (2008). English, rhetoric, democracy; Or, renewing English in Australia. *English in Australia, 43*(3), 35–44.

Grissmer, D., Flanagan, A., Kawata, J., & Williamson, S. (2000). *Improving student achievement: What state NAEP test scores tell us.* Santa Monica, CA: RAND Corporation.

Haack, S. (2004). Pragmatism old and new. *Contemporary Pragmatism, 1*(1), 3–42. doi:10.1163/18758185-90000126

Harpaz, Y. (2005). Teaching and learning in a community of thinking. *Journal of Curriculum and Supervision, 20*(2), 136–157.

Hartley, D. (2009). Personalisation: The nostalgic revival of child-centred education. *Journal of Education Policy, 24*(4), 423–434. doi:10.1080/02680930802669318

Hattie, J. A. C. (2009). *Visible learning: A synthesis of over 800 meta-analyses relating to achievement.* London, UK: Routledge.

Kubow, P. K., & Kinney, M. B. (2000). Fostering democracy in middle school classrooms: Insights from a democratic institute in Hungary. *The Social Studies, 91*(6), 265–271. doi:10.1080/00377990009602476

Moje, E. B. (2007). Developing socially just subject-matter instruction: A review of the literature on disciplinary literacy. In N. L. Parker (Ed.), *Review of research in education* (pp. 1–44). Washington, DC: American Educational Research Association.

Muijs, D., Harris, A., Chapman, C., Stoll, L., & Russ, J. (2004). Improving schools in socioeconomically disadvantaged areas – A review of research evidence. *School Effectiveness and School Improvement: An International Journal of Research, Policy and Practice, 15*(2), 149–175. doi:10.1076/sesi.15.2.149.30433

Nair, P. (2006). Design strategies for tomorrow's schools. In OECD (Ed.), *21st century learning environments*. Paris, France: OECD.

Peirce, C. S. (1931–1958). In C. Hartshorne & P. Weiss (Eds., Vols. 1–6) and A. W. Burks (Ed., Vols. 7–8), *Collected papers of Charles Sanders Peirce* (Vol. 8). Cambridge, MA: Harvard University Press.

Pintrich, P. (2004). A conceptual framework for assessing motivation and self-regulated learning in college students. *Educational Psychology Review, 16*(4), 385–407.

Pintrich, P. R., & De Groot, E. (1990). Motivated and self-regulated learning components of academic performance. *Journal of Educational Psychology, 82*(1), 33–40. doi:10.1037/0022-0663.82.1.33

Prain, V., Cox, P., Deed, C., Dorman, J., Edwards, D., Farrelly, C., Keeffe, M., … Yager, Z. (2014). *Adapting to teaching and learning in open-plan schools*. Rotterdam, The Netherlands: Sense Publishers.

Putnam, R. D. (2001). Community-based social capital and educational performance. In D. Ravitich & J. Viteritti (Eds.), *Making good citizens: Education and civil society* (pp. 58–95). London, UK: Yale University Press.

Putnam, R. D. (2004). *Education, diversity, social cohesion and "social capital"*. Paper presented at the meeting of OECD Education Ministry—Raising the Quality of Learning for All, March 18. Dublin, Ireland.

Pykett, J. (2010). *Personalised governing through behaviour change and re-education*. Paper presented at the Political Studies Association Conference, Edinburgh, Scotland, UK.

Rogers, S. (2013). Personalisation and student voice. *Insights, 7*, 1–4. Retrieved from http://www.bera.ac.uk/wp-content/uploads/2013/12/Insights-7-Personalisation-Student-Voice-for-web-2.pdf

Schlecty, P. (2003). *Inventing better schools: An action plan for educational reform*. San Francisco, CA: Jossey-Bass. (First published 1997)

Schreiner, C., & Sjøberg, S. (2007). Science education and youth's identity construction—two incompatible projects? In D. Corrigan, J. Dillon, & R. Gunstone (Eds.), *The re-emergence of values in the science curriculum* (pp. 231–247). Rotterdam, The Netherlands: Sense Publishers.

Seaton, A. (2002). Reforming the hidden curriculum: The key abilities model and four curricular forms. *Curriculum Perspectives, 22*(1), 9–15. Retrieved from http://www.andrewseaton.com.au/reform.htm

Sugarman, J., & Martin, J. (2011). Theorizing relational agency: Reactions to comments. *Journal of Constructivist Psychology, 24*(4), 321–323. doi:10.1080/10720537.2011.593472

Tomlinson, C. (2005). Grading and differentiation: Paradox or good practice. *Theory into Practice, 44*(3), 262–269. doi:10.1207/s15430421tip4403_11

WHO. (1996). *Promoting health through schools*. Geneva, Switzerland: WHO Global School Health Initiative, Health Education and Promotion Unit. Retrieved from http://www.who.int/iris/handle/10665/63367 - sthash.Mj72gAhw.dpuf

Wiggins, G., & McTighe, J. (1998). *Understanding by design*. Alexandria, VA: Association for Supervision and Curriculum Development.

Wittgenstein, L. (1972). *Lectures and conversations on aesthetics, psychology, and religious belief*. Berkeley, CA: University of California Press.

Zimmerman, B. (2008). Investigating self-regulation and motivation: Historical background, methodological developments, and future prospects. *American Educational Research Journal, 45*(1), 166–183. doi:10.3102/0002831207312909

CRAIG DEED

2. A MODEL OF TEACHER ADAPTATION TO OPEN-PLAN SETTINGS

KNOWLEDGE AND ADAPTATION

This chapter examines teacher adaptation to open-plan learning communities. Teacher adaptation is grounded in the practical knowledge and contextual awareness of teachers (Cochran-Smith & Lytle, 1999; Darling-Hammond, 2006; Kelly, 2006). Here, it is argued that adaptation is a pragmatist process of seeing differently in order to act differently (Schon, 1983; Verloop, Van Driel, & Meijer, 2001).

Teacher adaptation is conceptualised as an imaginative and dynamic (re)occupying of the open-plan learning environment, providing a bridging mechanism between narratives of the possibilities and constraints of prior experience, and projecting and enacting alternative learning experiences. This involves active interplay between individual and social knowledge, each informing the other (Borko, 2004). Exercise of teacher knowledge informs opportunities to shape and frame learning environments (Putnam & Borko, 2000).

A model is theorised that offers an explanation of teachers' adaptation to their working context. These interactions are drawn specifically from accounts of teaching practitioners' experience, and informed by literature about the relationship between practical knowledge and research. This chapter draws on pragmatist perspectives of knowledge as justified beliefs derived from analyses of experience (Dewey, 1938/2008). Teacher adaptive processes are conceptualised as a pragmatist sequence of problem recognition, including analysis of key elements, and development of possible solutions, trialling and review. Pragmatists are not seeking the truth but rather attempt to recognise the impact of a concept on practice through consideration of practical meaning and practical consequences (Misak, 2007).

The model provides an account of the complexity of practical adaptation to new spaces that are nested within institutional environments. It provides a more nuanced view of abstract models of adaptation, such as that put forward by Blackmore, Bateman, Loughlin, O'Mara, and Aranda (2011). Blackmore and colleagues (2011) proposed a four stage conceptual framework of four overlapping temporal phases: design, transition/implementation, consolidation, and re-evaluation/sustainability. Their model is a useful scrutiny of teacher and student inhabitation and engagement with alternative school learning environments.

This chapter contributes to ongoing discussion about teaching as situated and collective work (Borko, 2004; Grangeat & Gray, 2008; Shulman & Shulman, 2004), expert models of teaching knowledge (Shulman, 1987; Sternberg & Horvath, 1995), and professional learning communities as a means of teacher adaptation (Darling-Hammond, 2006; A. Hargreaves, 2003; Korthagen, 2010; Meirink, Imants, Meijer, & Verloop, 2010; Pridham, Deed, & Cox, 2013).

TEACHER PRACTICAL KNOWLEDGE AND INQUIRY

"Teaching is intentional – one must teach something – and the teacher must see what is being taught" (Clark, 2005, p. 296), leading to questions about whether the intentions have been achieved, or uncertainty about how to teach more efficiently. For the teacher, there is "relatively little hard evidence of 'what works'" (D. H. Hargreaves, 1997, p. 410). Teachers need a practice model that enables them to cumulatively build knowledge by drawing upon diverse perspectives to make meaning and gain insight from ongoing experiences (Korthagen, Loughran, & Russell, 2006).

Teacher theorising about the "complexity, artistry, and the demandingness of classroom teaching" (Clark, 1988, p. 11) is broadly referred to as practical knowledge (Elbaz, 1981). Connelly and Clandinin (1988) characterised this knowledge as emerging from past personal experience, informing current and future practice. Clandinin (1985) contends that practical knowledge is neither entirely theoretical nor simply practical. Rather, it is a contextually grounded dynamic blend of formal and informal knowledge (Hoekstra & Korthagen, 2011). This leads to the blending of technical knowledge with an intuitive or practised sense of what is likely to work – Darling-Hammond's (2010) "wisdom of practice", Berlin's (1996) "practical wisdom", or Buitink's (2009) "practical theories". It is what Lunenberg and Korthagen (2009, p. 226) identified as a capacity to "deal 'wisely' with particular situations in the course of teaching."

Elbaz (1981, p. 46) defined practical knowledge as "encompassing knowledge *of* practice as well as knowledge mediated *by* practice." This refers to knowledge that is constructed through ongoing experience and interaction with different perspectives about the meaning of that experience. In this way, a teacher's practical knowledge is developed through the practice of being a teacher and through integrated interaction with other teachers.

While teaching knowledge is exemplified as practical (what works), it also involves theorising about practice (what else might work). Cochran-Smith and Lytle (1999) describe this iterative knowledge building process as practical inquiry. Teacher, or practical, inquiry is relevant to address the questions, dilemmas and needs located in a teacher's day-to-day contextual interactions with other teachers and students (Grangeat & Gray, 2008; Richardson, 1994).

A principal driver of teacher knowledge development is the process of practitioner inquiry that sits on the "border between research and teaching" (Hammer & Schifter, 2001, p. 441). While practitioner inquiry is broadly congruent with the notion of teacher as researcher, it emphasises localised action rather than abstraction. One powerful form of practitioner inquiry is interactions with other teachers, hence recent consideration of professional learning communities (Grangeat & Gray, 2008). Lieberman and Mace (2010) identified two drivers for this trend: a move from isolated to collegial practice; changes in school learning space, including physical and virtual, affording an environment where teaching practice becomes more social and public. These collaborative levers have allowed informal and formal sharing of ideas, knowledge, values and orientation of teachers across a range of contexts; leading to questions about effectiveness of teaching approaches and means of improving standards and practice (Clark, 1988; Cochran-Smith & Lytle, 1999).

Hammer and Schifter (2001) identified that practitioner inquiry is directed towards action in immediate time and space, largely invisible, and reliant on observation and a sense of what is happening in the classroom. This inquiry is also not systematic, as the focus narrows onto a pressing issue, usually conducted in isolation, and involves personal and non-critical reflection. These informal processes offer important practice-based knowledge as a basis for teaching activity (Gallimore, Ermeling, Saunders, & Goldenberg, 2009).

Yet there is also a need for dynamic "iterative engagement in constructing and reconstructing professional knowledge using various perspectives" (Kelly, 2006, p. 509). This requires an intensity of thinking about the complexity, uncertainty, and unpredictability of the interaction between teaching and learning (Clark, 1988; Hoekstra & Korthagen, 2011; Zeichner, 2010). Borko (2004, p. 8) commented that the key question becomes "how can teachers represent the knowledge they acquire in a more principled and abstract form than in the past, while retaining its practical character?"

Investigating the narrative of teacher reasoning and practice "means delving into the subtle interplay between the intractability of social institutions and the options they offer for agents who have knowledge ... of how those institutions work" (Giddens, 1989, p. 298). One means of representing knowledge is through becoming a reflective practitioner (Schon, 1983; Yost, Sentner, & Forlenza-Bailey, 2000). Loughran (2002) makes the point that the framing and reframing of a problem is a crucial part of knowing about teaching. Reflecting on experience has the potential to change or clarify understanding, leading to reasoning about alternative activities (Boud, Keogh, & Walker, 1985). Collaboration through a practitioner inquiry process is envisaged here as the means to meld personal and social reflection with the generation of teacher practical knowledge. Practitioner inquiry involves a mindful awareness of current experience, opportunities and problems, and the reflective element makes "conscious and explicit the dynamic interplay between thinking and action" (Leitch & Day, 2000, p. 181).

Practitioner inquiry involves an examination of an experience in terms of physical, social and structural-contextual interactions (Clandinin, Pushor, & Orr, 2007). This approach recognises that personal, social, and cultural narratives are as significant as pedagogical content knowledge (Goodwin, 2010; Kelly, 2006).

Shulman and Shulman (2004, p. 259) propose a model of teacher communities that afford engagement in "theory-rich, open-ended, content-intensive classrooms." The model requires teachers to have a vision of what they want, be motivated to achieve this, understand contributing concepts and principles, be able to transform practice, be capable of learning by reflecting on experience, and to participate in a learning community (Shulman & Shulman, 2004).

This is consistent with Giddens' (1984, p. 71) definition of context as "strips of time-space" that are more widely connected to the "broader properties of social life" (Giddens, 1984, p. 119). This is another way of saying that while teacher knowledge is generated through personal practice, there are "elements of teacher knowledge that are shared by all teachers or large groups of teachers" (Verloop et al., 2001, p. 441). It is contextualised action that provides the possibilities and constraints influencing (as perceived and then reasoned into) teaching practice. This approach attempts to identify teacher conceptions and subsequent reasoned application of theorised ideas in practice, while being alert to the argument that educational transactions are "essentially contested" (Clark, 2005, p. 293).

TEACHER ADAPTATION THROUGH CONTEXTUALISED INQUIRY: A CASE STUDY

This case study is an account of the process of practitioner inquiry grounded in the dynamic process of adaptation to open-plan learning communities. Following Elbaz (1981), this case of practitioner inquiry demonstrates how teachers theorise about the possibilities and constraints of their practice, and how this theorising is mediated by their practice.

Problem Recognition

Dewey (1938/2008) claimed that problems are merely unclear situations, and inquiry is the process of seeking clarification. This stage of inquiry involves problem recognition, including identifying the sociocultural context, and relational interactions. "Problems which induce inquiry grow out of the relations of fellow beings to one another, and … the meanings which have developed in the course of living" (Dewey, 1938/2008, p. 42).

The process of practitioner inquiry was initiated within Grevillea College by the senior management team who were questioning whether the learning spaces were being used in an optimal way. The senior staff wanted teachers, when they were planning learning activities, to overtly think about how they were going to use the open-plan learning spaces. The shift was to broaden teacher thinking from content and pedagogy to consider the 'openness' concept and context.

The school had already instituted a lesson model, used by all teaching staff. This lesson model required teachers to address a series of questions related to the beginning of the lesson (e.g., what are your learning intentions and success criteria), explicit teaching (e.g., how will you teach the concept or skill?), guided practice (e.g., what activities will you ask students to undertake?), differentiation (e.g., which students do you anticipate will need additional support, and how will you provide it?), application (e.g., what independent practice will students undertake?), and review (e.g., how will you get students to reflect on their achievements?). The lesson model encouraged pedagogy of explicit teaching followed by application through independent or small-group activities, followed by guided review at the conclusion of the lesson. The implication was that explicit instruction would take place at the lesson's start and end, while students' learning activities would be afforded by the open-plan learning environment.

Analysis of Key Elements

Grevillea College held a learning spaces audit as a reference point for ongoing planning for professional learning. The author, part of the university-based Improving Regional Secondary Students' Learning and Wellbeing (IRL) team, became involved at this point.

Table 2.1 shows how each way of knowing (practice and abstract knowledge) can act as a resource in the interactions of a professional community of inquiry (Ottesen, 2007). The first column shows the questions identified by the senior staff members of the school. The questions had formed the basis of developing the local lesson-planning framework. The third column identifies the questions formulated by the IRL project team. These questions formed the basis of a number of different investigations and case studies. The central column is an integration of both practical (school staff members) and theoretical (university project team) perspectives; and acknowledges the distributed nature of expertise. The answers generated to these questions informed, to some extent, the resolution of both perspectives.

Table 2.1. *Integrating practical and abstract considerations*

Senior staff questions (Practical)	Practitioner inquiry (Integrated)	University researcher questions (Theoretical)
What works?	What main teaching strategies are currently used in the open-plan classroom?	What does quality learning look like in an open-plan environment?
How to use the classroom space more effectively?	What is the most successful strategy currently used in our open-plan classrooms?	How do open-plan environments interact productively with pedagogy?
	What are the main enablers and constraints of changes to our teaching?	

Trialling and Review

The trialling and review stage was action-oriented, based on inquiry into ongoing and possible practice. A survey was generated asking all teachers to identify a space they regularly taught in, what approaches they used, what approaches they would like to use, and what may afford or constrain effective teaching and learning in that space. From a population of 45 teachers, 32 responded to the survey. The survey provided an overview of practice that was discussed with senior staff members, with a focus on what they thought quality teaching was in an open-plan classroom context, and what practical wisdom they could pass on to teachers about working in this type of environment. This process asked teachers and senior staff members to draw directly on their experience and reasoning for practice. In the survey analysis each learning environment appeared to have a number of agreed routine pedagogical interactions, outlined in Table 2.2.

The different learning environments were seen as enabling a range of practices, with innovative practice a possibility. It was possible to identify a common narrative through the individual teacher theorising around shared experience in terms of physical, social, and structural contextual interactions (Clandinin et al., 2007):

> There is ample space to allow one to have to freedom to be fluid and flexible in one's approach… occasionally. (Teacher 28)

> Space-specific strategies were seen as emerging from conventional practice, rather than a radical shift. (Teacher 23)

> Good teaching will occur regardless; it is just more difficult if you are in the wrong environment. (Teacher 22)

In the neighbourhood the most common practice was to start with explicit teaching, usually based around a whiteboard, followed by small group or independent work with students more dispersed. Student choices appeared to be related to the type of task, where they conducted the task, and whether they worked individually or in small groups. Technology was used by students regularly. The large neighbourhood spaces enabled movement of students and the ability for students to move to a comfortable location for work:

> To have flexibility in drawing students in to provide explicit instruction, then to allow students to choose a space when given the opportunity to work on collaborative or independent activities. (Teacher 18)

The Socratic studio was mainly used for explicit teaching, media, and class discussion. There was a close link between the enclosed and relatively small space and its primary use for learning tasks requiring interaction and related noise. The Da Vinci studio, used mainly for science and art teaching, was used for project, inquiry and experiment-based learning approaches. Again, there was a link between the purpose-built nature of the space and the teaching and learning approach. The Einstein area was the least formally organised space, used as a break-out area for independent and small-group work.

A MODEL OF TEACHER ADAPTATION TO OPEN-PLAN SETTINGS

Table 2.2. A map of teacher practical knowledge

Learning environment	What currently works?	What might work?
Neighbourhood • Flexible teaching and learning practices • Varied furniture types and layouts	Explicit teaching Flexibility to allow students to choose space for work Social learning Use of technology	Increased sharing resources and ideas between colleagues Social learning Expanded use of technology Productive learning Self-directed learning
Socratic Studio • Enclosed teaching space • Audio-visual resources	Explicit teaching Use of media Class discussion	Use of interactive technology Increased student autonomy
Da Vinci Studio • Arts and Science learning • Project space	Explicit teaching Experiments Project-based learning Social learning	Exploring models of learning through experimentation Multi-disciplinary project work
Einstein Area • Breakout space • Main entry/exit to learning community	Independent and small-group work Break-out area Informal interaction	More opportunities for independent learning – (structured and scaffolded)

The teachers also had a common perspective about what they wanted to do in the spaces. Several teachers indicated they wanted to be involved in more team teaching or collegial practices such as sharing ideas and resources. They identified that these practices could be supported by strategic timetabling, more time for collaborative planning, observation, discussion, and reflection with other teachers:

> It is easy to be flexible, reflective and change your approach when you get to plan, teach and reflect in collaboration with others. The key thing is teaching together. (Teacher 3)

> The open learning spaces have allowed me to make regular informal observations of colleagues at work, picking up many strategies that I have successfully implemented into my classroom. (Teacher 6)

The teachers also indicated they wanted to enact more independent learning strategies including inquiry or project-based approaches. An increase in the use of technology, perhaps for social learning or interaction, was also indicated. The teachers thought that this could be enabled by access to specific instructions on how to structure and scaffold these approaches, and sharing practical suggestions on how to teach with the different spaces.

A key area for continued development was to improve the productivity of the learning spaces. There seemed to be a major emphasis on explicit teaching and controlling and shaping student activity as a precursor to student movement and use of the space for required learning tasks:

> Students lose focus due to the open and distractive nature of the open learning areas. (Teacher 13)

Teachers generally indicated a need to build student capacity for more autonomous work. A key teacher adaptation focus was therefore on balancing explicit teaching, which appears as a dominant pedagogical hinge for most learning activities, and the development of student autonomy. This was the basis for subsequent teacher development planning.

Explicit instruction was seen as the lynchpin, ideally providing a form of scaffold that shaped and focused student effort, but did not always tell students what, how, when, and where to complete a task (thus encouraging autonomy). The dilemma for senior staff members from the inquiry process was now precisely how to better incorporate the learning spaces into pedagogy?

The teacher responses indicated a conceptually-sensitive adaptation to the open-plan learning environment contexts (Deed, Lesko, & Lovejoy, 2014). These adaptations included the use of pedagogy that was contextually grounded, attempts to increase student agency, and some consideration to team- and collegial-teaching practice. Most apparent was the lack of aggression and conflict in the form of recurring student management issues, perhaps as a result of the humanising and democratising influence of the neighbourhood affordances. This was noted by all teachers during informal conversations as part of ongoing site visits and observations over the three years of the IRL project.

From Inquiry to Action

Based on the map of what was working and teacher perceptions of action possibilities, the senior staff members discussed how to effectively use the neighbourhood learning spaces. These discussions were influenced by university staff trying to resolve their own conceptual questions. As a result of these abstract and practical considerations the school and university jointly identified, as a starting point, a set of teaching strategies than were conducive to teaching in open-plan learning environments. These strategies represented a focus, generated through the inquiry process, for the next stage of on-the-ground teacher adaptation. The strategies emerged from the gap between *what* works and *what might* work, as identified in discussions between the teachers and university staff. The strategies were:

- moving from individual to collegial team-teaching by learning across disciplines, and extending learning within a discipline;
- increasing student autonomy by designing tasks that afford selecting, enacting, monitoring, and adapting personal learning strategies, and active construction of knowledge;

- increased student use of emerging technologies with an emphasis on social learning through virtual collaboration, and multi-media to represent and communicate what they have learnt;
- enactment of pedagogy for deep learning and critical thinking, including multiple solutions or solution pathways, and effortful elaborations and analysis;
- making teacher and student learning visible in the classroom by representation and communication of the learning experience, and explanation of the causes of learning success or failure.

The process reported here is somewhat circular, as each inquiry stage leads to further questioning and propositions about practice development. However, the case demonstrates how the general process of practitioner inquiry, grounded in the conceptual (university driven) and contextual interactions (practical knowledge and day-to-day activity), can inform localised and focused teacher learning and adaptation. As noted by Dewey (1938/2008, p. 140): "There is continuity in inquiry. The conclusions reached in one inquiry become means, material and procedural, of carrying on further inquiries."

A MODEL OF TEACHER ADAPTATION

Contemporary open-plan classroom spaces express and authorise conceptions of school-less space, humanism, democracy, agency, community and flexibility. Although not suggesting linear causality between space and pedagogy, there is a likely conceptually-sensitive adaptation to openness: different and experimental pedagogy, increased student agency, distributed expertise, interdisciplinary and team teaching within neighbourhoods, variable class size, and use of informal and irregular space and time for learning (Deed & Lesko, 2015). Following this, a model is proposed of teacher adaptation to their working environment.

The discussion is framed by a refined version of a model proposed by Lunenberg and Korthagen (2009) of a triarchic relationship between practical knowledge, theory, and contextualised experience. Lunenberg and Korthhagen's (2009) original model is represented by the shaded triangle, in Figure 2.1. In the refined version here, theory has been replaced by different perspectives, and an agency dimension added.

This model shows that teachers employ knowledge gained from both experience and interactions with different perspectives to inform and shape their actions. It also makes clear the role of agency as a means of reacting in different ways to a context. This model relies on its abstraction to achieve its purpose of identifying some of the key interactions in teacher development. It is acknowledged that these relationships and outcomes are open to ongoing negotiation and questioning (Schon, 1983). This model of knowledge development and action identifies some interactions that could be employed to strategically influence teacher adaptation (Bronkhorst, Meijer, Koster, & Vermunt, 2011). The model emphasises that specific practical knowledge is a requirement for making any change work (Mehta, 2013).

C. DEED

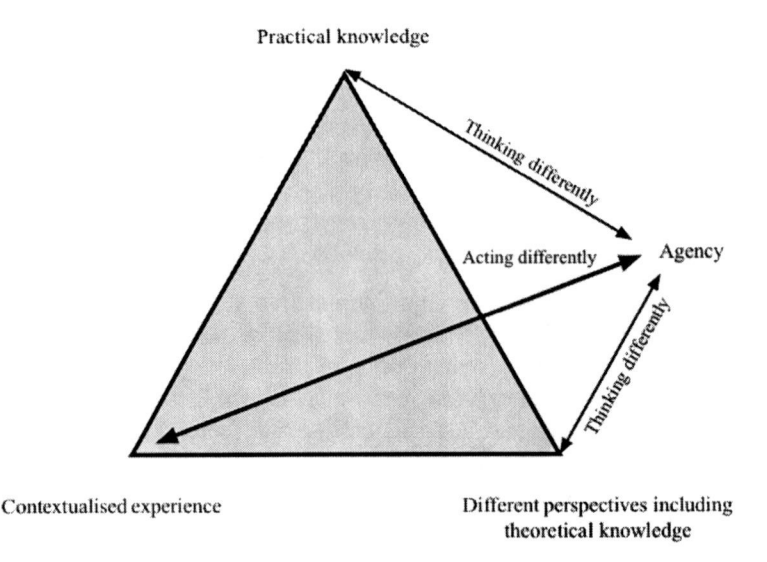

Figure 2.1. Teacher adaptation (context, knowledge & agency)

The model identifies that the practical question of what works can be resolved by consideration of the interaction between an individual's knowledge base, context, and the distributed expertise of peers and university staff. This does not suggest that a specific outcome of this process can be up-scaled or replicable. Rather, a model of the interactive process and critical elements of expert adaptation can be applied to different contexts. This accords with Mehta (2013, pp. 481–482) who asserts that this approach is appropriate for a study of teacher knowledge and learning, rather than the "clinical, relatively decision-free form we see in medicine … because the real-time demands are too great and the impact of any given decision is highly context dependent."

The axis from *practical knowledge* to *contextualised experience* applies to the immediacy of classroom interactions. This refers to intuitive decisions, routine action or instant reaction (Eraut, 1995). Teachers are bound by the day-to-day intensity of their practice, meaning there is an immediateness and concentration of concern with what works. The addition of *different perspectives* to this axis adds a degree of abstraction and criticality to the building of teacher knowledge. Different perspectives also include theoretical knowledge; provided in this case by university research staff. This interaction between individual teacher practical knowledge and different perspectives is a characteristic typical of a community of learning. These interactions can also be seen as reflective learning processes involving deliberate analysis, decision making and practice (Bronkhorst et al., 2011; Eraut, 1995). The authority for a community of practice is perhaps generated by the open-plan environment, allowing informal observation or discussion with other teachers within the learning neighbourhoods. More formal team planning, teaching, or review may also allow interaction with different perspectives. In the case reported here the use of the survey also enabled this interaction. The accessing of the distributed expertise of peers also ensures an informal validation or testing (or perhaps even a stimulus) process against the reality of daily routine work (Mehta, 2013).

An adaptive dimension is included in this model, identifying how *agency* is needed to enact knowledge-in-action. Imaginative manoeuvring to connect with the future is a significant characteristic of human agency (Dewey, 1981). This highlights the agentic orientation and underpinning of teacher adaptation as a contextualised activity; the tension and interplay between agency and structure must be accounted for in any examination of adaptability to workplace change (Emirbayer & Mische, 1998).

Each of these perceptions, possibilities and constraints, interactions and deliberations is grounded in contextual experience. Agency, as a driver of adaptation, is about deliberately shaping the learning environment by responding to the unique expressions and authorisations of experience of teaching and learning as part of that experience. The reflexive version of agency shown in the model balances realism or pragmatism of teaching with the action possibilities of open-plan learning environments. This is the contextualising of knowledge and action: teacher development grounded in practice. Exertion of individual agency in a social classroom context may also encounter different purposes requiring negotiation between staff or students to determine rules, roles and agendas (Alterator & Deed, 2013).

Agency has multiple meanings, but here it is conceptualised as a key component of teacher adaptation. This is demonstrated when a teacher makes a reasoned or knowledgeable choice that is sensitive to the context for action. The implication is that a teacher must be aware of their perceptions and reasoning, and have a view of their own learning as a process of resolving the contestability of different classroom contexts. The model outlined here assumes that teacher knowledge and action goes beyond individual activity, and includes collaborative and critical aspects, based on a disposition and capacity to engage with contextual expressions and authorisations (Deed & Lesko, 2015). Agency becomes transformative when it draws on and informs a collective knowledge base (Mehta, Gomez, & Byrk, 2012).

The case showed that teacher adaptation in new spaces is about acknowledging that the space is perceived and represented by multiple perspectives, contributing to a more complex framing and shaping of the learning environment. The use of what might be characterised as an informal and distributed professional-learning community model drew upon the breadth and depth of perspectives, including questions, needs and routines of teachers trying to make the spaces work on a day-to-day basis.

The model addresses the process of adaptation or "practicalising theoretical knowledge" (Cheng, Tang, & Cheng, 2012, p. 789). Cheng and colleagues (2012) suggested this process includes identifying, through experimentation, reflection and adaptation, strategies that are workable from multiple perspectives. In other words, agency, or the capacity to imagine and act differently, is inherent in the practicalising of teacher knowledge (otherwise referred to as teacher adaptation). Following Dewey (1896), knowledge, evident in teachers' practical reasoning, emerges from attempts to resolve practical questions from the classroom, melding of abstract with practical ideas. The model makes clear that it is individual and collective teacher's knowledge of their work and workplace that supports exercising judgement and discretionary decision making (Mehta, 2013).

IMPLICATIONS AND CONCLUSIONS

The process of teacher adaptation is conceived of within an action-oriented frame, grounded in a narrative of possibility and constraint as expressed and authorised by the open-plan learning environments. This is not an idealised model of collective transformation, rather a set of diverse individuals theorising and enacting practice. At the individual level, each teacher had to determine their readiness to engage with professional learning and address the question of how to situate inquiry within the narrative and culture of teaching and learning at that school.

Teacher adaptation is conceptualised and demonstrated in the case study as a dynamic alignment of context, knowledge (including perceptions of action possibilities and power to act differently), and institutional constraints. In many ways this precludes an orderly binding of the transition and consolidation phases (as conceived for example in the model proposed by Blackmore et al., 2011). Rather, there appears to be a space between these two phases, where agency is subject to the mitigating weight of institutional routine. This is not to offer a pessimistic version of adaptation. Rather, it suggests that a space does exist for thinking and acting differently, and that this is generated from the expressions and authorisations of the up-scaled open-plan environment (Deed & Lesko, 2015). Further research is required to examine in-depth the conditions and influences on the achievement of consolidated and sustainable stages of adaptation.

Based on the literature and this discussion, it is clear that the process of teacher adaptation and exercise of agency in open-plan learning communities has the following characteristics:

- while the abstract nature of open-plan learning environments affords a number of possibilities, these must be balanced with the day-to-day routines of school-based teaching;
- teacher adaptation is a personally and collectively contested processes, situated in specific contexts, although shaped by larger agendas of school and social change;
- adaptation refers to taking control over an experience through an intense (although largely practical) inquiry process;

- each teacher will make a reasoned choice about their teaching practice, balancing routine with difference;
- teacher reasoning about what might work will be based on their practical knowledge about what works;
- teacher adaptation involves moving from the immediacy of classroom interactions to building knowledge by seeking and critically interacting with diverse perspectives;
- although teacher adaptation is a personalised experience, these processes draw upon and inform a collective knowledge base

The university has a key role in teacher adaptation, in particular to:

- recognise university and school-based expertise as unique contributors to the knowledge building processes of practitioner inquiry;
- frame teacher adaptation through a critical examination of teacher perceptions and reasoning about contextualised experience;
- contest habitual practice through the introduction of a range of conceptual questions and strategies informed by research.

This chapter has demonstrated that the possibility of teacher adaptation being effective improves when it involves thinking and enactment of quality teaching practice grounded in contextual experience. Further, teacher adaptation to new contexts involves a focus on identified strengths and strategic imagining of different ways of being. This expression of agency is informed by an orientation to both adapt and critically question that adaptation.

REFERENCES

Alterator, S., & Deed, C. (2013). Teacher adaptation to open learning spaces. *Issues in Educational Research, 23*(3), 315–330. Retrieved from http://www.iier.org.au/iier23/alterator.html

Berlin, I. (1996). *The sense of reality*. London, UK: Chatto & Windus.

Blackmore, J., Bateman, D., Loughlin, J., O'Mara, J., & Aranda, G. (2011). *Research into the connection between built learning spaces and student outcomes: Literature review*, Melbourne, Australia: Department of Education and Early Childhood Development, East Melbourne, Victoria. Retrieved from http://dro.deakin.edu.au/eserv/DU:30036968/blackmore-researchinto-2011.pdf

Borko, H. (2004). Professional development and teacher learning: Mapping the terrain. *Educational Researcher, 33*(8), 3–15. doi:10.3102/0013189x033008003

Boud, D., Keogh, R., & Walker, D. (1985). *Reflection: Turning experience into learning*. London, UK: Kogan Page.

Bronkhorst, L., Meijer, P., Koster, B., & Vermunt, J. (2011). Fostering meaning-oriented learning and deliberate practice in teacher education. *Teaching and Teacher Education, 27*, 1120–1130. doi:10.1016/j.tate.2011.05.008

Buitink, J. (2009). What and how do student teachers learn during school-based teacher education? *Teaching and Teacher Education, 25*(1), 118–127. doi:10.1016/j.tate.2008.07.009

Cheng, M. M. H., Tang, S. Y. F., & Cheng, A. Y. N. (2012). Practicalising theoretical knowledge in student teachers' professional learning in initial teacher education. *Teaching and Teacher Education, 28*(6), 781–790. doi:10.1016/j.tate.2012.02.008

Clandinin, D. J. (1985). Personal practical knowledge: A study of teachers' classroom images. *Curriculum Inquiry, 15*(4), 361–385. doi:10.2307/1179683

Clandinin, D. J., Pushor, D., & Orr, A. M. (2007). Navigating sites for narrative inquiry. *Journal of Teacher Education, 58*(1), 21–35. doi:10.1177/0022487106296218

Clark, C. (1988). Asking the right questions about teacher preparation: Contributions of research on teacher thinking. *Educational Researcher, 17*(5), 5–12. doi:10.3102/0013189x017002005

Clark, C. (2005). The structure of educational research. *British Educational Research Journal, 31*(3), 289–308. doi:10.1080/01411920500082128

Cochran-Smith, M., & Lytle, S. L. (1999). The teacher research movement: A decade later. *Educational Researcher, 28*(7), 15–25. doi:10.3102/0013189x028007015

Connelly, F. M., & Clandinin, D. J. (1988). *Teachers as curriculum planners: Narratives of experience.* New York, NY: Teachers' College.

Darling-Hammond, L. (2006). Constructing 21st-century teacher education. *Journal of Teacher Education, 57*(3), 300–314. doi:10.1177/0022487105285962

Darling-Hammond, L. (2010). Teacher education and the American future. *Journal of Teacher Education, 61*(1–2), 35–47. doi:10.1177/0022487109348024

Deed, C., & Lesko, T. (2015). 'Unwalling' the classroom: Teacher reaction and adaptation. *Learning Environments Research.* doi:10.1007/s10984-015-9181-6

Deed, C., Lesko, T., & Lovejoy, V. (2014). Teacher adaptation to personalized learning spaces. *Teacher Development, 18*(3), 369–383. doi:10.1080/13664530.2014.919345

Dewey, J. (1896). The university school. *University Record (University of Chicago), 1,* 417–419.

Dewey, J. (1938/2008). Logic: The theory of inquiry. *The later works of John Dewey* (Vol. 12). Carbondale, IL: Southern Illinois University Press.

Dewey, J. (1981). The need for a recovery of philosophy. In J. J. McDermott (Ed.), *The philosophy of John Dewey* (pp. 58–97). Chicago, IL: University of Chicago Press.

Elbaz, F. (1981). The teacher's "practical knowledge": Report of a case study. *Curriculum Inquiry, 11*(1), 43–71. doi:10.2307/1179510

Emirbayer, M., & Mische, A. (1998). What is agency? *The American Journal of Sociology, 103*(4), 962–1023. doi:10.1086/231294

Eraut, M. (1995). Schon shock: A case for refraining reflection-in-action? *Teachers and Teaching: Theory and Practice, 1*(1), 9–22. doi:10.1080/1354060950010102

Gallimore, R., Ermeling, B., Saunders, W., & Goldenberg, C. (2009). Moving the learning of teaching closer to practice: Teacher education implications of school-based inquiry teams. *The Elementary School Journal, 109*(5), 537–553. doi:10.1086/597001

Giddens, A. (1984). *The constitution of society: Outline of the theory of structuration.* Cambridge, MA: Polity Press.

Giddens, A. (1989). A reply to my critics. In D. Held & J. B. Thompson (Eds.), *Social theory of modern societies: Anthony Giddens and his critics.* Cambridge, England: Cambridge University Press.

Goodwin, A. L. (2010). Globalization and the preparation of quality teachers: Rethinking knowledge domains for teaching. *Teaching Education, 21*(1), 19–32. doi:10.1080/10476210903466901

Grangeat, M., & Gray, P. (2008). Teaching as collective work: Analysis, current research and implications for teacher education. *Journal of Education for Teaching, 34*(3), 177–189. doi:10.1080/02607470802212306

Hammer, D., & Schifter, D. (2001). Practices of inquiry in teaching and research. *Cognition and Instruction, 19*(4), 441–478. doi:10.1207/S1532690XCI1904_2

Hargreaves, A. (2003). *Teaching in the knowledge society: Education in the age of insecurity.* Maidenhead, England: Open University Press.

Hargreaves, D. H. (1997). In defence of research for evidence-based teaching: A rejoinder to Martyn Hammersley. *British Educational Research Journal, 23*(4), 405–419. doi:10.1080/0141192970230402

Hoekstra, A., & Korthagen, F. A. (2011). Teacher learning in a context of educational change: Informal learning versus systematically supported learning. *Journal of Teacher Education, 62*(1), 76–92. doi:10.1177/0022487110382917

Kelly, P. (2006). What is teacher learning? A socio-cultural perspective. *Oxford Review of Education, 32*(4), 505–519. doi:10.1080/03054980600884227

Korthagen, F. A. (2010). Situated learning theory and the pedagogy of teacher education: Towards an integrative view of teacher behavior and teacher learning. *Teaching and Teacher Education, 26*(1), 98–106. doi:10.1016/j.tate.2009.05.001

Korthagen, F. A., Loughran, J., & Russell, T. (2006). Developing fundamental principles for teacher education programs and practices. *Teaching and Teacher Education, 22*(8), 1020–1041. doi:10.1016/j.tate.2006.04.022

Leitch, R., & Day, C. (2000). Action research and reflective practice: Towards a holistic view. *Educational Action Research, 8*(1), 179–193. doi:10.1080/09650790000200108

Lieberman, A., & Mace, D. P. (2010). Making practice public: Teacher learning in the 21st century. *Journal of Teacher Education, 61*(1–2), 77–88. doi:10.1177/0022487109347319

Loughran, J. (2002). Effective reflective practice: In search of meaning in learning about teaching. *Journal of Teacher Education, 53*(1), 33–43. doi:10.1177/0022487102053001004

Lunenberg, M., & Korthagen, F. A. (2009). Experience, theory, and practical wisdom in teaching and teacher education. *Teachers and Teaching: Theory and Practice, 15*(2), 225–240. doi:10.1080/13540600902875316

Mehta, J. (2013). From bureaucracy to profession: Remaking the educational sector for the twenty-first century. *Harvard Educational Review, 83*(3), 463–488. Retrieved from http://search.proquest.com.ez.library.latrobe.edu.au/docview/1434423566?accountid=12001

Mehta, J., Gomez, L., & Byrk, A. S. (2012). Building on practical knowledge: The key to a stronger profession is learning from the field. In J. Mehta, R. B. Schwartz, & F. M. Hess (Eds.), *The futures of school reform* (pp. 35–64). Cambridge, MA: Harvard Education Press.

Meirink, J. A., Imants, J., Meijer, P., & Verloop, N. (2010). Teacher learning and collaboration in innovative teams. *Cambridge Journal of Education, 40*(2), 161–181. doi:10.1080/0305764X.2010.481256

Misak, C. J. (2007). *New pragmatists*. Oxford, England: Oxford University Press.

Ottesen, E. (2007). Teachers "in the making": Building accounts of teaching. *Teaching and Teacher Education, 23*, 612–623. doi:10.1016/j.tate.2007.01.011

Pridham, B., Deed, C., & Cox, P. (2013). Workplace-based practicum: Enabling expansive practices. *Australian Journal of Teacher Education, 38*(4). doi:10.14221/ajte.2013v38n4.7

Putnam, R. T., & Borko, H. (2000). What do new views of knowledge and thinking have to say about research on teacher learning? *Educational Researcher, 29*(1), 4–15. doi:10.3102/0013189x029001004

Richardson, V. (1994). Conducting research on practice. *Educational Researcher, 23*(5), 5–10. doi:10.3102/0013189x023005005

Schon, D. (1983). *The reflective practitioner: How professionals think in action*. New York, NY: Basic Books.

Shulman, L. S. (1987). Knowledge and teaching: Foundations of the new reform. *Harvard Educational Review, 57*(1), 1–21.

Shulman, L. S., & Shulman, J. H. (2004). How and what teachers learn: A shifting perspective. *Journal of Curriculum Studies, 36*(2), 257–271. doi:10.1080/0022027032000148298

Sternberg, R. J., & Horvath, J. A. (1995). A prototype view of expert teaching. *Educational Researcher, 24*(6), 9–17. doi:10.3102/0013189x024006009

Verloop, N., Van Driel, J., & Meijer, P. (2001). Teacher knowledge and the knowledge base of teaching. *International Journal of Educational Research, 35*, 441–461. doi:10.1016/s0883-0355(02)00003-4

Yost, D. S., Sentner, S. M., & Forlenza-Bailey, A. (2000). An examination of the construct of critical reflection: Implications for teacher education programming in the 21st century. *Journal of Teacher Education, 51*(1), 39–49. doi:10.1177/002248710005100105

Zeichner, K. (2010). Rethinking the connections between campus courses and field experiences in college- and university-based teacher education. *Journal of Teacher Education, 61*(1–2), 89–99. doi:10.1177/0022487109347671

CRAIG DEED

3. USING A GAME-DESIGN PROJECT TO AFFORD TEACHER AND STUDENT AGENCY

AGENCY

How is agency imagined and enacted by teachers and students as the restraints of the enclosed classroom are peeled away? This question is considered here by drawing on socio-cultural theories to examine the mutuality of teacher and student agency in a personalised learning environment. This discussion takes into account the literature and is demonstrated by a case study of the complex interplay of expectations and perceptions of self and others during teaching and learning.

Agency is a complex interplay between the teacher and student and the active affordances and constraints of the context. This chapter starts with Giddens' (1984) notion of agency, broadly characterised as the capacity to *act differently*. This introduces the notion of capacity and power, key cultural constructs useful in any consideration of building capacity of low socio-economic students. In this case, the construct of agency frames an examination of teacher and student interactions within a personalised learning context that affords an "imaginative distance from (habitual responses)" (Emirbayer & Mische, 1998, p. 1006).

Here, agency is considered in terms of personalised learning. In a personalised learning environment, the students' developmental needs, capabilities, perspectives, and approaches to learning are addressed (Prain et al., 2014). In this context, influences on teacher and student agency are multi-faceted and complexly inter-related. While teachers and students have routine ways of acting in a conventional classroom, a personalised learning context affords different, non-routine, versions of agency (Johnson & Liber, 2008). This is of particular relevance to an examination of agency as a lever of teacher and student engagement and learning. This is consistent with the argument that, in new or alternative contexts, agents "must explain and underpin their actions and choices by 'rational' arguments rather than by referring to 'traditional' ways of doing things" (Brannen & Nilsen, 2005, p. 416).

It is useful to apply Edwards' (2007, p. 7) discussion of "relational agency" to any rationalisation of the exercise of teacher and student agency. In particular, the tendency for both to demarcate, and then continuously and reflexively redefine, relative spheres of influence (Edwards, 2011). Relational agency acknowledges the role of individual capacity and purpose, but makes the point that interaction (student-student, student-teacher, teacher-teacher) contributes to a dynamic common knowledge. Reflexive mutuality is evident as teachers and students engage with the others' intentions and actions in the classroom. In the case examined in this chapter, this mutuality occurs between the teacher's design and implementation of a personalised curriculum, and an expectation that students take responsibility for their learning. This chapter addresses the question therefore, of the nature and scope of both teacher and student agency, sphere of influence, and its exercise; and how this contributes to the creation, sustainability, and refinement of the culture of personalised learning.

Student agency is grounded in their experience, enactment, and knowledge of the conventions of the classroom context. Conventions are usefully seen as a loose set of understandings allowing considerable scope for students to react in a range of ways (King, 2000). Teaching approaches, such as those based on theories of cognitive constructivism, may assume inherent student agency. Constructs like student autonomy, self-regulated learning, and mastery approaches to learning, require agency in terms of different (and usually more complex) learning behaviours: for example, non-linear approaches to problem- solving (Scardamalia & Bereiter, 1991; Zimmerman, 2002).

Teacher agency emerges from a dynamic blend of theoretical, formal, practical, and informal knowledge and reasoning about teaching and learning (Clandinin, 1985; Hoekstra & Korthagen, 2011). Teacher practice knowledge is simultaneously drawn upon and rebuilt through day-to-day classroom activity and is evident in past experience, present thinking and action, and future planning (Connelly & Clandinin, 1988; Elbaz, 1981). Teacher agency may be characterised as somewhat practical in nature, based on perceptions about *what works* in their own classroom context (Hargreaves, 1997). However, there is also an element of projection in terms of *what might work*. Teacher agency then, is generated through perceptions, reactions, questioning, and adaptation to contextual activity (Cochran-Smith & Lytle, 1999). As noted by Ottesen (2007) and others, making sense of practice is continuous as teachers adapt to contextually ground experiences.

Agency for both teachers and students is an interaction between individual knowledge of conventional action, awareness of action possibilities for acting differently: and the opportunistic reasoning for realising this capacity. This can be characterised as an interdependent relationship between teacher, student and context (Campbell, Robinson, Neelands, Hewston, & Mazzoli, 2007). Consider, for example, the agency required when students engage in reflective problem-solving discussion (Paris & Paris, 2001). In terms of agency, students are likely to project themselves according to how they understand the context, as socially constructed through teacher and student interaction. In this example the teacher's capacity to afford reflection and the student's ability to be reflective will become apparent to each other and subsequently afford more refined versions of agency.

Teacher and student agency is nested within institutional, pedagogical, and sociocultural constraints, evident in perspectives of teaching and learning routines and roles and responsibilities (Prain et al., 2014). This is coherent with Greeno's (2009, p. 273) argument that "the context of an activity is constructed by participant(s) as a framing in the kind of social and discourse practice the participant(s) understand(s) her- or himself or themselves to be engaged in, rather than treating the context as something that is given in the situation." The teacher and students must imagine how they can and will adapt reflexively to the possibilities and constraints of classroom-based activity.

Agency can be characterised as a variable individual contestation of habitual teaching or learning practices in different learning spaces through a deliberate seeking of, and interaction with, other refined affordances, interpretations, and perspectives.

PERSONALISED LEARNING AND GAME DESIGN PEDAGOGY

There has been recent appreciation of how game design can inform approaches to effective pedagogy (see for example Gee, 2003). There is an emerging theoretical conceptualisation of the relationship between motivation, engagement, and complex problem-solving during game-based learning, including game design and play (Eseryel, Law, Ifenthaler, Ge, & Miller, 2014). Certainly the motivational aspects of digital game-based learning are well recorded (Hwang & Wu, 2012).

Game design and play requires knowledge of the skills and processes to simultaneously design, image, and critique a gaming experience (Salen, 2007). Digital game design includes problem-solving, strategic thinking, information processing, negotiation, collaborative investigation, and decision-making and self-regulation (Gros, 2007). There is particular emphasis on digital identity, online communities, and networks (Salen, 2007).

Game design characteristics are largely congruent with the principles and strategies of personalised learning (O'Neil, Wainess, & Baker, 2005). Specific features typical of game design include student negotiation of aspects of content, modes of investigative and problem-based learning, and peer review and assessment (D. Edwards, Deed, & Edwards, 2014). In this case, a key cultural affordance of agency is the way the teacher conceptualises how they will support student autonomy in relation to analytical discussion, research, and reflection (Gros, 2007). Building learner competence in new spaces is complex because the scaffolds tend to be collective and include the teacher as well as peers and web-based resources.

The pervasive use of social networking technology in game design and play accentuates the use of informal learning environments (Dabbagh & Kitsantas, 2012). This networked or collective intelligence affords use of multi-modal representation, accessing diverse opinions, and purposefully building knowledge through iteratively accessing, questioning, and applying ideas and experiences (Deed & Edwards, 2013).

The use of technology in game design allows students to shape their own learning, although this may be somewhat incoherent, or may be perceived as a disruption to the formal purposes of the teacher (Selwyn, 2009). Online gaming networks provide distributed environments that are easy to access and useful for building social and community identity, networking, and learning, and afford educational purposes including communication, collaboration, and resource sharing (Mazman & Usluel, 2010).

Learning afforded by technology is "unconstrained by time, place, or formal learning structures" (Oblinger, 2004, p. 4). Computers are frequently based in classrooms, or at designated learning stations or laboratories. Students also have access to mobile technology, including tablets and smart-phones. Although a dynamic concept, mobile learning environments typically include those created by an individual or group to achieve a learning purpose through the use of mobile technology (Collinson, 1999; Solvberg & Rismark, 2012). This afford new conceptions of learning as personalised, learner-centred, situated, collaborative, and ubiquitous (Collinson, 1999; Sharples, Taylor, & Vavoula, 2010).

In essence, a game design project sanctions teachers and students to exert new forms of agency, making choices about different teaching and learning structures and relationships (Collinson, 1999).

CASE STUDY: GAME DESIGN PROJECT

A game design case study demonstrates the complexity of the relational and nested interactions between agency and pedagogical approaches affording personalised learning. The purpose is to provide an example of how agency was projected and enacted by teachers and students. This case study focused on the teacher and 25 Years 9–10 male students in a Programming elective class unit, over a ten-week term at Grevillea College. Students elected to complete this unit based on either prior experience or an interest in programming; the aim was for students to design and create a digital game. As part of the process students had to enact core elements of game-design, including creating a storyline, rules and levels, and balancing gameplay with learning activities.

Data were collected through two interviews with the teacher, one in 2011 during an earlier iteration of this elective about planning and design for the following year, and one mid-term in 2012. Classroom observations were conducted for two hours a week over ten weeks in 2012. During the observation period, students were informally interviewed about their project, their interactions with peers and the teacher, their approach to problem-solving, and their evaluation of the project. In addition, students were asked to complete a brief survey identifying problems they had encountered and how they resolved these.

For the data analysis all observation and interview notes were transcribed. The broad categories of learning environment, personalised learning strategies, and teacher and student agency were used to inform the initial data review. Within each category a number of structural codes relating to choices and reasoning were identified (Saldana, 2009). The initial categories and codes were reviewed in a second and final analytical sweep of these data by the researchers. The key themes emerging were related to the linkages and relationships between teacher and student agency and personalised learning strategies.

Table 3.1 shows the Personalised Learning Experience Questionnaire (PLEQ) data (student perceptions of the extent to which their learning environment was personalised) for 2011–12, mean score for each of the nineteen scales, for males, Years 9–10, at Grevillea College (for a full discussion of the PLEQ please refer to Prain et al., 2014; Waldrip et al., 2014). These data indicate the general male student cohort perception of experienced learning practices at the school where the case study was located. Students who elected to enrol in the game design project were drawn from this cohort. Female students were not excluded from enrolling, but none did during the data collection period.

The scales with the lowest scores refer to practice that is experienced infrequently. It may be inferred that these practices are either: (a) the most difficult for a teacher to encourage; (b) the most difficult for a student to undertake; or (c) a combination of these two. This provides an indicative map of the context for teaching and learning affordances and constraints, and suggests a typical cohort experience. It is noted that each learning activity is both grounded in, and can act to modify these learning experiences.

Table 3.1. Grevillea college, years 9–10 males, 2011–12

Scales	Mean	N	Standard Deviation
Self-control	3.80	211	0.67
Self-management	3.70	216	0.62
Peer relations	3.53	211	0.92
Academic efficacy	3.44	212	0.89
Cognitive engagement	3.43	214	0.77
Desire for learning	3.37	209	0.80
Congruence with planned learning	3.32	217	0.80
Transparency	3.26	211	0.92
Behavioural engagement	3.23	216	0.87
Teacher support	3.20	213	0.95
Opportunities for personal development	3.17	209	0.96
Emotional engagement	3.10	211	0.99
Student negotiation	3.08	212	0.94
Authenticity	2.91	215	0.92
Personal relevance	2.90	216	0.94
Individualisation	2.84	201	0.85
Shared control	2.73	215	0.96
Student consultation	2.68	216	0.97
Self-reported disruptive behaviour	2.58	207	1.03

The five highest scoring scales were: self-control (mean = 3.80), self-management (3.70), peer relations (3.53), academic efficacy (3.44), and cognitive engagement (3.43). These scales indicate considerable student experience in some elements of agency, including: self-directed learning; positive and supportive peer relations; problem-solving and coping with challenging work; and making an effort to understand.

Excluding self-reported disruptive behaviour, the five lowest scoring scales were: authenticity (mean = 2.91); personal relevance (2.90); individualisation (2.84); shared control (2.73); and student consultation (2.68). These scales indicate students have limited experience in enacting certain elements of agency including: applying tasks to real life everyday situations outside of school; making choices about topics, use of materials or activities; and co-planning learning activities and assessment tasks with teachers. It may also be argued that teachers also typically struggle to afford a learning environment where these aspects of agency may flourish.

The game design project was designed to provide a personalised learning experience. While it did not explicitly address the low scoring scales above, it did focus on the use of a variety of resources, scaffolding for individual learning needs and approaches, teaching in a variety of ways, and enacting different teacher and student roles. This is coherent with Prain and colleagues (2014) who identified that personalised learning approaches are effective when there is a reasonable fit between individual learning perspectives, approaches to learning and capacity, and the demands of the learning activities. In relation to affording agency, the teacher, Jason, wanted students to take increased responsibility for their learning, and to develop collaborative learning and problem-solving skills. He reasoned that the game design project would: allow him to trial innovative pedagogy; improve his knowledge of how to effectively use flexible classroom spaces; and appeal to the learning preferences of contemporary students.

Jason assumed that his students would be able to take more control over their learning activities and approaches. Students had to develop an understanding of game design mechanics and then develop a storyline using a programming language. Project design was largely an independent process, supported by online materials and tutorials. There were also opportunities for whole-class explanations and demonstrations.

Students were provided with computer work stations to work on their product. Jason explicitly required students to practise skills of collaboration, communication, problem-solving, and research. This meant that students could use a wide array of resources, including: peers; online communities of game designers or specific programming language sites; other online resources, and the teacher. Jason expected that this expansive network of resources would augment the conventional top-down teacher-directed approach to learning.

Jason tended to explain and demonstrate material and resources using an interactive whiteboard at the front of the room. This occurred on a needs basis, such as when Jason noticed common questions in the online forum. Students functioned as a class unit for a small percentage of their time. Students were generally free to move about the room to work with, assist, or seek assistance from peers.

Virtual learning spaces were used in a variety of ways. Jason used a learning management system where he posted links to online tutorials and support materials for the programming language, as well as other information about the task. An online forum was also available for students to post questions of class peers. Jason monitored the forum and occasionally contributed. Students were encouraged to conduct research online to locate other resources to support their game design task. This included using YouTube clips, which they had to view off-site because the school had banned in-school access. In addition, students were encouraged to join online game design special interest group forums. If students located any useful links or resources they could post these in the learning management system.

Students tended to work individually and had a high degree of control over the selection and employment of learning strategies. The planning and design of the game prior to programming were important stages and required students to use imagination, representation and communication, and negotiation skills as they developed their storyline.

Higher-order thinking and metacognition were visibly evident in the online forums, class discussions and demonstrations, and individual game design coding and revision. This included students planning, enacting, monitoring and adapting their own cognitive strategies in order to effectively complete the task (Zimmerman, 2008). Metacognitive processes are critical for the development of agency through students autonomously analysing problems, examining personal thinking, and explaining and justifying individual reasoning processes.

Problem-solving was a particular indicator of the shared control aspect of agency. As expected by the teacher, student use of programming language created a constant set of issues for students. During the data collection, students were asked to identify who they would ask for help to resolve a problem during the game design and creation. The students' responses indicated that their primary strategy was to try, through trial and error, to independently solve the problem. The second most common strategy was talking to other students in the class, followed by talking to the teacher. Using online resources for problem-solving was usually tried after independent, peer- or teacher based strategies.

One example of problem-solving is provided by Mitchell, who had been working on his game at home and was ready to test it. As he played the game he realised there was a coding error that had resulted in the 'Home' button not working. Mitchell read over the programming code and tried various changes. Although frustrated, he continued to work by himself using trial and error. Eventually he went online and found a game design site. He posted his question and over the week had several responses. Generally, Mitchell was not happy with the usefulness of the responses, and he resumed his trial and error approach. This continued for the remainder of the project as he worked alone trying different means of resolving the programming issue. This example was unusual in that there was little peer collaboration – a key feature regularly observed.

The students were generally reluctant to use the online tutorials and tended to learn about programming language using trial and error. Initially there was a high degree of off-task behaviour with students playing games or chatting. Jason circulated and strategically talked to students one-on-one to get them focused. As the term progressed Jason continually reminded the students about the project timeline and the task requirements.

DISCUSSION

Consideration of the dynamic and contextual nature of agency involves investigation of how the teacher and students jointly create, work in, and reflexively maintain a space that affords quality learning. This includes taking account of the reflexive interactions between individuals and the context and conditions within which they make choices and experience the consequences of those decisions and understandings (Brannen & Nilsen, 2005). As was evident in the survey reported in Table 3.1, students taking part in the game design project had limited experience in enacting elements of agency including: applying tasks to real life everyday situations outside of school; making choices about topics, use of materials or activities; and co-planning learning activities and assessment tasks with teachers. Some of these elements of agency featured in the learning practices experienced by both the teacher and students during the game design project. Students were involved in choices about topics as they created their own game, and were responsible for assessment as their peers determined if a completed game was comprehensible, workable and interesting to play.

While the task did not afford the co-planning of learning activities this is an indication of the complexity of personalised learning. It also provides direction for the ongoing development of quality teaching and learning tasks that further develop teacher and student agency.

In drawing on the literature and case study findings it is possible to identify how agency is projected and dynamically enacted through teacher and student interactions in an environment affording personalised learning. Essentially agency is a shared orientation and ongoing negotiation contributes to a culture supporting learning. This required an awareness of each other's intentions, motives, values, and purposes. Further, both teacher and students had to be responsive to the possibilities and constraints or uncertainties of the physical, virtual and social learning environment. Teacher and student agency can be conceptualised as a set of ongoing reflexive choices about personalised learning grounded in context. The perceived affordances of personalised learning interact to produce teacher and student expectations and perceptions about their own and each other's choices and actions.

Teacher agency, evident in the actions taken to project, create and maintain a learning environment conducive to personalised learning can be characterised as:

- being willing to enact different approaches to teaching and learning;
- using flexible learning spaces, both physical and virtual;
- providing students with a task structure that supports making choices about topics, use of materials and activities, based on personal interest and experience;
- providing scaffolding in the form of in- and out-of-class resources including a learning management system that was maintained by the teacher but included sharing of student identified resources and exemplar material;
- Supporting the development of student agency, including co-regulation of activities and application of problem-solving approaches. Regular individual and social reflection activities are used to monitor student progress, engagement with the task and to provide the teacher with information about the efficacy of teaching and learning strategies and approaches.

Student agency can be characterised as:

- personal knowledge of learning strengths and preferences as a basis for adaptation to the project requirements and context;
- effortful application of higher-order thinking and metacognitive skills;
- co-regulation (peer-peer and peer-teacher) of learning activities, including application of problem solving skills;
- active and autonomous learning through an orientation to task requirements and expectations, goal-setting and monitoring, awareness and selection of learning strategies, responsiveness to feedback, and reflection on their learning approach and achievement;
- proficiency in their use of Web 2.0 technology to support their learning. They are able to seek and apply information, use analytical and evaluative strategies to determine the most useful and practical sites and processes, and to demonstrate learning through the use of multi-modal representations and communication.

The case study presented here details momentary contextual transactions of agents in personalised learning spaces. The analysis considers the teacher and students' conceptualisations of teaching and learning, and perceptions of learning-related intentions and transactions in that environment.

Edwards' (2005) notion of relational agency provides an explanatory frame that emphasises the mutuality of agency. This is evident in the reflexive monitoring by both students and the teacher, and is symbolic of the rich reciprocity between student, teacher, task, and contextual interactions. These perceptions and resulting choices are immediate, continuous, reactive, and typically complexly grounded in the environments affording agency.

In the case study, the teacher created a learning culture that encouraged student autonomy. This was evident in the task design, and included modelling of co-regulation, and framing and authorising the use of distributed expertise within and external to the classroom (Hadwin, Miller, & Winne, 2011). The teacher made choices to realise a personalised curriculum. This included supporting a culture of co-regulatory relationships, encouragement of student responsibility and problem-solving, use of flexible learning spaces, and networking and interactivity. By requiring students to develop their individual games, the game design project addressed differences in student preferences, abilities, interests, and readiness.

The task design afforded student agency. The teacher was a key influence in this sense of agentic possibility by effectively facilitating the use of various learning spaces and designing pedagogy sympathetic to personalised learning. The task design centred on the regular class meetings, where the teacher explicitly provided direction, explanation, and modelling.

The task design encouraged students to seek and apply multiple strategies for game design and creation, and to find solutions for problems. These strategies are consistent with those suggested by Stefanou, Perencevich, DiCintio, and Turner (2004) to support cognitive autonomy. The teacher had to come to terms with allowing students to exert agency and recognise that, at times, the students' expertise would exceed that of the teacher. Of course, some students were more competent than others. The dynamic mutuality of agency meant that the teacher could encourage independence in all students but support those who needed more assistance. In response, the students generally showed a capacity to make choices and take actions that were appropriate within the teaching and learning context, although it is important to note that these achievements were not universal.

This approach assumed that students would be autonomous problem-solvers. The progress of the task was associated with increasingly difficult and complex problems. Students used a variety of strategies, including: interaction with peers, online tutorials, class forums, and gamer networks. As problems became increasingly complex, students sought support and guidance from the teacher. This required careful balancing of teacher and student agency in order to maintain a frame of productive activity without removing autonomy. This was consistent with the view of teacher and student agency as a complex and dynamic interplay between individual capacity and the affordances and constraints of prior experience, generated by the related teaching and learning culture established for this task (Archer, 2003; Emirbayer & Mische, 1998).

IMPLICATIONS AND CONCLUSIONS

The reflexive mutuality of teacher and student agency demonstrates several aspects of the complex contextual interaction between teaching and learning. Student agency was evident when students engaged with the action possibilities of the pedagogical intent of the teacher. The level of investment students made in realising the affordances of the personalised learning context was particularly evident in their problem-solving approaches and strategies. Teacher agency was apparent in the deliberate co-regulation of learning, creating a culture that supported independent student problem-solving and the management of teaching and learning processes. The mutuality was observed in each agent's sense of the other's investment in learning. A question emerges here, as a basis for future research, about the balance between allowing students to self-manage their own developing agency and the co-regulation of this development by educators. The balance is most important when increasingly challenging tasks result in the possibility of greater depth and breadth of learning.

This case study demonstrates that the teacher has considerable responsibility for designing a high-quality curriculum that affords a culture of agency. This is successful when the social processes of learning include intentional and purposeful activities that question and reform classroom routines (Deed, Lovejoy, Prain, & Waldrip, 2014). A number of implications are apparent for affording teacher and student agency in open-plan personalised learning environments.

- Teachers must intentionally work to develop a classroom culture supporting agency – for example giving students increased responsibility for planning, monitoring, and reflection.
- Teachers and students need to explicitly model and explicate their teaching and learning choices relating to the use of flexible classroom spaces and personalised learning strategies. This makes visible the higher order thinking and metacognitive processes being employed by both teacher and students.
- Student exemplars of task design and enactment, with emphasis on subsequent problem-solving approaches and strategies can be used as models of agency in practice.
- Models of complex problem-solving can be identified based on student examples of practice. These can provide a frame for discussions about establishing and maintaining agency.
- Models of distributed expertise can likewise be identified. These will explicitly draw on resources within and external to the classroom. This will raise questions about efficacy in dealing with formal and informal information and learning resources.
- Constraints on the exercise of teacher and student agency should be explicitly identified and noted in classroom discussion of the learning process—questions and perspectives about the impact of these constraints are likely to inform productive projections of agency.

Our discussion of agency provides a conceptual frame for an examination of building capacity to change the classroom and school culture. The case study and literature show that this is a mutual and reflexive process. However, there needs to be some degree of overt intention from both teacher and student to enact these processes in order for both to engage in what might be characterised as quality learning—commencing with engagement.

Conversations like these should be about the efficiency and effectiveness of emerging agency, with a focus on teacher and student reasoning for reflexive choices and strategic actions. The workability and durability of acting differently should be attended to, as the investment of teachers and students in innovative learning-activity design and enactment is often considerable.

REFERENCES

Archer, M. (2003). *Structure, agency and the internal conversation.* Cambridge, England: Cambridge University Press.

Brannen, J., & Nilsen, A. (2005). Individualisation, choice and structure: A discussion of current trends in sociological analysis. *The Sociological Review, 53*(3), 412–428. doi:10.1111/j.1467-954x.2005.00559.x

Campbell, R., Robinson, W., Neelands, J., Hewston, R., & Mazzoli, L. (2007). Personalised learning: Ambiguities in theory and practice. *British Journal of Educational Studies, 55*(2), 135–154. doi:10.1111/j.1467-8527.2007.00370.x

Clandinin, D. J. (1985). Personal practical knowledge: A study of teachers' classroom images. *Curriculum Inquiry, 15*(4), 361–385. doi:10.2307/1179683

Cochran-Smith, M., & Lytle, S. L. (1999). Relationships of knowledge and practice: Teacher learning in communities. *Review of Research in Education, 24*, 249–305. doi:10.2307/1167272

Collinson, V. (1999). Redefining teacher excellence. *Theory into Practice, 38*(1), 4–11. doi:10.1080/00405849909543824

Connelly, F. M., & Clandinin, D. J. (1988). *Teachers as curriculum planners: Narratives of experience.* New York, NY: Teachers' College.

Dabbagh, N., & Kitsantas, A. (2012). Personal learning environments, social media, and self-regulated learning: A natural formula for connecting formal and informal learning. *Internet and Higher Education, 15*(1), 3–8. doi:10.1016/j.iheduc.2011.06.002

Deed, C., & Edwards, A. (2013). Knowledge building in online environments: Constraining and enabling collective intelligence. In P. Ordonez de Pablos, H. O. Nigro, R. D. Tennyson, S. E. G. Cisaro, & W. Karwowski (Eds.), *Advancing information management through semantic web concepts and ontologies.* Hershey, PA: IGI Global.

Deed, C., Lovejoy, V., Prain, V., & Waldrip, B. (2014). Personalised learning in the open classroom: The mutuality of teacher and student agency. *International Journal of Pedagogies and Learning, 9*(1), 66–75. doi:10.1080/18334105.2014.11082020

Edwards, A. (2005). Relational agency: Learning to be a resourceful practitioner. *International Journal of Educational Research, 43*, 168–182. doi:10.1016/j.ijer.2006.06.010

Edwards, A. (2007). Relational agency in professional practice: A CHAT analysis. *Actio: An International Journal of Human Activity Theory, 1*, 1–17.

Edwards, A. (2011). Building common knowledge at the boundaries between professional practices: Relational agency and relational expertise in systems of distributed expertise. *International Journal of Educational Research, 50*(1), 33–39. doi:10.1016/j.ijer.2011.04.007

Edwards, D., Deed, C., & Edwards, A. (2014). Learning in technologically-mediated spaces in open-plan settings. In V. Prain, P. Cox, C. Deed, D. Edwards, C. Farrelly, M. Keeffe, … Z. Yager (Eds.), *Adapting to teaching and learning in open-plan schools* (pp. 79–94). Rotterdam, The Netherlands: Sense Publishers.

Elbaz, F. (1981). The teacher's "practical knowledge": Report of a case study. *Curriculum Inquiry, 11*(1), 43–71. doi:10.2307/1179510

Emirbayer, M., & Mische, A. (1998). What is agency? *The American Journal of Sociology, 103*(4), 962–1023. doi:10.1086/231294

Eseryel, D., Law, V., Ifenthaler, D., Ge, X., & Miller, R. (2014). An investigation of the interrelationships between motivation, engagement, and complex problem solving in game-based learning. *Educational Technology & Society, 17*(1), 42–53.

Gee, J. (2003). *What video games have to teach us about learning and literacy.* New York, NY: PalGrave-McMillan.

Giddens, A. (1984). *The constitution of society: Outline of the theory of structuration.* Cambridge, MA: Polity Press.

Greeno, J. (2009). A framework bite on contextualizing, framing, and positioning: A companion to son and goldstone. *Cognition and Instruction, 27*(3), 269–275. doi:10.1080/07370000903014386

Gros, B. (2007). Digital games in education: The design of games-based learning environments. *Journal of Research on Technology in Education, 40*, 23–38. doi:10.1080/15391523.2007.10782494

Hadwin, A., Miller, M., & Winne, P. (2011). *Socially-shared metacognition: Convergence and co-construction CSCL planning.* Paper presented at the European Association for Research in Learning and Instruction Conference, Lyon, France.

Hargreaves, D. H. (1997). In defence of research for evidence-based teaching: A rejoinder to Martyn Hammersley. *British Educational Research Journal, 23*(4), 405–419. doi:10.1080/0141192970230402

Hwang, G. J., & Wu, P. H. (2012). Advancements and trends in digital game-based learning research: A review of publications in selected journals from 2001 to 2010. *British Journal of Educational Technology, 43*(1), E6–E10. doi:10.1111/j.1467-8535.2011.01242.x

Johnson, M., & Liber, O. (2008). The personal learning environment and the human condition: From theory to teaching practice. *Interactive Learning Environments, 16*(1), 3–15. doi:10.1080/10494820701772652

King, A. (2000). The accidental derogation of the lay actor: A critique of Giddens's concept of structure. *Philosophy for the Social Sciences, 30*(3), 362–383. doi:10.1177/004839310003000302

Mazman, S. G., & Usluel, Y. K. (2010). Modeling educational usage of Facebook. *Computers & Education, 55*(2), 444–453. doi:10.1016/j.compedu.2010.02.008

Oblinger, D. G. (2004). The next generation of educational engagement. *Journal of Interactive Media in Education, 8*, 1–18. doi:10.5334/2004-8-oblinger

O'Neil, H. F., Wainess, R., & Baker, E. L. (2005). Classification of learning games: Evidence from the computer games literature. *The Curriculum Journal, 16*(4), 455–474. doi:10.1080/09585170500384529

Ottesen, E. (2007). Teachers "in the making": Building accounts of teaching. *Teaching and Teacher Education, 23*, 612–623. doi:10.1016/j.tate.2007.01.011

Paris, S. G., & Paris, A. H. (2001). Classroom applications of research on self-regulated learning. *Educational Psychologist, 36*(2), 89–101. doi:10.1207/S15326985EP3602_4

Prain, V., Cox, P., Deed, C., Dorman, J., Edwards, D., Farrelly, C., Keeffe, M., ... Yager, Z. (2014). *Adapting to teaching and learning in open-plan schools.* Rotterdam, The Netherlands: Sense Publishers.

Saldana, J. (2009). *The coding manual for qualitative researchers.* Los Angeles, CA: Sage.

Salen, K. (2007). Gaming literacies: A game design study in action. *Journal of Educational Multimedia and Hypermedia, 16*(3), 301–322.

Scardamalia, M., & Bereiter, C. (1991). Higher levels of agency for children in knowledge building: A challenge for the design of new knowledge media. *The Journal of the Learning Sciences, 1*(1), 37–68. doi:10.1207/s15327809jls0101_3

Selwyn, N. (2009). Faceworking: Exploring students' education-related use of Facebook. *Learning, Media and Technology, 34*(2), 157–174. doi:10.1080/17439880902923622

Sharples, M., Taylor, J., & Vavoula, G. (2010). A theory of learning for the mobile age. In B. Bachmair (Ed.), *Medienbildung in neuen Kulturraumen* (pp. 87–99). Wiesbaden, Germany: VS Verlag fur Sozialwissenschaften.

Solvberg, A., & Rismark, M. (2012). Learning spaces in mobile learning environments. *Active Learning in Higher Education, 13*(1), 23–33. doi:10.1177/1469787411429189

Stefanou, C. R., Perencevich, K. C., DiCintio, M., & Turner, J. C. (2004). Supporting autonomy in the classroom: Ways teachers encourage student decision making and ownership. *Educational Psychologist, 39*(2), 97–110. doi:10.1207/s15326985ep3902_2

Waldrip, B., Cox, P., Deed, C., Dorman, J., Edwards, D., Farrelly, C., ... Yager, Z. (2014). Student perceptions of personalised learning: Validation and development of questionnaire with regional secondary students. *Learning Environments Research, 17*(3), 355–370. doi:10.1007/s10984-014-9163-0

Zimmerman, B. (2002). Becoming a self-regulated learner: An overview. *Theory into Practice, 41*(2), 64–70. doi:10.1207/s15430421tip4102_2

Zimmerman, B. (2008). Investigating self-regulation and motivation: Historical background, methodological developments, and future prospects. *American Educational Research Journal, 45*(1), 166–183. doi:10.3102/0002831207312909

CATHLEEN FARRELLY AND VALERIE LOVEJOY

4. A WHOLE-SCHOOL APPROACH TO ADOLESCENT WELLBEING IN OPEN-PLAN SCHOOLS

INTRODUCTION

In this chapter we report on the attempts of one Bendigo Education Plan (BEP) school to respond to identified wellbeing issues by developing a whole-school approach to foster the wellbeing needs of their Years 7–10 students. The school has a cohort of students from lower than average socio-economic backgrounds. Research points to the necessity of a multi-layered approach to building a positive school culture to improve student wellbeing. We agree that a whole-school coordinated approach is needed to foster the connectedness and relationships that are foundational to improved learning outcomes. However, the literature is generally speculative about the practical ways of achieving this and reticent about ways of tracking the effects on students of wellbeing measures taken. Quantitative data drawn from our multi-dimensional model of learning and wellbeing in open-plan settings (Prain et al., 2014) and qualitative data from student and teacher interviews are used in this chapter to track the effects of measures taken to improve wellbeing in our case study schools. The chapter highlights the challenges of setting up structures, processes, and curriculum content that work in an integrated way to enhance student wellbeing. In discussing one whole-school approach to meeting these challenges, we recognise that no one way of addressing issues of wellbeing is paramount because wellbeing is culturally specific and impacted by individual capacity.

THEORETICAL UNDERSTANDINGS OF WELLBEING AND SCHOOLING

The Role of Schools in Promoting Wellbeing

The powerful role middle schools can play in nurturing safe and supportive relationships for young people is widely recognised among educational researchers who have found a significant link between positive student wellbeing and improved learning (Seligman, Ernst, Gilham, Reichvich, & Linkins, 2009; Fredrickson, 1998; Bolte, Goschke, & Kuhl, 2003; Fredrickson & Branigan, 2005; Rowe, Hirsch, Anderson, & Smith, 2007; Isen, Rosenzweig, & Young, 1991; Kuhl, 1983, 2000). These research findings increase the imperative on schools to develop integrated policies and practices that assist adolescents to negotiate a complex real and virtual world in which easy access to fast food, drugs, bullying, violence, and pornography present daily challenges to their physical and mental health at a time when their self-identity is still being formed. Adolescents from low socio-economic backgrounds are particularly vulnerable to these challenges that are associated with low levels of social capital and community cohesion. A perception of connectedness or belonging to a school community has been associated positively with engagement, academic success, and completion rates of secondary schooling (Bond et al., 2007) as well as the development of a positive adult sense of self (Youngblade et al., 2007). Researchers also recognise that to nurture school connectedness, schools must consider themselves as an integral part of broader communities. The quality of the connections among the multiple groups that contribute to a school community, such as students, teachers, families, professionals from community agencies, and other involved local groups and individuals, reflects the degree of social capital in the school environment. Kawachi and Berkman, (2000), Putnam, (1993) and Wilkinson (1996) define social capital as cohesiveness characterised by strong social bonds, high levels of trust and reciprocity. An accumulation of social capital leads to the promotion of democratic systems to manage conflict, and associations to bridge social divisions, thus reducing social conflict and bullying (Kawachi & Berkman, 2000).

Threats to Student Wellbeing

It is acknowledged that attending school on a regular basis underpins academic, social, and language development, lessening the likelihood of dropping out of school, or future criminal activity, and increasing the likelihood of future financial independence through employment (Christenson & Thurlow, 2004; Wilson & Tanner-Smith, 2013). An indication of an absence of wellbeing is reflected in chronic absenteeism. Policies and practices that encourage attendance by promoting connectedness are important in reaching out to school-avoiding and school-refusing students. Addressing this issue is complex because the reasons for non-attendance are complex. They may originate from the child, the family, the school environment, or a combination, such as an underlying medical condition, separation anxiety, feelings of lack of safety at school because of unsatisfactory social relationships, trouble with teachers, peer rejection or bullying, or feelings of inadequacy because of lack of academic progress.

The highly visible nature of the open-plan settings that form the context for our study has the potential to exacerbate problems of exclusion and cyber-bullying. Girls appear to be more active on social media than boys and more covert in relational aggression. They appear to report more cyber-bullying than boys (Cassidy, Jackson & Brown, 2009; Walgrave & Wannes, 2011) with greater perceived negative effects on their wellbeing in terms of reputation, ability to concentrate, ability to make friends and suicidal thoughts. Cassidy, Jackson, and Browne (2009) suggest that a trajectory of relational aggression can be changed to one of relational support and mutual care by embedding a school culture that builds strong, caring relationships in an environment that is attentive to the voices of students.

The Multi-Dimensional Nature of Wellbeing

Understandings of wellbeing incorporate various notions of happiness, life satisfaction, flourishing, a balanced or meaningful life, reaching one's true potential, freedom and choice, resilience, emotional literacy, engagement, a positive sense of self, and the active pursuit of physical, mental, emotional, and spiritual health (Australian Catholic University (ACU) and Erebus International, 2008; Coleman, 2009). The complex nature of wellbeing is theorised by Allardt (1976, 1981, 1989) as being a state in which it is possible for a person to satisfy his or her material and non-material needs. Drawing on Allardt (1989) and Konu and Rimpelä (2002) these needs fall into three categories with objective and subjective indicators: 'having' (material and interpersonal needs, indicated objectively by the level of living and environmental conditions and subjectively by the degree of satisfaction with one's living conditions); 'being' (personal growth needs indicated objectively by people's relation to society and nature and subjectively by their personal experience of alienation or connectedness); and 'loving' (the need to relate to others and develop social identities indicated objectively by relationships with others and subjectively by their feelings of happiness or unhappiness with social relations).

BENDIGO EDUCATION PLAN CONTEXT

According to the Index of Socio-Educational Advantage (ICSEA)[1], three of the four Bendigo Education Plan Year 7–10 colleges are below the Victorian state average. Community health and welfare statistics paint a picture of significant and entrenched adolescent health and wellbeing problems in a context of poverty and disadvantage. Experiences of bullying, rates of psychological distress, teenage pregnancies, and incidents of self-harm are all higher than the state average, while feelings of positive psychological wellbeing are lower than the state average (Bendigo Loddon Primary Care Partnership, 2012, p.99). However, this depressing picture represents only one side of the story. The BEP steering committee, which was set up in 2005 to guide the rebuilding of Bendigo schools, recognised that Bendigo students are also highly resilient with strong community networks, and support from passionate and committed parents, teachers, and community members who work hard to increase their life chances (BEP Steering Committee, 2005; Prain et al., 2014). Our survey data over three years from 2011–2013 revealed that students in the BEP schools have high levels of self-efficacy and self-control, suggesting that students have a positive sense of their own ability to cope with school tasks (Prain et al., 2014). Self-efficacy and social competence were identified by Rutter (1990, p. 311) as "robust predictors of resilience".

Prior to the establishment of the BEP, a survey of 421 Year 10 students revealed that 25% left school without good memories (BEP Steering Committee, 2005). Attitudes to School Survey data from 2004 and 2005 were consistent with these findings.[2] The lower the academic achievement, the lower the level of satisfaction with school, and the more frequently students represented the school negatively. Criticisms of disengaging pedagogy, lack of challenge, and lack of subject choice were matched by requests for breadth, choice, and good teaching in an 'adult environment'.

The Bendigo Education Plan aimed to improve both the academic performance and wellbeing of Bendigo Years 7–10 students. The first step to achieving this aim was the rebuilding of four Years 7–10 schools between 2008 and 2012 (see Prain et al., 2014). All schools had an open, flexible design incorporating spaces that dissolved the boundaries between formal and informal education (Reh, Rabenstein, & Fritzsche, 2011), provided more freedom and independence for personalised learning experiences (McGregor, 2004a, 2004b), and offered an attractive setting for larger learning communities, team-teaching and multi-age groupings.

To counter possible negative effects on student wellbeing of large open-plan settings on some students, each school was structured into four learning communities, comprising two learning neighbourhoods of 150–300 students. These neighbourhoods were further divided into teacher advisor groupings of 25 students with the aim of providing a core groups of peers and teacher with whom all students could develop ongoing stable and close relationships. The learning communities were differently structured according to local school preferences. At Ironbark College for example, each learning community was vertically structured (comprising Years 7–10 students) and divided into junior (Years 7 and 8) and senior (Years 9 and 10) neighbourhoods.

TRACKING STUDENT WELLBEING IN BEP SCHOOLS

Our research aimed to understand student perceptions of learning in these new open-plan settings and their impact on wellbeing. To this end, we surveyed approximately 3000 students across all year levels (Years 7–10) in the four BEP schools each year from 2011 to 2013 using our Personalised Learning Experience Questionnaire (PLEQ) (Prain et al., 2014). The schools' annual Attitudes to School Survey data were also examined for the years 2010 to 2013. We aimed to gain insight into the factors influencing wellbeing in these open-plan settings, and to understand how students and teachers perceive wellbeing in these settings. As a further dimension, our research also explored perceptions of student wellbeing through student interviews undertaken in all of the BEP schools.

Attitudes to School Survey

In Victoria, all students' opinions on their schools are gathered on an annual basis through the "Attitudes to School Survey" (DEECD, 2014). The survey consists of 11 scales covering wellbeing (student morale and student distress), learning and teaching (teacher effectiveness, teacher empathy, stimulating learning, school connectedness, students motivation and confidence), and student relationships (connectedness to peers, classroom behaviour and student safety.

Table 4.1 includes data from the Attitudes to School survey for the Year 7 student cohort in 2010 and again when they were in Year 10 in 2013. Most of students in this cohort had experienced at least three of their four years in the new open-plan settings. Grevillea and Whirrakee were the last to complete their building program and as a result, their data includes a small cohort that did not relocate to the open-plan settings until mid 2011. The values in the table are the difference between the average cohort score and the state average. The arrows indicate where the differences were above (↑), below (↓) or within 0.1 (→) of the expected values based on state-wide data.

Table 4.1. Student relationships and wellbeing for cohort who commenced year 7 in 2010 and completed year 10 in 2013 in all BEP schools (the values are the difference between the average cohort score and the state averages)

School	Year 7 in 2010		Year 10 in 2013	
	Student relationships	Wellbeing	Student relationships	Wellbeing
Ironbark	−0.18	−0.29	−0.16 →	−0.05 ↑
Whirrakee	0.01	−0.29	0.15 ↑	0.40 ↑
Grevillea	−0.23	−0.24	−0.49 ↓	−0.74 ↓
Melaleuca	−0.30	−0.36	−0.26 →	−0.27 →

Table 4.1 indicates that students in all schools, except Grevillea College, showed at least some improvement, albeit minor in the case of Melaleuca and Ironbark, in perceptions of student relationships. Similarly the students' ratings of their own wellbeing improved in all schools except Grevillea compared to the state average.

THE PERSONALISED LEARNING EXPERIENCE QUESTIONNAIRE (PLEQ)

We developed a model based on our PLEQ survey that identified relationships among factors that indicated the perceived quality of the learning experience in the open-plan settings including factors that indicated student wellbeing: peer relationships (loving), self-report of disruptive behaviour (being), individualisation in tailoring learning tasks to students' interests and abilities (having), and opportunities for personal and social development (having) (Prain et al., 2014). Our model reflected the complexity of the environment and the relationship between key factors in the environment and wellbeing. Some factors in our model overlap with those in Konu and Rimpelä's (2002) model that drew on Allardt's theory of welfare although the context in which our model was tested was very different. Our multi-dimensional model revealed that the learning environment (including teacher support) and self-efficacy were positively associated with wellbeing. The results of the PLEQ from 2011–2013 suggest that there is a complex interplay of factors influencing school wellbeing and that changing only one or two factors will not necessarily provide a direct effect on wellbeing. As in the Attitudes to School Survey, there was no significant change in student wellbeing in our case study schools over the survey period. However, age-based differences were found in the PLEQ results, with a decline in wellbeing from Year 7 to Year 8 followed by a gradual increase to approximate Year 7 scores by Year 10 (see Prain et al., 2014).

The results of the PLEQ survey also revealed significant gender differences. Scores from aggregating the four wellbeing scales (i.e., peer relations, self-report of disruptive behaviour, individualisation, and opportunities for personal and social development) in the PLEQ revealed a slight improvement in wellbeing for male students and a slight decrease in wellbeing for female students from 2011 to 2013. However, the wellbeing scores were slightly higher across all the survey years for female students than those for the males (Prain et al., 2014). When each of the wellbeing scales was examined, female students had significantly lower self-reporting of disruptive behaviour, and higher perceptions of opportunities for personal and social development, while males reported significantly more positive perceptions of peer relations. These results support Quenzel and Hurrelmann's (2013) argument that adolescent males are more likely to have more friends and spend more of their free time with them than females who are more socialised towards academic success. Though difficult to isolate from other factors, the physical environment may contribute to perceptions of wellbeing, particularly among male students. At Ironbark College, our survey analyses revealed a significant increase in perceptions of teacher support and peer relations for males in the new open-plan settings. However, there was a slight decrease in perceptions of teacher support and peer relations for females. These outcomes suggest that males are perhaps more responsive to changed school environments than are females and that it cannot be assumed that all changes will affect all students in the same way.

The multi-dimensional nature of the PLEQ may need to be further refined to account for the complexity of the interplay between factors impacting on student wellbeing. In a review of the literature regarding the measuring of wellbeing in a schooling context, Fraillon (2004) identified 12 aspects of intrapersonal and interpersonal dimensions of wellbeing that should be included in such an instrument. The PLEQ was necessarily limited in its size, both to ensure students could complete the survey, and to incorporate perceptions of students' learning.

STUDENT INTERVIEWS

We conducted 61 interviews with Years 7 and 10 students in the BEP schools. Our questions sought their opinions of the open-plan setting, the quality of their relationships and learning, and their sense of wellbeing at school. Most students reported that they liked the open-plan learning spaces mainly because of the greater sense of freedom of movement they create, but also because of the potential for improved relationships. They appreciated the opportunities the space provides to mix with a larger range of students and learn from a variety of teachers who have different skills and teaching styles:

> You are not with the same people all the time. You meet more students and when you have one teacher they are good at one thing and not at another thing. (Year 7 boy)

However, favourite spaces at school, linked to informal times of the school day, were generally intimate outside spaces where students socialised in their own 'territory' with a few friends. Cross-community friendships were common by Year 10.

Most students reported positive feelings of wellbeing in the open-plan learning environments. Common adjectives to describe Year 7 feelings included "happy", "relaxed", "good" and "safe", concentrating on the physical environment, while the more complex responses of Year 10 students suggested their feelings were closely linked to relationships with peers and teachers "relaxed", "calm", "belonging", "grateful", "respected", and "challenged". This sense of safety was also apparent in data from the Attitudes to School Survey. Students commented that the teachers spoke more quietly and tended to raise their voices far less than they had in the traditional classrooms, something that the students agreed created a much better social environment.

At Ironbark College organising the school into Years 7–10 learning communities had a positive effect on student wellbeing. This sense of belonging and connectedness to a community afforded students more consistency in their relationships because they stayed in the same learning community with the same teachers for four years:

> I think it's really good because you can connect and bond with the same people throughout your whole school life. It's good that we have the same teacher so you get more confident to talk to them about anything that's happening in school and with other classmates as well. (Year 8 girl)

Some students also identified the value of having older students and even siblings in the same learning community:

> Its good having older kids in there as well to try and help you out, its good having older kids and younger kids, its good having a bit of a range…my brother was in the same community as me [when I came in Year 7] so he was in the class next door which was completely open so he could help me. It was good. (Year 10 girl)

The visibility of the spaces seems to have lessened overt bullying so that most students feel safe and happy at school, confirmed by interviews with the principals and teachers. The presence of TA groups (see Chapter 10) gives students a sense of belonging. TA groups were established to mitigate the possible alienating effects of larger communities and open learning environments by the personal connections students could establish in these groups of 25 students.

> I could probably name every single person. I'm always friendly to people and smile, so I guess I know them quite well. (Year 10 girl)

Though friendship groups were much smaller (5–10), all Year 7 and Year 10 students felt they knew the students in their TA well, and reflecting their longer time at school, Year 10s had a much broader acquaintance with others in their community:

> I know a lot of people but they have their own friends. My friends have grown quite a bit over the years. We wind each other up and have fun. (Year 10 girl)

While both Year 7s and Year 10s suggested that new students need to work at making friends in order to fit in, Year 10s' stronger sense of identity was reflected in advice to new students to "be yourself".

Positive effects of new learning environments on relationships with teachers were evident in Year 10 advice to students. They warned of the consequences of "dumbing yourself down" on academic grades, showing off as "giving the wrong impression" and "being scared of the teachers" as missing an opportunity for assistance. The strong advice to "ask teachers" suggested a confidence in teacher/student relationships:

> We have a lot of fantastic teachers here who would do anything for students. A lot of people write them off and don't get to know them. Teachers are willing to do a lot for you. (Year 10 boy)

The biggest differences students noticed in the new learning environments were the improved teacher/student relationships (Year 7, 12 comments, Year 10, 12 comments):

> If you're having a few social issues, like you've got things going on at home, I've noticed they're nicer to you. They're easier on you and they ask you how you are going all the time. They really do care. (Year 7 girl)

Year 10 students were more aware than Year 7 students of the physical effect of the learning environment on teacher/student relationships:

> I think they can be more free such as us being more free. They feel they can interact better with the kids…you can actually have a chat with them about what they're doing at the weekend. The buildings have changed the people—it's good. (Year 10 boy)

Good relationships with teachers were particularly important for Year 7 students (11 of 33) whose advice to teachers included "to listen", to be "kind and helpful", to "give everyone a fair go" and importantly to "try and stay happy even if you're not feeling that way so kids don't think it's their fault". Year 10s were more likely to value a teacher who had established a respectful, egalitarian relationship with them: "he talks to me like I'm a friend—like we're equal" and one who is willing to "put in the extra yards" of availability beyond class time. A sense of humour is a highly valued attribute at both year levels and both appreciate an enthusiastic, "joyful" teacher who communicates their passion to the students.

Open-plan settings do not suit every student's needs though few students expressed negative feelings. Adjectives such as "nervous", "scared" and "edgy" reflected the new status of Year 7s in the school, while negative Year 10 responses such as "frustrating", "disappointing" and "angry" reflected disappointment in their learning experience.

The interview data indicated that there was considerable overlap between the TA and the Physical, Health and Sport Education curriculum (PHASE), although this did not seem to be orchestrated. There may be opportunities to strengthen the links between these two areas in order to provide improved sequencing and time allocation to discrete topics. The extension of participatory learning strategies in both areas (see page 15 for further discussion) will be of considerable value in improving student perceptions of wellbeing.

Our tracking of student wellbeing in the case study schools demonstrates that these schools face major challenges in improving students' perceptions of their wellbeing. While in interviews, the students reported experiencing improved relationships with peers and teachers, and a sense of safety and even happiness in flexible open-plan settings, the survey data shows less definitive satisfaction. Interviews by their nature are personalised and informal, and allow teasing out of responses. Surveys and questionnaires are valuable as they enable the gathering of large datasets, but the language in which questions are framed can be misinterpreted and responses tend to be muted.

THE WHO HEALTH PROMOTING SCHOOLS FRAMEWORK (HPS)

A multi-dimensional view of wellbeing suggests that, to improve student wellbeing, a multi-dimensional approach is needed that has a purposeful and systematic focus on wellbeing as a primary aim of schooling. The lens of the WHO Health Promoting Schools Framework (HPS) is applied to our case study school (WHO, 1996). The HPS framework is based on worldwide research that suggests that successful promotion of health and wellbeing can be achieved through three interrelated areas in schools: (1) organisation, ethos, and environment; (2) curriculum, teaching, and learning; and (3) partnerships and services (Clift & Jensen, 2005; Rowe & Stewart, 2009; Sun & Stewart, 2007). Rather than focusing on the individual components of the approach, Rowe and Stewart's (2009) focus on the interactions of a whole-school approach across all levels of the school community serves to demonstrate the powerful influence of the HPS model on school connectedness with positive effects for students' wellbeing, health and academic achievement.

CASE STUDY IRONBARK COLLEGE

School Organisation, Ethos, and Environment

At Ironbark College, interviews with the school principal, deputy principal, school chaplain, community leaders, teacher advisor coordinator, school engagement officer, and teacher advisors garnered descriptions of school ethos, organisation, and policies and were universally enthusiastic responses to the whole-school approach taken at this school to improve student wellbeing. The organisation of the school into four Years 7 to 10 communities was designed to address issues of wellbeing through creating a sense of connectedness and belonging. Students, and as far as possible, staff, remain in these communities for their four years at the school. The community design encourages a familial relationship among staff and students. Staffrooms are integrated into the community, students are welcome in their communities at all times, and bathroom facilities are shared. Therefore, staff and students mingle in formal and informal community spaces. As mentioned earlier in this chapter, each community is divided into Years 7 and 8 and Years 9 and 10 neighbourhoods. In Years 7 and 8 all classes are taken within the learning community, with teachers from their own community, while in Years 9 and 10 students join with students from other communities in a variety of specialist, elective subjects while their core subjects continue to be studied in their own community. Each student belongs to a teacher advisory class in which they remain for four years, The pivotal role of the teacher advisors in creating an accepting and nurturing environment for their students is discussed in chapter 11. Students are encouraged in their sense of connectedness by the close long-term relationships with peers and teacher advisor that they establish in these surroundings.

A welfare structure provides support for staff and students at this school. As the teacher who has the closest relationship with the students in their care, the teacher advisor is the first port of call for students and classroom teachers. However, teacher advisors are also supported by the neighbourhood and community leaders who guide and mentor them in issues arising with their students. In addition, a wellbeing team, consisting of social workers, a chaplain, a psychologist, a nurse, an indigenous worker, an attendance officer, and an intellectual disabilities coordinator, provides a framework of support. The referral system ensures that all teacher advisors and students are able to access the wellbeing team at any time, and that when necessary, the wellbeing team is able to refer students to the best external services available. Student referrals to the wellbeing team are discussed at executive level and involve the child psychologist, assistant principal, wellbeing coordinator, and attendance officer. They identify the best course of action, agency, or service for the referred student.

Policies and procedures and a positive school culture support the new structures. The ethos of the school is focussed on positive and respectful relationships (Principal interview). For example, student behaviour-management is based on a system of restorative action (RA), a form of conflict resolution which seeks to make clear to the miscreant that their behaviour is not condoned, while at the same time being supportive and respectful of the individual (McCluskey et al., 2011; Morrison, 2007). In a staged response to poor student behaviour, classroom teachers take initial responsibility for dealing with the problems. If necessary, the teacher advisor is involved to provide, with their more intimate relationship with the student, both context and advocacy. The central premise of RA, that the community as a whole is harmed when one person belonging to it causes harm to another, is imparted to students, promoting a sense of responsibility in restoring community harmony (McCluskey & Lephalala, 2010). Community leaders support the teacher advisors, and the assistant principal, or principal, is the last step, usually in extreme situations. This provides for greater shared responsibility for students. School uniform policies are couched in ways that take into consideration the home circumstances of students who are not wearing school uniform and confidential guidance and assistance is offered where the family's financial or other circumstances warrant such intervention. Such policies contribute to the promotion of student and staff wellbeing.

Procedures for student management are perceived to be extremely important in developing a school culture of consistency and security. Explicit teaching about the school's core values relates to behaviour within the school community, making the most of opportunities, respect in relationships, and behaviours relevant to their expectations and achievements, including working hard, being organised, always persisting and doing one's best. Constant reference to these values when talking with students enhances the shared culture. One teacher suggested that, although the learning communities tended to function like four mini-schools due to variations in how teachers were implementing the procedures, there was enough consistency to ensure that all students and staff were aware of the expectations for learning and behaviour. Staff members knew what to expect from week to week and this allayed past fears about managing student behaviours. This sense of consistency is important for students' sense of security and fairness.

Clearly the development of this positive social environment within the learning communities requires more communication and connection among teachers and students. Discussion about school and community values encourages teachers to recognise their own strengths and weaknesses, to reflect on their development needs and to draw on their colleagues' knowledge and skills. Community leaders and teacher advisors model communication strategies, or the implementation of TA learning activities, for their colleagues and then discuss these experiences. Such professional learning opportunities hone teachers' communication skills as they rehearse and practise them in a context of growing relational agency, (Edwards, 2011; Prain et al., 2014). The learning-team members learn from each other leading to new ways to understand and respond to student needs. One staff member who has been involved in student wellbeing for many years noted that referrals to the wellbeing team had decreased over the past few years. He put this down to improved relationships, communication, and shared responsibility for students.

Where possible, the wellbeing team works with the families of students and this assists in developing a closer relationship with the school. In answer to a question regarding where the line is drawn between the responsibilities of the school and others, the school chaplain stated that:

> [There is] no line [between school and home]. We deal with or work [with] the families. Myself, and I know other wellbeing team members, make a lot of home visits. Usually, or if not always, we speak to the parents in relation to what's happening at school with the students. If their behaviour is really questionable then usually the TAs have rung them, and often it will be a referral to the chaplain or wellbeing team to follow up, and then we keep in touch with parents.

While the community structures within the open-plan settings were designed to improve relationships and the overall culture of the school, the physical environment, including the design of the open-plan learning spaces, also contributes to students' wellbeing. The changes to the school's built environment were, and continue to be, welcomed by the students. A lack of graffiti and damage to the learning spaces is further testament to student appreciation. All the teachers interviewed commented on the significant decline in student misbehaviour in these new spaces.

The protocols for the use of inside spaces are perceived as contributing to a sense in students that their school cares about them. In interviews, while most students nominated outside spaces, some students referred to inside spaces as their favourites, including the library and the couches in the Einstein areas. Staff reported that another significant outcome of this arrangement was a decrease in problems in the school grounds during lunch and recess.

The physical environment outside the learning communities is considerable in size. Areas between the buildings are landscaped as passive recreation areas and spaces further from the buildings provide opportunities for major games such as netball, basketball, cricket, and football. In interviews, students from both Year 7 and Year 10 highlighted the lack of playing equipment. Playground equipment has been identified as inducing physical activity, thereby contributing to the physical and social health of students (Ramstetter, Murray, & Garner, 2010; Parrish, Okely, Stanley, & Ridgers, 2013). The assistant principal acknowledged that students did not suddenly lose interest in playing games when they come to secondary school and down-ball squares, which had been introduced to meet this need, were extremely popular with the junior students.

A male leading teacher recalled being on edge when he was on yard duty in this first year of teaching at the school.

> I was always looking for trouble. Whereas now, my yard duty consists of playing down-ball with the kids or wandering around and having chats with little groups of kids who are basically sitting around having their lunch and talking. So it's a really good feeling.

Curriculum, Teaching and Learning

Research points to the school curriculum, an often neglected component of student health and wellbeing, as a vital link in the whole-school approach. Through their formal and informal learning in the settings, students learn awareness of issues that affect theirs and others' lives and the consequences of life style choices. In classroom discussions with peers and teachers, students consider a range of viewpoints and learn to deepen their understanding, reasoning, and judgment. The consequences of neglecting curriculum are that students do not learn, in a safe environment, the social and emotional skills that will enable them to manage relationships and academic learning at secondary school, as well as the critical health literacy that will enable them to make healthy life choices and prepare them to manage their future health and wellbeing needs. Ironbark College takes a two-pronged approach to student health and wellbeing through the school curriculum.

The TA program in this school (discussed in detail in Chapter 11) focuses on the development of close, positive, and supportive relationships between teachers and students, and between students. The informal social and emotional education that occurs in a cohesive small and supportive group, that remains together over a period of four years, is complemented by a formal curriculum in which students discuss issues relevant to their personal lives, and learn key generic skills that assist them in their academic subjects. The commitment to, and scope of, the formal curriculum is an indication of the value attached to the teacher advisory program as an integral part of the students' wellbeing at this school. Students report high levels of satisfaction with their TAs and almost always identify them as a key support person to whom they take their problems and concerns. These positive and caring relationships set the tone for the culture of care across the whole school.

Ironbark College also provides Physical, Health and Sport Education (PHASE) as a compulsory subject for Years 7 and 8 and elective health and physical education subjects for Years 9 and 10. Students at all levels are required to participate in sports with the opportunity for students to experience a variety of sports. Students are also encouraged to participate in community sporting clubs, and the school intentionally does not run school-based teams in most sports to support community-based sporting clubs. The teachers perceive sport and physical education as contributing to social, teamwork, and leadership skills, as well as physical health. The emphasis, in harmony with the ethos of the school, is on participation rather than excellence in performance. PHASE also includes the range of topics found in most health education programs including anatomy, fitness, body image, mental health, drugs and alcohol, and sexuality education.

Some overlap of content in the PHASE curriculum with the TA curriculum is indicated in interviews. Yet the approaches are complementary, with the former concerned with encouraging physical good health, and the latter concerned with developing social and emotional health. The intention of both is to contribute to student wellbeing. The development of health literacy is an important aspect of PHASE, enabling adolescents to understand, negotiate, and manage information sources pertaining to their own health needs and interests. In their teacher advisory sessions (see Chapter 11 for more detail) students participate in embodied learning activities, role plays, circle time and small-group discussions with a familiar group of peers to learn to consider a variety of opinions, to value their own experience, and that of their teacher advisors and peers in broadening their perspectives on a range of relevant issues, deepening their reasoning and decision-making ability. Initial reluctance from TA teachers to employ participatory strategies because of time restrictions, concern about loss of control, and lack of training and confidence and lack of time (see Cahill et al., 2013; Ennett et al., 2003; Natvig et al., 2003; Stead et al., 2007; Tappe et al., 1997) has been largely overcome at Ironbark College as through practice, working in teams of two, and professional learning activities, teachers have improved "their understanding of the educational purpose of the activities" and their confidence in "their pedagogical function in promoting student engagement and their capacity to control the class" (Cahill et al., 2013).

Considerable research evidence (see Cahill et al., 2013; Herbert & Lohrmann, 2011; Durlak et al., 2011) suggests that participatory learning strategies or, learning strategies that employ student-to-student interaction rather than just teacher-to-student interaction, are integral to successful health education. These types of learning strategies include role-play and simulation, small-group problem- solving, discussions, critical thinking tasks, skills development exercises, and themes games (Cahill et al., 2013, p. 2). Such strategies serve a range of epistemological functions through the invitation to students to actively engage in their learning. In drug education, participatory learning tasks prompt students to explore drug-use norms of their age mates (often overestimated by adolescents), pressures and risks related to drug use, and require students to examine choices and options relevant to a range of authentic situations. Furthermore, participatory learning strategies allow students to practice strategies and solutions to minimise the harm they might otherwise experience in these situations. Through role play students develop skills in risk analysis, problem-solving and ownership of solutions; they engage empathetically with a particular predicament and acquire the help seeking or refusal skills needed to realise particular choices. Cahill et al. (2013) claim that role play in particular "assists student to identify the gap that might exist between the theory about what they would or could do, and challenge of application" (p. 3).

Partnerships and Services

Schools are not isolated entities but are part of the broader community that has resources to support the school and broaden the horizons of students. Contributing to the community and drawing on its resources is part of a culture that values connectedness and reciprocity. Ironbark College is part of a very close-knit community with fierce traditional community pride and loyalties. The school's close identification with its community is visually signified by a shared totem and colours (school uniform and local sporting teams).

Each morning a free breakfast is made available to all students. Many of the students would otherwise start their school day without having had breakfast. The preparation and supply of the breakfast is another source of connectedness to the community. The breakfast is staffed by community volunteers and the school chaplain and the food is sourced from the local *Foodshare* organisation, a community volunteer organisation. A local youth worker often attends the breakfast and runs lunchtime games as well, using the time to build relationships with the students and inviting them to attend youth club activities in the local community.

The community connections of the school begin with the families of students. The wellbeing team works with families to develop close, comfortable relationships. Through the teacher advisor, who gets to know each parent through telephone calls and home visits, the parent always has a familiar point of contact with the school, a person they can talk over issues with. The broader wellbeing team also understands that student wellbeing depends on fostering a close partnership with the families of students and follows up with home visits to keep in touch with parents. This relationship is particularly important with disengaged students or those who refuse school.

It is a sign of the school ethos that Ironbark College ensures "no one gets lost or forgotten" (student engagement officer interview). Though there is no funding allowance, a student engagement worker, a teacher skilled in counselling 'at risk' students, has been employed to reconnect these students with the school. The student engagement worker's role is to work one-on-one with these students to provide the motivation and skills to return to school, and to work in partnership with parents where possible. This often involves phone conversations before school, or actually going to a student's home to coax him/her out of bed. The student engagement officer develops a trusting relationship with parents that sometimes results in parents gaining the confidence to assert themselves with their adolescent child. The engagement officer also prepares students for their return to school by coaching them on how to deal with the situations they are likely to face. Perhaps the biggest challenge for the student engagement worker is to create a teacher culture that understands the difficulties students experience beyond school and values students' rights to return and be respected in the same way as more motivated students.

Sometimes it is not possible to work with families as a number of disengaged students live in Out-of-Home-Care, with foster parents or in residential care homes. Some have been involved with the justice system. For these students the wellbeing team at Ironbark College maintains strong relationships with relevant service agencies in order to ensure suitable and relevant education plans are put in place for these students. The sphere of influence of school staff in this context clearly extends beyond their traditional roles and beyond the school boundaries. Development of relational agency (Edwards, 2005, 2007, 2011; Prain et al., 2013) among teachers, principals, the student engagement worker, and those from outside services is necessary if student wellbeing for these at risk students is to be maximised.

Curriculum opportunities beyond the school boundaries have also been explored at this school to broaden student horizons. Some senior students visit local primary schools or pre-schools once a week in a cross-age tutoring program to assist the teachers and act as buddies and mentors to younger children. Students visit local aged care facilities to read to and talk to the residents. A dance troupe that links indigenous students with the local Aboriginal leaders, has led to improvements in indigenous students' engagement and wellbeing. Senior students can negotiate to undertake fundraising projects or community service projects for local community organisations as part of an elective subject. The students learn skills of negotiation, time management, responsibility and communication in planning for and projects such as collecting food to distribute to needy families or walking dogs to raise money for the RSPCA. Community members are also welcomed into the school to share their skills and expertise with students. Some are involved in a program that encourages success for boys by sharing their ICT and literacy expertise over breakfast and encouraging boys to see education as a vital preparation for the workforce. Others come to talk about their careers and show students possible future pathways. Community sports enthusiasts are also involved in assisting physical education teachers to instruct the students.

Positive signs are emerging of a whole school approach to wellbeing. Our case study, survey and interview data suggests that: (1) a focus on the school ethos and environment, (2) a focus on curriculum and teaching including social and emotional learning, (3) and partnerships with the parents and the community are essential to improved student wellbeing.

CONCLUSION

It is evident that student wellbeing is not something that can be enhanced through knowledge and skills development alone, although this tends to be the focus in many schools. Positive and caring relationships developed between staff and students underpin a whole-school approach where all aspects of the school experience are geared towards enhanced wellbeing. The physical environment can create spaces that are pleasing to the eye, provide students with a sense that they are valued, reduce areas traditionally associated with bullying, and create a sense of both security and informality which enhance relationships.

The overall ethos driven by the school philosophy and policies can contribute to shared expectations for both staff and students, increased staff awareness of their role in student wellbeing and, draw attention to staff professional development that might be required to enhance the supportive ethos of the school. Shared expectations leads to consistent responses to student issues that arise providing a sense of security for both staff and students. Making time in the curriculum for social and emotional learning, personal development skills and relationship building such as was observed in the Teacher Advisory program also creates opportunities for individualised support and high expectations for all students. It is evident in our case study school, that stronger connections between the Teacher Advisory program and the Physical, Health and Sport Education (PHASE) curriculum are possible and indeed preferable. It is apparent also that a comprehensive, developmental health and wellbeing curriculum that employs highly dialogic and participatory learning strategies can contribute to improved student wellbeing outcomes.

Strong partnerships built between the school, parents, and a range of agencies within the community are essential to ensuring students' wellbeing needs are met. In addition, stronger relationships with students' families can contribute to improved shared understandings about students' needs between parents and staff, as well as improved wellbeing in families. Strengths within the local community can be acknowledged, valued and drawn upon in the quest for improved wellbeing.

NOTES

[1] ICSEA is calculated using family background data including occupation, adults in family unemployed, educational level and single parent family status. The ICSEA values are produced on a scale that has a mean of 1000 and a standard deviation of 100. ICSEA scores range from about 500 representing schools with extremely disadvantaged students, to approximately 1300, representing schools with students from very educationally advantaged backgrounds (Australian ACARA, n.d.). Scores for all schools are available at the My School website http://www.myschool.edu.au

[2] In Victoria, all students' opinions on their schools are gathered on an annual basis through the "Attitudes to School Survey" (DEECD, 2014). The survey consists of 11 scales covering wellbeing (student morale and student distress), learning and teaching (teacher effectiveness, teacher empathy, stimulating learning, school connectedness, students motivation and confidence), and student relationships (connectedness to peers, classroom behaviour and student safety).

REFERENCES

Allardt, E. (1976). Dimensions of welfare in a compartative Scandinavian study. *Acta Sociologica, 19*, 227–240. doi:10.1177/000169937601900302

Allardt, E. (1981). Experiences from the comparative Scandinavian welfare study, with the bibliography of the project. *European Journal of Political Research, 9*, 101–111. doi:10.1111/j.1475-6765.1981.tb00591.x

Allardt, E. (1989). *An updated indicator system: Having, loving, being.* Working papers 48. Helsinki, Europe: University of Helsinki, Department of Sociology.

Australian Catholic University & Erebus International. (2008). *Scoping study into approaches to student wellbeing: Final report.* Sydney, Australia: Australia Catholic University, Erebus International.

Bendigo Education Plan Steering Committee (BEP). (2005). *Bendigo education plan.* Bendigo, Victoria, Australia: Loddon Mallee Region, DEECD. Retrieved from http://www.weeroona.vic.edu.au/site-content/strategic-plans/BEP.pdf

Bendigo Loddon Primary Care Partnership (BLPCP). (2012, June). *Community health and wellbeing profile - June 2012.* Bendigo, Victoria, Australia: Bendigo Loddon Primary Care Partnership. Retrieved from http://www.blpcp.com.au/BLPCP%20Community%20Profile%2022%20November_2012.pdf

Bolte, A., Goschke, T., & Kuhl, J. (2003). Emotion and intuition: Effects of positive and negative mood on implicit judgements of semantic coherence. *Psychological Science, 14*(5), 416–421. doi:10.1111/1467-9280.01456

Bond, L., Butler, H., Thomas, L., Carlin, J., Glover, S., Bowes, G., & Patton, G. (2007). Social and school connectedness in early secondary school as predictors of late teenage substance use, mental health and academic outcomes. *Journal of Adolescent Health, 40*(4). doi:10.1016/j.jadohealth.2006.10.013

Cahill, H., Coffey, J. E., Lester, L., Midford, R., Ramsden, R., & Venning, L. (2013). Influences on teachers' use of participatory learning strategies in health education classes. *Health Education Journal*, 1–12. doi:10.1177/0017896913513892

Cassidy, W., Jackson, M., & Brown, K. N. (2009). Sticks and stones can break my bones, but how can pixels hurt me? Students experiences with cyber-bullying. *School Psychology International, 30*(4), 383–402. doi:10.1177/0143034309106948

Christenson, S. L., & Thurlow, M. L. (2004). School dropouts: Prevention considerations, and challenges. *Current Directions in Psychological Science, 13*(1), 36–39. doi:10.1111/j.0963-7214.2004.01301010

Clift, S., & Jensen, B. B. (2005). *The health promoting school: International advances in theory, evaluation and practice*. Copenhagen, Denmark, Europe: Danish University of Education Press.

Coleman, J. (2009). Well-being in schools: Empirical measure, or politician's dream? *Oxford Review of Education, 35*(3), 281–292. doi:10.1080/03054980902934548

DEECD. (2014). *Attitudes to school survey*. Retrieved from http://www.education.vic.gov.au/school/principals/management/Pages/performsurveyat.aspx

Durlak, J. A., Weissberg, R. P., Dymnicki, A. B., Taylor, R. D., & Schellinger, K. B. (2011). The impact of enhancing students' social and emotional learning: A meta-analysis of school-based universal interventions. *Child Development, 82*(1). doi:10.1111/j.1467-8624.2010.01564.x

Edwards, A. (2005). Relational agency: Learning to be a resourceful practitioner. *International Journal of Educational Research, 43*(3), 168–182. doi:10.1016/j.ijer.2006.06.010

Edwards, A. (2007). Relational agency in professional practice: A CHAT analysis. *Actio: An International Journal of Human Activity Theory, 1*, 1–17.

Edwards, A. (2011). Building common knowledge at the bourndaries between professional practices: Relational agency and relational expertise in systems of distributed expertise. *International Journal of Educational Research, 50*(1), 33–39. doi:10.1016/j.ijer.2011.04.007

Ennett, S. T., Ringwalt, C. L., Thorne, J., Rohrbach, L. A., Vincus, A., Simons-Rudolph, A., & Jones, S. (2003). A comparison of current practice in school-based substance use prevention programs with meta-analysis findings. *Prevention Science, 4*(1), 1–14. doi:10.1023/A:1021777109369

Fraillon, J. (2004). *Measuring student well-being in the context of Australian schooling* (Discussion paper). Melbourne, Australia: MCEETYA.

Fredrickson, B. L. (1998). What good are positive emotions in positive psychology? *Review of General Psychology, 2*(3). doi:10.1037/1089-2680.2.3.300

Fredrickson, B. L., & Branigan, C. (2005). Positive emotions broaden the scope of attention and thought-action repertoires. *Cognition & Emotion, 19*(3), 313–332. doi:10.1080/02699930441000238

Herbert, P. C., & Lohrmann, D. K. (2011). It's all in the delivery! An analysis of instructional strategies from effective health education curricula. *Journal of School Health, 81*(5), 258–264. doi:10.1111/j.1746-1561.2011.00586.x

Isen, A. M., Rosenzweig, A. S., & Young, M. J. (1991). The influence of positive affect on clinical problem solving. *Medical Decision Making, 11*(3), 221–227. doi:10.1177/0272989X9101100313

Jackson, M., Cassidy, W., & Brown, K. (2009). You were born ugly and youl die ugly too: Cyber-bullying as relational aggression. *In Education, 15*(2). Retrieved from http://ineducation.ca/ineducation/article/view/57/538

Kawachi, I., & Berkman, L. (2000). Social cohesion, social capital and health. In I. Kawachi & L. Bermann (Eds.), *Social epidemiology* (pp.174–190). New York, NY: Oxford University Press.

Konu, A., & Rimpelä, M. (2002). Well-being in schools: A conceptual model. *Health Promotion International, 17*(1), 79–87. doi:10.1093/heapro/17.1.79

Kuhl, J. (1983). Emotion, cognition, and motivation: II. The functional significance of emotions in perception, memory, problem-solving, and overt action. *Sprache & Kognition, 2*, 228–253.

Kuhl, J. (2000). A functional-design approach to motivation and self-regulation: The dynamics of personality systems interactions. In M. Moekaerts, P. R. Pintrich, & M. Zeidner (Eds.), *Handbook of self-regulation* (pp. 111–169). San Diego, CA: Academic Press.

McCluskey, G., & Lephalala, M. (2010). A person is a person because of others: Challenges to meanings of discipline in South African and UK schools. *Power and Education, 2*(1), 18–30. doi:10.2304/power.2010.2.1.18

McCluskey, G., Kane, J., Lloyd, G., Stead, J., Riddell, S., & Weedon, E. (2011). Teachers are afraid we are stealing their strength: A risk society and restorative approaches in school. *British Journal of Educational Studies, 59*(2), 105–119. doi:10.1080/00071005.2011.565741

McGregor, J. (2004a). Space, power and the classroom. *Forum, 40*(1), 13–18. doi:10.2304/forum.2004.46.1.2

McGregor, J. (2004b). Spatiality and the place of the materials in schools. *Pedagogy, Culture & Society, 12*(13), 347–372. doi:10.1080/14681360400200207

Morrison, B. (2007). Schools and restorative justice. In G. Johnstone & D. W. Van Nessl (Eds.), *Handbook of restorative justice* (pp. 325–351). Oxon, UK: Willan Publishing.

Natvig, G. K., Albrektsen, G., & Qvarnstrom, U. (2003). Associations between psychological factors and happiness among school adolescents. *International Journal of Nursing Practice, 9*(3), 166–175. doi:10.1046/j.1440-172X.2003.00419.x

Parrish, A. M., Okely, A. D., Stanley, R. M., & Ridgers, N. D. (2013). The effect of school recess interventions of physical activity. *Sports Medicine, 43*(4), 287–299. doi:10.1007/s40279-013-0024-2

Prain, V., Cox, P., Deed, C., Dorman, J., Edwards, D., Farrelly, C.,... Yager, Z. (2013). Personalised learning: Lessons to be learnt. *British Educational Research Journal, 39*(4), 654–676. doi:10.1080/01411926.2012.669747

Prain, V., Cox, P., Deed, C., Dorman, J., Edwards, D., Farrelly, C., . . . Yager, Z. (Eds.). (2014). *Personalising learning in open-plan schools*. Rotterdam, The Netherlands: Sense Publishers.

Putnam, R. D. (1993). The prosperous community: Social capital and public life. *The American Prospect, 4*(13), 35–42.

Quenzel, G., & Hurrelman, K. (2013). The growing gender gap in education. *International Journal of Adoelscence and Youth, 18*(2), 69–94. doi:10.1080/02673843.2012.665168

Ramstetter, C. L., Murray, R., & Garner, A. S. (2010). The crucial role of recess in schools. *Journal of School Health, 80*(11), 517–526. doi:10.1111/j.1746-1561.2010.00537.x

Reh, S., Rabenstein, K., & Fritzsche, B. (2011). Learning spaces without boundaries? Territories, power and how schools regulate learning. *Social & Cultural Geography, 12*(1), 83–98. doi:10.1080/14649365.2011.542482

Rowe, F., & Stewart, D. (2009). Promoting connectedness through whole-school approaches: A qualitative study. *Health Education, 109*(5), 396–413. doi:10.1108/09654280910984816

Rowe, G., Hirsh, J. B., Anderson, A. K., & Smith, E. E. (2007). Positive affect increases the breadth of attentional selection. *PNAS Proceedings of the National Academy of Sciences of the United States of America, 104*(1), 383–388. doi:10.1073/pnas.0605198104

Rutter, M. (1990). In J. Rolf, D. Mastein, D. Cicetti, K. Neuchterlain, & S. Weintraub (Eds.), *Psychosocial resilience and protective mechanisms*. New York, NY: Cambridge University Press.

Seligman, M. E. P., Ernst, R. M., Gilham, J., Reivich, K., & Linkins, M. (2009). Positive education: Positive psychology and classroom interventions. *Oxford Review of Education, 35*(3), 292–311. doi:10.1080/03054980902934563

Stead, M., Stradling, R., MacNeil, M., MacKintosh, A., & Minty, S. (2007). Implementation evaluation of the blueprint multi-component drug prevention programme: Fidelity of school component delivery. *Drug & Alcohol Review, 26*(6), 653–664. doi:10.1080/09595230701613809

Sun, J., & Stewart, D. (2007). How effective is the health-promoting school approach in building social capital in primary schools? *Health Education, 107*(6), 56–574. doi:10.1108/09654280710827948

Tappe, M., Galer-Unti, P., & Bailey, K. (1997). Evaluation of trained teachers' implementation of a sex education curriculum. *Journal of Health Education, 28*(2), 103–108. doi:10.1080/10556699.1997.10608600

Walgrave, M., & Wannes, H. (2011). Cyberbullying: Predicting victimisation and perpetration. *Children and Society, 25*(1), 59–72. doi:10.1111/j.1099-0860.2009.00260.x

WHO. (1996). *Promoting health through schools*. Geneva, Switzerland: WHO Global School Health Initiative, Health Education and Promotion Unit. Retrieved from http://www.who.int/iris/handle/10665/63367-sthash.Mj72gAhw.dpuf

Wilkinson, R. G. (1996). *Unhealthy societies: The afflictions of inequality.* London, UK: Routledge.
Wilson, S. J., & Tanner-Smith, E. E. (2013). Dropout prevention and intervention programs for improving school completion among school-aged children and youth: A systematic review. *Journal of the Society for Social Work and Research, 4*(4), 357–372. doi:10.5243/jsswr.2013.22
Youngblade, L. M., Theokas, C., Schulenberg, J., Curry, L., Huang, I.-C., & Novak, M. (2007). Risk and promotive factors in families, schools, and communities: A contextual model of positive youth development in adolescence. *Pediatrics, 119*(2), S47–S53. doi:10.1542/peds.2006-2089H

VAUGHAN PRAIN, VALERIE LOVEJOY AND DEBRA EDWARDS

5. "IT'S NOT A PLUG-IN PRODUCT"

Making Digital Technologies Serve Learning in a School with an Open-Plan Setting

OPTIMISING COMPUTER AFFORDANCES

As noted by Jonassen (2014), computer use has evolved over the last thirty years, deeply diversifying how students learn. This resource now functions variously as a learning guide or tutor (as in access to web-based tutorials and information sites), as a communicative tool with self and others for reasoning, inquiring, and creating or disseminating knowledge (as in the programs in computer games, English, science, and mathematics outlined in other chapters in this book), and as an organiser through which students can self-manage, reflect upon, and enact/improve their learning in systematic ways (as in learning dashboards).

Learning dashboards, as used in schools, are digital systems designed to "capture data about learner activities and visualise these data to support awareness, reflection, sense-making, and impact" (Verbert, Govaerts, Duval, Santos, Assche, Parra, & Klerkx, 2014, p. 1501). They have evolved from early designs as a digital visual display of a database to organise information (as in an early warning system to alert teachers and students to a student's lack of progress with learning or behavior, mirroring malfunction alerts in a car dashboard). Now they are expected to serve multiple functions around quality learning. These systems can also be designed to enable access to this information for students, teachers, and parents. Verbert and colleagues (2014) identified a variety of dashboards currently in use internationally that reinforce face-to-face, virtual, and blended learning. While these dashboards all monitor student-learning activities and assessment, Verbert et al. (2014) and others, (Britzman, 1991; Kress & van Leuwen, 2001; Mårell-Olsson, 2012), also note the potential of this digital technology to make learning visible to students and teachers in ways not previously available. This technology now enables a convergence in one place of goal-setting records, student reflections, student assessment and progress data, portfolios of achievement, and access to resources for students to understand and represent their learning processes and outcomes.

These changes to the role of learners in learning pose demanding challenges for teachers. According to Edwards (2014), drawing on Engestrom (2005, p. 324), both teachers and students need to develop "collective intentionality capital". By this she means a shared view of what counts as enablers and evidence of quality learning, while recognising that these collaborations are "fragile, open, and literally under construction" (p. 324). The dashboard is a prime site or tool where this fluid knowledge about shared teacher and student intentions (and strategies) is built, reviewed, and distributed.

For Verbert et al. (2014), student learning from learning dashboards poses many research questions about user actions, purposes, and preferences, and the particular dashboard features most conducive to student reflection and knowledge about what best supports their learning, and why. These questions move the focus from what types of resources (and their display) support student reflection and learning to what kinds of interactions with the resources enable this learning, and why. Does knowing these data motivate students to refine past learning strategies or does it have no inevitable effects? For example, does access to these data make them willing to identify strengths and weaknesses in how they learn across different subjects, and experiment with new approaches? Can the learning and experiencing self influence the remembering self? Kahneman (2011) makes the deflating claim that the remembering self tends to dominate an individual's narrative of his or her life, and this is probably true of students' reactions to assessment. The result often erases the process, and the student moves on. This suggests that insightful reflection on performance is a significant challenge for adults, and even more so for adolescents.

Verbert et al. (2014) sensibly suggest that a fruitful starting point for engaging students on these issues is to ask them about their expectations, experiences, and practices in using dashboards. What suggestions would they make about improvements, and why? What advice (whether their teacher's or their own) has enabled them to improve their work, or how they approach learning tasks? What prompts deepen their reflection on the experiencing self in the act of tackling these tasks? What makes them change tack? These questions also have significant implications for teachers as expert learning coaches.

In this chapter we report on the development over several years of a learning dashboard at Whirrakee College, noting its initial and added functions, its impact on student learning, and its evolution to serve more purposes. We claim that this dashboard can personalise student learning and enhance the quality of this learning under certain conditions. We draw on analyses of quantitative data (student academic performance in literacy and numeracy at Whirrakee College, 2008–2014, and distribution of scores across all subjects 2009–2011) and qualitative data (teacher and student interviews, 2011–2015) to support these claims. We have seen over extended time that this dashboard sets high expectations of students, encouraging them to be responsible for organising and being accountable for their learning. We have noted how it functions for some students as a motivator to greater effort because they are able to measure their progress against themselves, their class, and state averages.

We do not claim the dashboard optimises all possible functions of such a device, given current and future rates of technical innovation and adaptation, and future changes to assessment practices. Rather, we think it continues to evolve to address real challenges around personalising learning and learning support in a large open-plan school of over 1200 students in four learning communities. These challenges include: providing a user-friendly learning platform that informs, motivates, tracks, supports, and archives individual students' academic goals, performance, and progress; and establishing an effective means to meet mandated administrative requirements that schools monitor and report on attendance, academic performance, and wellbeing of all their students. In an up-scaled learning community of 300 students, where there may be a risk of some aspects of an individual student's progress or needs being overlooked, the dashboard provides a practical solution to address this potential problem.

RESEARCH AIMS AND METHODS

In this study we aimed to: (1) track the evolution of the dashboard design and its effects on teacher and students' teaching and learning practices; and (2) analyse these effects in relation to understanding the practice and theory of personalising learning. Research methods included analyses of quantitative data and qualitative data (interviews with principal (6 interviews, 2011–15), teachers (10 interviews), and students (20 interviews with 10 Year 7 and 10 Year 10 students). Quantitative data were analysed for trends over the three years of the research project, and qualitative data were analysed for key themes and by drawing on theoretical constructs from the relevant literature, including affordance theory (Gibson, 1977), Edwards' relational agency (2011), and Engestrom's (2005) account of challenges in activity systems.

FINDINGS

The Whirrakee Dashboard

The College expects all students to succeed, and the dashboard was devised as a practical way to support this outcome. Through an individualised approach to learning trajectories, students devise, implement, share and track their own personalised learning plans (PLPs), as prescribed in the BEP (Prain et al., 2014). From its inception the dashboard was expected to facilitate learner independence by encouraging student ownership and self-regulation of learning through transparent, timely sharing of information between students and teachers. The dashboard was intended to provide a detailed current account of student performance that students could analyse and act upon, supported by their teachers. Available on the school's intranet, data were accessible to all students, teachers, and parents 24 hours a day. This information about individual student learning and progress was to be organised in one place to enable students and teachers to plan and monitor goal-setting. Collective monitoring of these data could also enable the principal and teachers to plan and monitor subject and school goals.

Each student's results were displayed for every subject and their academic progress points (against state-based standards) in literacy and numeracy were monitored weekly. A summary appeared on their home page that indicated their current level of achievement in literacy and numeracy, and whether they were achieving at a pass, credit, or honours level in each subject area. These points were also graphed for students against expected levels of progress, and against all other students in that year level. All learning assessment tasks were listed together with completion dates to help students plan their work. Students knew that their achievement levels were updated weekly depending on when tasks were due. The student learning button contained subject-based resources to assist students with learning tasks. Daily bulletins, personal notices, emails, and displays of outstanding student work were also included. The dashboard also reminded students of the College's expectations about their development as well-rounded community members, with opportunities to plan and report on co-curricular and extra-curricular participation, entailing such activities as sports days and community work. These features were intended to encourage students to become competent self-managers of their own learning, where they could know precisely their current levels of achievement across multiple areas, and take informed action and remediation.

Teachers had access to a portal that required them to enter results for every learning assignment on the dashboard within two weeks of the due date. This enabled them to follow individual student performance closely, as well as check on the progress of assigned students (see Figure 5.1). The teacher portal enabled teachers individually and collectively, to follow individual and group student progress.

Through the dashboard, teachers could also have a snapshot view of all student data to enable targeted review of the effectiveness of their teaching, with scope for informed action (see Figure 5.2).

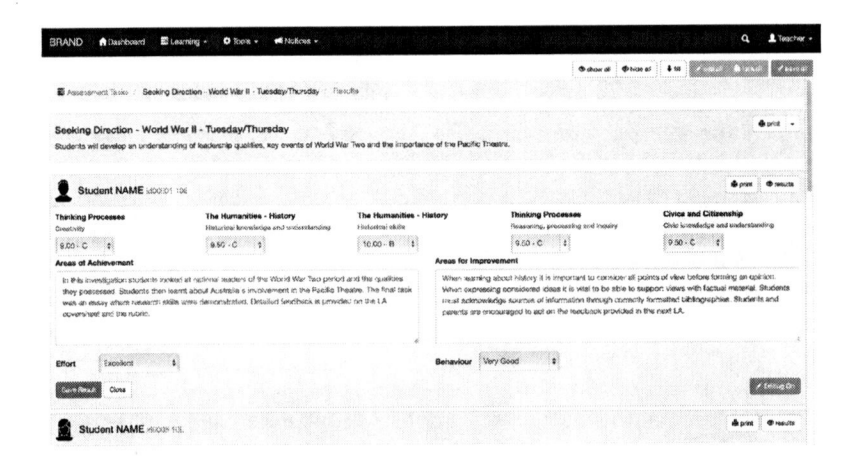

Figure 5.1. The teacher portal

"IT'S NOT A PLUG-IN PRODUCT"

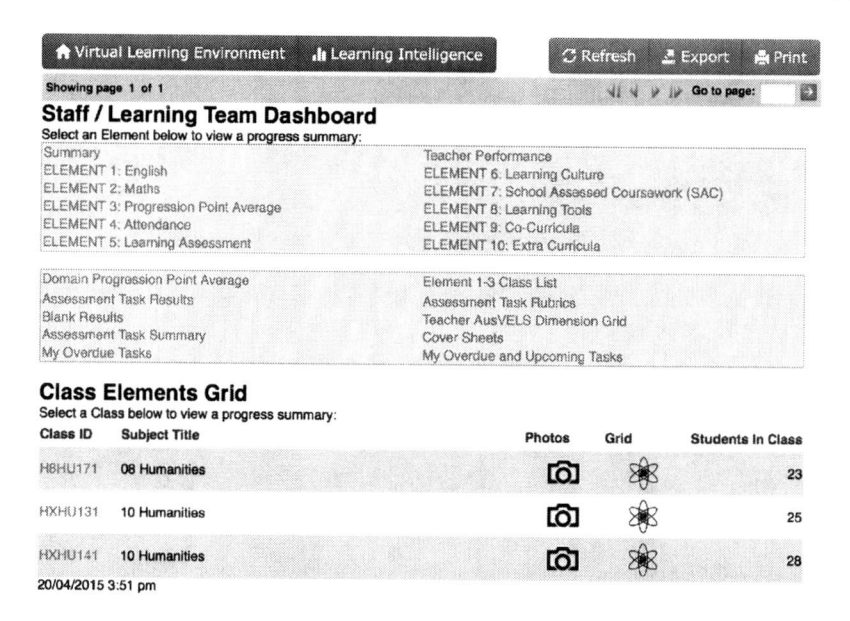

♠ Virtual Learning Environment ▪ Learning Intelligence	⟳ Refresh ⤓ Export 🖶 Print

Showing page 1 of 1

Staff / Learning Team Dashboard
Select an Element below to view a progress summary:

Summary	Teacher Performance
ELEMENT 1: English	ELEMENT 6: Learning Culture
ELEMENT 2: Maths	ELEMENT 7: School Assessed Coursework (SAC)
ELEMENT 3: Progression Point Average	ELEMENT 8: Learning Tools
ELEMENT 4: Attendance	ELEMENT 9: Co-Curricula
ELEMENT 5: Learning Assessment	ELEMENT 10: Extra Curricula
Domain Progression Point Average	Element 1-3 Class List
Assessment Task Results	Assessment Task Rubrics
Blank Results	Teacher AusVELS Dimension Grid
Assessment Task Summary	Cover Sheets
My Overdue Tasks	My Overdue and Upcoming Tasks

Class Elements Grid
Select a Class below to view a progress summary:

Class ID	Subject Title	Photos	Grid	Students In Class
H8HU171	08 Humanities	📷	⚛	23
HXHU131	10 Humanities	📷	⚛	25
HXHU141	10 Humanities	📷	⚛	28

20/04/2015 3:51 pm

Figure 5.2. The teacher view of all student data

DASHBOARD MODIFICATIONS

Over the last three years dashboard modifications have aimed to enhance its practicability and efficiency. While many of the original features have been retained, some modifications to the dashboard have been made. The current student dashboard (2015) has ten elements, preserving many original features, but adding new ones to specify and prompt learner analyses of their current progress (see Figure 5.3). These elements are: (1) a graphed record of each student's literacy level, (2) a graphed record of the numeracy level, (3) AusVELS requirements and expected levels, (4) attendance records that students can scan in, using their ID cards, (5) an assessment record on work handed in on time to the office, (6) a ready-to-learn category around being an organised learner, including coming to class with the appropriate equipment, uniform, and demonstrated punctuality (with a three warnings system, and subsequent parent contact), (7) a record of tests and essays written in class within a two-week period in each subject per semester, where students receive an S or N score; (8) learning tools, including an online planner, class-based activities, and a reflection requirement on work completed; (9) co-curricular involvement, entailing attendance at sporting events, parent/teacher interviews, and awards for extra leadership in representing the College in various ways; and (10) extra-curricular activities outside the school as part of wider community participation.

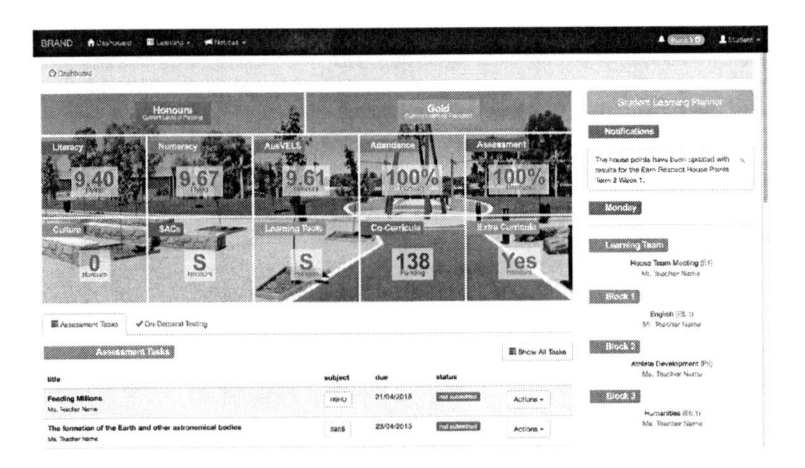

Figure 5.3. The 2015 student dashboard homepage

There are interfaces for students, teachers, and parents, and both public and private spaces on the dashboard. Both teachers and students can enter information about student progress, goals developed with the student, home and school assistance to reach goals, student responsibilities or strategies, and other reporting information. This information provides the basis for students to self-regulate their approach to learning, as well as to plan and monitor goals and outputs with teachers. Students (as well as their parents) are able to see for themselves when they are struggling, on track, or exceeding goals across all assessed areas, rather than this information being held and distributed by their teachers. The dashboard also provides a larger map of achievement than previously possible that teachers and students can analyse and act upon.

These changes over time to the look and functions of the dashboard have arisen from multiple inputs and for multiple reasons. User feedback from students and teachers prompted changes to the look of the dashboard to enhance navigability and ease of access. A carousel approach to each of the elements has been replaced by a summary page of all ten elements (see Figure 5.3) each one of which allows for more sophisticated drilling down to further detail by hovering over the element (see Figure 5.4).

Student requests for more detailed feedback led to changes to increased information about assessment results and attendance data. Other changes have aimed to enhance student motivation. For example, privileges such as participation in extra sports training can be undertaken by students if they maintain pass grades in other areas of the dashboard.

Planned changes include web-based access for parents to be informed in detail about their child's progress, and an increased range of capacities built into the

"IT'S NOT A PLUG-IN PRODUCT"

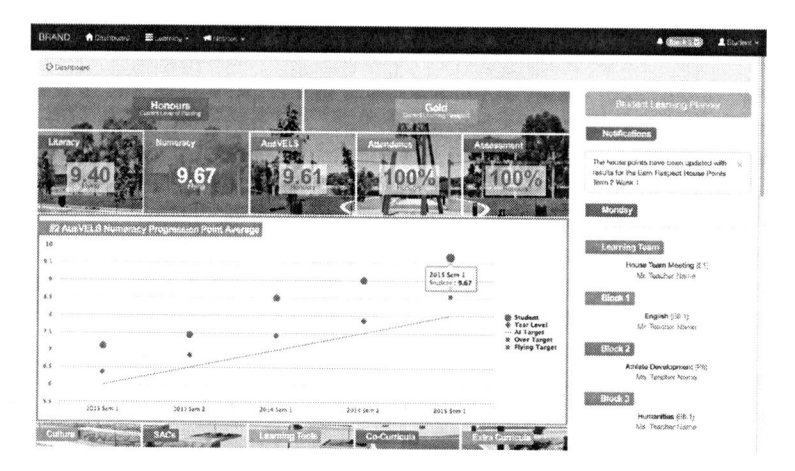

Figure 5.4. Record of individual student progress in element 2, numeracy

platform, such as an individual student learning portfolio as an on-going record of student attainment, and increased prompts and opportunities for student to record reflections on how they learn. Rather than the initial checklists of deadlines and timely submissions of work, and performance scores, additional elements have been added, such as detailed study-skills information, and the expectation that students will devise individual wellbeing plans rather than simply record participation in co- and extra-curricular activities. Students and parents will have access to online scanning of attendance, and have more information about student levels of attainment and growth in NAPLAN results. Next year, the College intends to create a learning platform for elements 1(Literacy), 2 (Numeracy) and 3 (AusVELS), where all resources will be provided online. There will be a continuum of learning, where students will progress at their own pace, and be responsible for their progress, with built-in checks along the way. Access to the resources provided, their learning portfolio, and their learning journal, are intended as integral parts of this learning. These changes point to the broad intention of increasing the dashboard's capacity to function as a personalised learning tool to identify and address individual learner needs.

A companion teacher dashboard is planned for 2015 as a contribution to staff professional learning and development. As noted by the principal, "if we are asking this of the kids, then it is only reasonable to ask this of staff too". From his perspective, the teachers should be under the same level of self- and peer-scrutiny and expectation of learning gains as their students, and should have the goal of improving their professional knowledge and learning as teachers. This development also points broadly to the intention of increasing critical analyses of what teacher-student learning experiences and what staff and student reflections best serve enhancement of student and teacher learning.

STAFF AND STUDENT VIEWS AND USE OF THE DASHBOARD

Given the evolutionary nature of the Whirrakee dashboard's capacities, it is difficult to assess impacts of old or new specific features and functions, either individually or collectively, against a shifting set of extended purposes. In addition, parallel to the dashboard's evolution, the College has also introduced and experimented with a wide range of ICTs, including interactive whiteboards, internet and computer-based programs, including google docs, blogs, podcasts, wikis, mind-map tools, and particular software design programs, such as comic life, and garageband. These resources have been promoted by staff as key student learning tools within and across different subjects, where engaging with their affordances is envisaged as a driver and cause of new student learning processes and content acquisition (see Chapters 6, 7, and 8 for examples of these processes and outcomes across BEP schools).

Students believe they learn in many ways within and outside school. These processes include learning through internet-based research on information and "published handy hints", observation, inquiry-based conversations with friends, peers, parents, classroom groups, adults and online experts, rehearsal and practice, enactments, following their teachers' short-cuts and clarifications, individual mental calculations, memorising mnemonics, intuition, guestimates, happenstance, luck and chance, thought experiments, purposeful manipulation of symbolic and actual tools, participation in simulated and actual experiences, and guided imitation of expert others (Barsalou, 2008; Prain et al., 2013, 2014). Learning through precise reflection on experience and practice, while strongly and broadly advocated in educational research (Black & Wiliam, 2009; Hattie, 2009), is not necessarily a preferred, automatic, well-deployed, well-understood student option. The school's prioritising of the goal of independent self-directed student learning, particularly through ICTs, has therefore deeply influenced students' perceptions of what enables and demonstrates learning across the mandated curriculum, and the potential and actual use of the dashboard in this process. The following comments by teachers, students, and the principal (who has been a strong advocate of the dashboard since its inception) reflect broad recurrent themes on the dashboard's perceived value and usage. They also reflect the evolution of student and teacher engagement with different versions of this resource.

Staff Views and Use of the Dashboard

Based on interviews, the teachers valued: (a) the administrative short-cuts enabled by the dashboard, where traditional time-consuming paper-based approaches to roll-calls, and tracking/reporting of student attendance, performance, and misbehaviour were streamlined; (b) improved access to precise data on individual and group student performances; (c) targeted conversations about learning effectiveness with students, especially when students initiate these conversations themselves; (d) the continuity of teacher practice, in that new or replacement teachers knew exactly the progress of classes in any particular subject; and (e) the student support, motivation, and self-management of learning enabled by the dashboard. The following comments from Teachers A, B, D and E provide a very brief snapshot of staff views, indicating their reasoning on these points:

> If a student is away for two weeks with tonsillitis they can access the learning button with support material and powerpoints, associated websites, youtube, video, worksheets all on there for them. They can get access to their assessment, front cover sheet, rubric, and other information. (Teacher A, 2011)

> Our college has a very strong assessment and reporting focus to support staff, students and parents. No longer is it the 'pretty' work. All students know what they need to do to get a certain mark or a VELS progression point. The learning assessment cover sheet supports this with students knowing what VELS is being assessed, what the requirements are, or the elements of the learning assessment task so they know exactly what's required. No longer do parents and students wait until the end of semester to get feedback on their assessment. (Teacher D, 2011)

> The students have a lot of information up there from their learning activities. So it's about goal-setting. The unit's called effective learning so it's what's a rubric, what are learning assessments, what are the systems at this school to help you learn, on-demand testing results, so you can set goals and things like that. Sometimes they use the computers to present their work, sometimes they use it to create or to visualise their thinking. We're doing a lot on graphic organisers. (Teacher A, 2011)

> A rubric is also given to students so that all students know what's required at each VELS level and they certainly should know their mark before they even submit the work according to the descriptions on the rubric. All students reflect on their learning and how they're going to apply their learning to a new situation in the future. (Teacher D, 2011)

> Our ability to provide a whole range of data and keeping students and their families up-to-date with that data is crucial for students to be able to manage their own learning and to get feedback. This includes their engagement, their actual VELS levels, and the curriculum delivery. The students have access to online resources, task requirements, and support material. (Teacher B, 2012)

> Parents are now messaged every time a student doesn't come into class with the right materials. On the spot they know, they're kept up to date and as soon as a student hasn't handed in a learning assessment, parents are notified. (Teacher B, 2012)

> If I'm a new teacher and I pick up a class semester 2, I'm able to access the information of any student I'm going to be teaching to find out where they're

at, what they're capable of, and use this information to support the student. (Teacher D, 2011)

They can go to their website and it shows them their results … and there's a target … history so they can see where they are going and what they need to get in order to achieve honours. So they are coming to me and saying, "Miss, Miss, my progression point average needs to go up by 0.2 in order to get honours, What do I have to do?" (Teacher A, 2011)

The dashboard puts all important information for a student on one site. With parents' contributions, more people are investing in each student. (Teacher E, 2015)

The site is a history of the student's progress at the school, and provides a context for current progress. It can also catch worrying trends, problems for students, early. (Teacher E, 2015)

These comments indicate a strong administrative, instrumental flavour to the teachers' perceptions of the dashboard's value and use as a student assessment organiser and teacher feedback system. The teachers broadly assumed that it complemented other ICTs that students used to inquire, pose questions, make records, communicate, collaborate, and represent learning individually and in groups in all subjects. As noted by Teacher B (2012), "the students have left the teachers behind in their ability to do the actual tasks", perhaps implying that student learning was being personalised by default, in that teachers were not able to over-prescribe learning pathways, representational choices, or narrow versions of success. However, the teachers' comments also reasonably indicate that they considered that assessment and reporting was now accessible in a timely fashion, more targeted, more precise, more distributed between teachers, and personalised to the goals and performance of every learner. There was not strong evidence that the dashboard was altering how teachers taught, but parallel to teacher motivation of students, it functioned as a personal targeted motivator.

Refinements and additional functions for the dashboard have aimed to enhance the capacity for students to use the platform as an advanced thinking and problem-solving analytical tool. Teacher B claimed that students were very competent in using many software programs to organise their understanding of topics into polished multi-modal presentations, but were less effective in using the platform to deepen independent inquiry, speculative reasoning, problem-seeking or as a collaborative tool/space to show deeper learning, and informed insightful reflection. She viewed this partly as a problem of how teachers reflected on their own roles in promoting learning and their capacity to anticipate and judge the design, challenges, and intended outcomes of the learning activities they set, oversaw and assessed:

I think it's limited by the quality of the task the teacher is setting. I said before about the scaffolding of inquiry and independence. That's something our teachers need to come to terms with and develop. What does a quality task look like? What opportunities are there for students to do learning in different ways to pursue their area of interest inside the theme or concept? (Teacher B, 2012)

Reflecting on over three years of student and staff dashboard usage in his school, the principal concurred with this concern. He claimed the dashboard was "not a plug-in product" that produced a quick fix to achieve learning excellence. Rather, its value depended on a significant long-term "cultural shift" in teachers' understandings and expertise in their roles as co-learners and supporters of student learning (Principal, 2015). Teachers needed to yield learning ownership from themselves to the students. In this challenging shift in the division of labour, detailed student feedback to teachers was a crucial element in making learning tasks, goals, and feedback more deeply generative for learning. Students could then be more innovative in how they personalised, and reflected upon, how they learnt. The goal was not standardised pathways and templates for every student's learning trajectories, but rather a shared wisdom/language about varied means to achieve diverse quality outcomes. Therefore, according to the principal, student feedback to teachers needed to shift from notions of "personal" assessment (of a teacher's style or personality) to assessment of the quality/usefulness of the tasks, task support, including ICT resources, and prompts, provocations, and questions that led to deeper learning, insightful reflection, informed action, and risk-taking. For the principal, the recent changes to the dashboard and setting up a companion teacher dashboard represent a move to "open accountability" for both students and teachers as learners. For him, data visibility for all participants means that there can be no excuses or alibis for lack of effort or evidence in trying to understand and improve quality learning. He considers that the dashboard can be the critical site for a sustained focus on the question of "what does good learning look like?" (Principal, 2015), and how and why is it achieved.

Taken as a whole, these comments by staff and the principal indicate that the dashboard has functioned effectively as a site for timely feedback to students on their progress across many performance areas. However, there would seem to be further scope to expand its role as an analytical tool where students and staff develop shared knowledge about how to identify and act upon effective teaching and learning strategies generally, and for different topics and different learners.

Student Use and Views of the Dashboard

In 2011, Year 7 students were accessing the dashboard from almost daily to a few times a week, and Year 10 students were accessing it two to four times daily for assessment requirements. Most students accessed their learning button most days. By 2011 every student had a laptop computer through which the dashboard could be utilised. Given the diversity of dashboard functions (initially and over time), it is difficult to sum up all students' views on the relative value of these functions for different year-level students now or initially. The following Year 10 students' comments in 2014, based on several years of interactions with the evolving platform, are indicative of broader student perspectives. Students were asked to identify patterns in their current purposes for use of the dashboard and to nominate possible improvements. Their comments echo teachers' claims about the dashboard's value as an individualised planner that enables students to monitor task requirements and performance, and self-manage learning demands and progress:

> It's easy to keep on track, you can use it as a personal organiser, and everything you need at school is on one website. (Student A, 2014)

> It's a useful tool for knowing what your assessment tasks are, and motivational, because you can see if you are falling behind and need to do extra work to get back to where you want to be. (Student B, 2014)

> It's good that the information is specific to you. It's good to see your marks and how they are improving. (Student C, 2014)

> As a learning and research tool, I find that worksheets for each subject are easily accessed so that you can download anything you may have missed. (Student C, 2014)

Student C claimed she did all her research on the internet and therefore did not use the dashboard "for learning". In reviewing her learning goals, as set at the beginning of the year, she claimed the dashboard was "a gateway to learning" rather than the main enabler of learning processes. This widespread view aligns with the teachers' perspectives that subject-specific and generic ICTs were key tools for developing student content, processes, and reporting of learning as well as promoting student independence as learners, rather than the dashboard. When asked about possible improvements to the dashboard, most students could offer no suggestions. This perhaps further indicates acceptance of a functional division between the dashboard and other ICTs, or that students had not seen any untapped potential in teacher-student insight-sharing on how to optimise return for effort by analysing past learning experiences and outcomes. The few suggestions for improvement were about increased program-tracking support, such as teachers putting "all their lessons and resources on the learning button, not just some, to make it easy to catch up if you miss a class" (Student A).

QUANTITATIVE FINDINGS

As reported in chapter 1, the results in national testing in reading and numeracy (2008–2014) in Year 9 (see Figures 5.5 and 5.6) indicate that all the BEP schools gained against like schools, with Whirrakee College making significant gains in both areas over that time.

Clearly many factors influenced these gains. These include extended review of existing programs, and teachers team-teaching a more coherent, robust multi-level

"IT'S NOT A PLUG-IN PRODUCT"

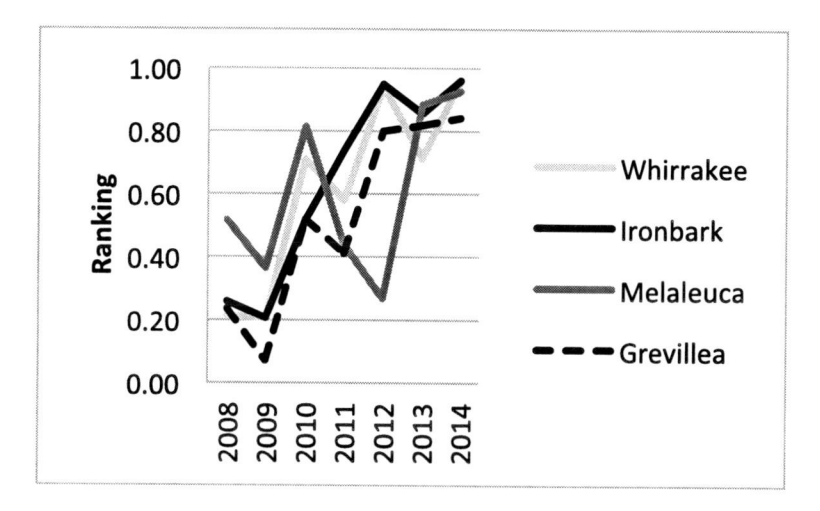

Figure 5.5. Year 9 Reading scores in BEP schools compared to like schools 2008–2014

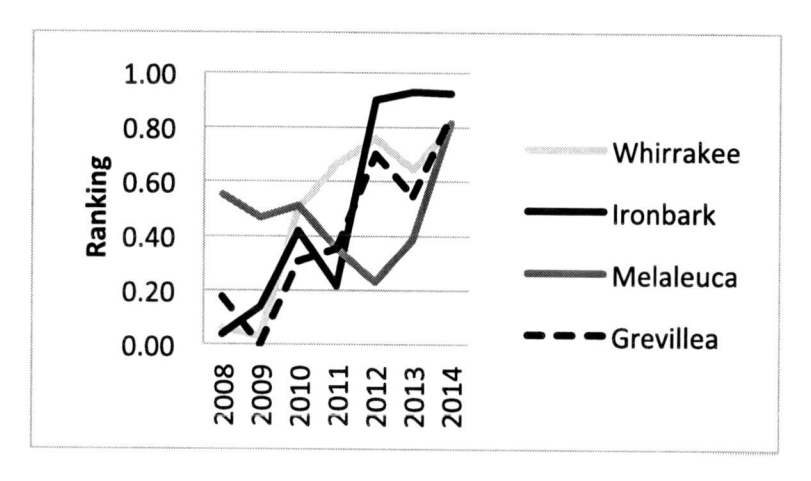

Figure 5.6. Year 9 Numeracy scores in BEP schools compared to like schools 2008–2014

curriculum, particularly in these subjects. However, it is reasonable to suggest that the dashboard has provided precise feedback to motivate and inform student effort, and therefore contributed to these gains. Table 5.1 shows evidence of an increase in student academic performance after the introduction of the dashboard in 2011 with a greater percentage of students performing at honours or credit levels. While the immediate effect was notable, the gains in student performance have been generally sustained over the four years since the dashboard's introduction. Past research on large-scale curricular innovations indicates that there can be both a lag in terms of

89

Table 5.1. Percentage of years 7–10 students performing at different levels 2009–2011

Year	Semester	Honours	Credit	Pass	Exempt	Pending	Participation	Unknown
2009	1	12.6%	14.2%	26.3%			46.9%	
2009	2	23.2%	16.6%	26.0%			34.2%	
2010	1	15.7%	13.6%	28.7%			42.1%	
2010	2	14.0%	12.9%	28.0%			45.0%	
2011	1	23.4%	18.9%	17.8%			36.6%	3.4%
2011	2	33.3%	15.1%	20.9%			30.5%	0.2%
2012	1	30.5%	18.9%	16.2%		8.3%	23.5%	2.7%
2012	2	35.0%	18.0%	23.5%			23.4%	
2013	1	21.3%	23.7%	26.5%		7.9%	18.3%	2.3%
2013	2	29.3%	22.3%	33.0%	3.0%	0.1%	11.6%	0.9%
2014	1	26.2%	24.1%	26.6%	0.2%	5.4%	14.3%	1.2%
2014	2	29.1%	22.5%	35.3%	1.4%		10.5%	1.2%

Note: Before 2011 students who had an unknown level of passing were recorded at "Participation" level.

immediate impacts, and yet sustained gains may occur over a longer period (Adey, Shayer, & Shayer, 2006).

Taken together, these academic results reflect immediate and sustained gains that can be reasonably attributed to a broad mix of contributing influences, including student use of the dashboard.

DISCUSSION

This case study of Whirrakee's dashboard indicates that both staff and students perceived that it informed and motivated student effort, and that this has contributed to improved academic performance over time. In providing a site to personalise and enhance student learning, this case study also sheds light on ongoing challenges, opportunities, and conditions likely to enhance this outcome in this setting. These challenges include establishing a shared view (common knowledge and expertise) between teachers and students about: (a) the dashboard's ultimate purpose of supporting students to develop as self-disciplined learners who are successful, independent, and strategic; and (b) the roles of both students and teachers in this process. Beyond being motivated, students are expected to develop tactical insights into how to optimise their focus (and gain from effort) in interacting with the dashboard. Teachers are expected to build a culture conducive to student engagement in learning activities in subjects generally, and also provide, and learn from, timely support and feedback on student self-assessment. The further challenge is to build a culture where this mutual intentionality is accepted, broadly practised, and drives recognised gains by all participants.

Current and new practices in student and staff dashboard usage can provide opportunities to address these challenges. In their own reflections on student feedback on what helps students learn, teachers may have opportunities in the new teacher dashboard to model for colleagues and students how they refine their practices in the light of this feedback. These reasoning processes can then inform students' own analytical reflections. This building of shared knowledge could further clarify the roles of teachers in co-regulating student learning as a basis for more independent student-initiated approaches. In chapter 6 we report on teacher attempts to enact this approach to enriching student learning experiences in English at Whirrakee through guided group-work and scope for independent student assessment of multi-modal learning in this subject. This strategy points to the need for teachers to continue to review the extent to which their current designed curricular processes, activities, and assessment support all students' learning needs and capabilities, and for teachers to be open to program change and refinement.

This case study also implies that multiple conditions need to be met to optimise the likelihood of students personalising their learning through interacting with the dashboard. These conditions include: (a) access to a robust curriculum that is strongly engaging for students; (b) tasks that are targeted to enable all learners to experience success; (c) student access to timely, expert feedback on their performance; (d) the invitation to, and development of skills that enable learners to interpret and learn from this feedback; (e) student willingness to try to improve; and (f) access to teachers who can contribute expertly to all phases of these processes. The Whirrakee dashboard strongly meets some of these conditions, especially (b) and (c), but the other conditions are in a state of evolution.

In this regard, our study points to ways to address a major concern in the broadly optimistic literature on feedback (Black & Wiliam, 2009), namely the significant problem of achieving a deep alignment of student and teacher intentions and shared understandings about the how and why of learning. This knowledge entails not only motivational influences, but also generic and subject-specific skills about strategies to engage with (as well as track) learning purposes, strategies, and outcomes. In achieving alignment between student and teacher aims and methods, private, individual, and group approaches to effective learning and expertise acquisition need to be discussed explicitly, analysed, and distributed, as part of building common knowledge between teachers and students. This knowledge will link personal and collective strategic reasoning on the what, how, and why of meaningful learning.

Our case study also implies that personalising learning is not simply a binary possibility that students either achieve or fail to achieve. Rather, there are gradations or degrees of personalisation as felt by students inside and out of school and across different subjects and topics. If students are intensely interested in (and successful at) a topic or subject, they are more likely to explore additional ways to increase their knowledge and expertise in this area, drawing on multiple pathways, sources, and forms of repeated practice. This may feed and intensify a sense of personalised meaningfulness of learning experiences in this area and in intrinsic motivation. Knowing the precise current levels of performance in subjects (and past learning strategies) can also contribute to this personalising process by building informed motivation. This can lead to student adoption of strategies that are felt either as personalised or simply viewed to be strategically viable to promote success, without students particularly valuing their learning or its application to their lives. As we claimed in chapter 1, this suggests that a sense of personalised learning can vary for students across topics, subjects, and over time, affecting their motives and adoption of strategies to maintain and improve their academic performance.

An effective dashboard encourages a sense of mutual responsibility between participants, both teacher and students, to enact Edwards' (2011) notion of "relational agency" effectively. Under these conditions, both groups willingly share insights into what practices, frameworks, and affordances motivate, extend, reward and sustain learning gains for mutual benefit. This knowledge, to judge from this chapter, can sometimes remain fragmented into perceived boundaries around each group's expected contributions to the teaching-learning partnership. Each group needs to practise more the demanding task of analysing their experiencing selves as learners rather than their remembering selves. As noted by Kahneman (2011, pp. 317–20), the remembering self is motivated by "risk aversion", and only wants to simplify and encapsulate the past as a global set of positive and/or negative memories. The activity system of teacher-student roles and routines in the new open-plan settings, as noted in other chapters, creates new objects (or intentions for learning) and new means to learn. In such a context, the networked dashboard can be both a highly personalised space for individual learners, but also a prompt for a much larger conversation on and beyond individual sites, promoting prudent risk-taking and gains for participant students and teachers.

CONCLUDING REMARKS

Our account of the aims and outcomes of the Whirrakee dashboard is a story of significant new and complex demands on students and teachers. They are now expected to take more risks, and to take very seriously opportunities to become more expert as learners and co-learners. However, the story is also one of promise and optimism that this ICT can enable quality learning processes and outcomes. We do not view this intensification of a learning focus as a trivialised move to the "learnification of education" (Biesta, 2009, p. 3), where students are merely busy with endless small and inconsequential hurdle requirements. We also resist the interpretation of this "open accountability" as detrimental, intrusive surveillance of student and staff behaviour (Markus, 1993). Rather, we claim that where a robust, challenging multi-level curriculum is enacted in an open-plan setting, then a tool such as the Whirrakee dashboard provides timely targeted support for personalising student learning in these settings, and the potential for (once private) powerful common knowledge to be created and shared. As noted by the principal, the meaning and value of this platform depends on the school's culture around the purposes and means of promoting quality learning, and teacher and student buy-in.

REFERENCES

Barsalou, L. W. (2008). Grounded cognition. *Annual Review of Psychology, 59*, 617–645. doi:10.1146/annurev.psych.59.103006.093639

Biesta, G. (2009). Good education in an age of measurement: On the need to reconnect with the question of purpose in education. *Educational Assessment, Evaluation and Accountability, 21*(1), 33–46. doi:10.1007/s11092-008-9064-9

Black, P., & Wiliam, D. (1998). Assessment and classroom learning. *Assessment in Education, 5*(1), 7–74. doi:10.1080/0969595980050102

Britzman, D. P. (1991). Decentering discourses in teacher education: Or, the unleashing of unpopular things. *Journal of Education, 173*(3), 60–80. Retrieved from http://www.jstor.org/stable/42742229

Edwards, A. (2011). Building common knowledge at the boundaries between professional practices: Relational agency and relational expertise in systems of distributed expertise. *International Journal of Educational Research, 50*(1), 33–39. doi:10.1016/j.ijer.2011.04.007

Edwards, A. (2014). Epilogue: The end of the beginning. In V. Prain, P. Cox, C. Deed, D. Edwards, C. Farrelly, M. Keeffe, … Z. Yager (Eds.), *Adapting to teaching and learning in open-plan schools*. (pp. 205–210). Rotterdam, The Netherlands: Sense Publishers.

Engeström, Y. (2005). Knotworking to create collaborative intentionality capital in fluid organisational fields. In M. M. Bayerlein, S. T. Bayerlein, & F. A. Kennedy (Eds.), *Collaborative capital: Creating intangible value* (pp. 307–336). Amsterdam, The Netherlands: Elsevier.

Gibson, J. J. (1977). The theory of affordances. In R. Shaw & J. Bransford (Eds.). *Perceiving, acting, and knowing: Toward an ecological psychology* (pp. 67–82). Hillsdale, NJ: Erlbaum.

Hattie, J. A. C. (2009). *Visible learning: A synthesis of over 800 meta-analyses relating to achievement*. London, UK: Routledge.

Herbert, P. C., & Lohrmann, D. K. (2011). It's all in the delivery! An analysis of instructional strategies from effective health education curricula. *Journal of School Health, 81*(5), 258–264. doi:10.1111/j.1746-1561.2011.00586.x

Hill, H. C., Rowan, B., & Ball, D. L. (2005). Effects of teachers' mathematical knowledge for teaching on student achievement. *American Educational Research Journal, 42*(2), 371–406. doi:10.3102/00028312042002371

Hillocks, G. (2010). "EJ" in focus: Teaching argument for critical thinking and writing: An introduction. *English Journal, 99*(6), 24–32. Retrieved from http://www.jstor.org/discover/10.2307/20787661?uid=3737536&uid=2&uid=4&sid=21106496826893

Hoekstra, A., & Korthagen, F. A. (2011). Teacher learning in a context of educational change: Informal learning versus systematically supported learning. *Journal of Teacher Education, 62*(1), 76–92. doi:10.1177/0022487110382917

Horn, I. (2010). Teaching replays, teaching rehearsals, and re-visions of practice: Learning from colleagues in a mathematics teacher community. *Teachers College Record, 112*(1), 225–259.

Hwang, G. J., & Wu, P. H. (2012). Advancements and trends in digital game-based learning research: A review of publications in selected journals from 2001 to 2010. *British Journal of Educational Technology, 43*(1), E6–E10. doi:10.1111/j.1467-8535.2011.01242.x

Isen, A. M., Rosenzweig, A. S., & Young, M. J. (1991). The influence of positive affect on clinical problem solving. *Medical Decision Making, 11*(3), 221–227. doi:10.1177/0272989X9101100313

Jackson, A. W., & Davis, G. A. (2000). *Turning points 2000: Educating adolescents in the 21st century*. New York: Teachers College Press.

Jackson, M., Cassidy, W., & Brown, K. (2009). You were born ugly and youl die ugly too: Cyber-bullying as relational aggression. *In Education, 15*(2). Retrieved from http://ineducation.ca/ineducation/article/view/57/538

Jenkins, E. W. (2006). The student voice and school science education. *Studies in Science Education, 42*(1), 49–88. doi:10.1080/03057260608560220

Jonassen, D. H. (2014). Mindtools (productivity and learning). In R. Gunstone (Ed.), *Encyclopedia of science education*. (pp. 1–7). The Netherlands: Springer. doi:10.1007/978-94-007-6165-0_57-1

Kagan, J. (2009). *The three cultures: Natural sciences, social sciences, and the humanities in the 21st century*. Cambridge, England: Cambridge University Press.

Kahneman, D. (2011). *Thinking, fast and slow*. London, UK: Penguin Books.

Kress, G., & van Leeuwen, T. (2001). *Multi-modal discourse: The modes and media of contemporary communication*. London, UK: Oxford University Press.

Markus, T. (1993). *Buildings and power: Freedom and control in the origins of modern building types*. London, UK: Routledge.
Mårell-Olsson, E. (2012). *Att göra lärandet synligt? Individuella utvecklingsplaner och digital dokumentation* [Making learning visible? Personal development planning and digital documentation.] (Unpublished dissertation). Umea, Sweden: Umea University.
O'Brien, M. L., & Johnson, K. (2002). *School is for me: Student engagement and the fair go project: A focus on engaging pedagogies in primary classrooms in low socio-economic status communities in south-western Sydney*. Paper presented at the Australian Association of Research in Education Conference, Brisbane. Retrieved from http://www.aare.edu.au/data/publications/2002/obr02357.pdf
Prain, V., Cox, P., Deed, C., Dorman, J., Edwards, D., Farrelly, C., Keeffe, M., ... Yager, Z. (2013). Personalised learning: Lessons to be learnt. *British Educational Research Journal, 39*(4), 654–676. doi:10.1080/01411926.2012.669747
Prain, V., Cox, P., Deed, C., Dorman, J., Edwards, D., Farrelly, C., Keeffe, M., ... Yager, Z. (2014). *Adapting to teaching and learning in open-plan schools*. Rotterdam, The Netherlands: Sense Publishers.
Verbert, K., Govaerts, S., Duval, E., Santos, J., Assche, F., Parra, G., & Klerkx, G. (2014). Learning dashboards: An overview and future research opportunities. *Personal and Ubiquitous Computing, 18*(6), 1499–1151. Retrieved from http://research.acer.edu.au/aer/3

SECTION 2
CURRICULUM CASE STUDIES

VALERIE LOVEJOY, LUCY MOW, STEPHANIE DI PALMA,
VAUGHAN PRAIN AND DEBRA EDWARDS

6. CREATING AND ANALYSING MULTI-MODAL TEXTS IN ENGLISH CLASSES IN OPEN-PLAN SETTINGS

CONCEPTUALISING QUALITY TEACHING AND LEARNING IN 21ST CENTURY ENGLISH CLASSES

S18: I think it just gets the point across more, the sound. Like, just knowing what he says.

S14: Yeah but, like, when I was listening to it, you could hear what was going on but you couldn't really picture it. Yeah, you could hear all these sirens and you could hear the children cheering but you couldn't really tell that the president was going past and stuff.

S13: But the guy said that 'that's Mandela'.

S14: Yeah, but that was afterwards.

S13: Yeah, but after that you could picture it. You could picture that he's driving past with a police escort.

S14: No but you couldn't really tell about the separation of the two groups. All you could hear was the white coach talking to tell that they were separated.

As in other countries, the aims, rationale, and content of the English curriculum in Australia are hotly contested (Edwards, 2010; Green, 2008; Kress, 2006). Teachers disagree about the degree to which equity outcomes for all students are addressed and the extent to which state and national documents enshrine, or should enshrine, past and/or future versions of literacy (Goodwyn, Reid, & Durrant, 2013; Peel, Patterson, & Gerlach, 2000; Turner, 2007). Reviewing state and national syllabi, Golsby-Smith (2013) also noted ongoing squabbles over ideological investments. Enthusiasts for cultural studies approaches, utilitarian/functional, critical, aesthetic, multi-literacy, and economic rationalist accounts jostle for discursive supremacy (Edwards & Potts, 2008; Edwards, 2010). Beavis (2013), Goodwyn (2012), and Goodwyn, Reid, and Durrant (2013), and others point out the continued discrepancy between how teachers in Australia and England perceive English should be taught, what should count as learning, and the outcomes embedded in current English curriculum and actual classroom practice.

In addressing what should count as quality in middle years English, we acknowledge that we are adding our own claims to broader debates about the purpose of English in school (Edwards & Potts, 2008; Green, 2008; Kress, 2006). These debates typically centre on questions relating to desirable versions of literacy (Edwards & Potts, 2008), the role of English in shaping future citizenry (Green, 2008), and the legitimacy of teaching and learning from different types of texts (Cazden et al., 1996). In so doing, we also acknowledge the political, cultural and social significance of claims about quality learning in English (Green, 2008; Kress, 2006) and recognise that our own perspectives are situated within the context of 21st century versions of learning and literacy, ideas that are continually evolving and adapting to keep pace with societal and technological change.

In these 21st century versions of learning, generic skills such as the ability to collaborate with others, negotiate difference, problem-solve, and adapt to new situations are seen as desirable for the development of an engaged, productive citizenry (Barr et al., 2008; Schleicher, 2013). In the Australian Curriculum, these skills, amongst others, are reflected in several general, cross-curricular "capabilities" designed to inform approaches to curriculum in all subject areas (Australian Curriculum and Assessment Reporting Authority (ACARA), 2014b). These capabilities include critical and creative thinking, personal and social capability, and literacy as some key generic skills (ACARA, 2014b). In the version of quality learning that we propose, these skills are embedded in English curricula through an emphasis on reasoning and collaboration as processes informing both students' critical and creative approaches to texts. The two case studies that we present suggest some broad, general strategies to enact these kinds of tasks in the classroom:

- interpretive and creative interactions with texts (in this case multi-modal texts) are framed as reasoning events;
- tasks are relatively open-ended, requiring that students negotiate and use reasoning to make their thinking explicit;
- students are encouraged to solve problems relating to signification and meaning;
- collaboration is encouraged through semi-structured small-group interactions.

From this perspective, we perceive that "up-scaled" (Prain et al., 2014, p. 5), open-plan settings afford practices that can lead to quality learning in English in several ways. As a primary affordance, the altered conditions created by the space are seen to necessitate revised spheres of influence, teacher and learner roles, and group configurations, creating opportunities for experimentation with more varied models of interaction (Prain et al., 2014). The extent to which, and the manner in which, these opportunities are acted on depends on teacher take-up and interpretation of these primary affordances, as well as teacher and student alignment with particular learning goals (Prain et al., 2014). We have chosen to focus on several key affordances of these up-scaled learning communities that we consider as being particularly valuable for designing learning experiences of the kind described above. These include more varied kinds of interactions in which:

- students engage with a broader range of people, perspectives and ideas;
- students participate in groups that are mixed age or mixed ability;
- teachers model collaborative reasoning and present varied interpretations of texts;
- designated spaces are allocated for dialogic or collaborative work;
- whole-school approaches to collaboration and reasoning are visible to all students as a consistent learning practice.

Our emphasis on reasoning follows an emerging trend that has been explored extensively in other domains, (Kuhn, 2009; Lemke, 1993; Osborne, 2010) but which has not yet been clearly developed or articulated in English. There is a broad body of literature to support the idea that reasoning and critical thinking should be taught explicitly in the Language Arts (Hillocks, 2010; Rex et al., 2010; Warren, 2010). Argumentation, it is argued, is increasingly becoming the "dominant mode" for assessment in English (Warren, 2010, p. 41) and is, along with critical reasoning, perceived as a valuable skill for participation in social life (Hillocks, 2010; Rex, et al., 2010; Warren, 2010). These ideas are broadly applicable to English teaching across the globe. However, as Warren notes (2010), the teaching of critical reasoning skills that are essential for academic success is often a "daunting" task for English teachers who may "have little or no training in formal logic" (p. 41). It may also be the case that in English, quality reasoning is associated with persuasive writing with less attention directed towards identifying and exploring the features involved in the process of logical reasoning or argumentation more broadly (Hillocks, 2010). In our first case study, reasoning is used as a platform for apprenticing students into the social practice of film interpretation, while in the second case study it is applied as a justificatory process for creating multi-modal texts as a creative response to literature.

Our version of quality learning in English is also underpinned by our conviction that the teaching of 'reading' in schools can no longer be confined to the study of print texts alone. In keeping with multi-literacy perspectives (Cazden et al., 1996), we suggest that quality education for 21st century literacy must account for the broader ways in which meanings are configured through visual, aural and multi-modal 'texts', and through a diverse range of media. Rather than assuming that, as "digital natives" (Prensky, 2001), students are competent readers of multi-modal texts, we suggest that an explicit focus on reading multi-modality supports students to develop a broader range of reading roles (Luke & Freebody, 1999; Serafini, 2012) that are both critically and creatively enabling. An explicit orientation in the semiotic vocabulary and forms of reasoning that inform the production of multi-modal meanings is an important step in scaffolding these kinds of competencies.

Finally, we suggest that including collaborative and multi-modal reasoning in the design of English curriculum can personalise the learning experience for students of English in three ways. First, reasoning presents students with a framework for understanding that can be generalised across various texts, equipping them with skills that enable them to self-regulate their reading practices. Second, because reasoning prompts students to apply higher-order thinking skills to their study of textual and multi-modal meaning-making, learning in this way can also become personalised by providing an appropriate level of demand for students who require learning extension, such as the middle-to-higher-end students involved in these case studies. Third, in keeping with the non-isolationist version of personalisation outlined in the introductory chapter of this book (see Chapter 1), we suggest that students view learning as being meaningful when it involves meaningful connections to others. The development of collective goals and the use of interaction as a means of sharing ideas and evaluating content also encourages the development of student agency and accountability, creating experiences that are relevant and meaningful for individual learners.

We claim, drawing on Dewey (1902), Nay-Brock (1984), Freebody, Barton, and Chan (2014), Edwards (2011), Beavis (2013), and Morgan, Comber, Freebody and Nixon (2014), among others, that quality English teaching and learning should enable students to develop culturally-valued knowledge, skills, and dispositions around constructing and interpreting a range of texts, including multi-modal collaborative ones. This extends teaching and learning beyond a narrow focus on test-coaching and restricted curricular prescriptions, by engaging learners in rich purposes and development as literate citizens, and developing learners as creative, critical, literate problem-solvers. This set of goals implies the need for a robust, in-depth curriculum. To this end, we consider that the prescribed curriculum and mandated assessment methods in the Australian context provide some useful diagnostic, formative, and summative guidelines for designing tasks to address student capabilities. We view them as indicative leads to consider in group-based and personalised student learning in terms of goals and outcomes. In this way, we resist reducing curriculum to a competency-based, standards-driven 'one size fits all' imperative that has no space for learners' diverse collective and personalised learning needs. However, national testing regimes such as that in Australia tend to push teachers towards focusing on what is specifically assessed by such national testing at the expense of a rich curriculum (Pendergast & Main, 2013). In addition the pressure to assess student-learning gains against age-based standards has potential to depersonalise learning experiences (see Rogers, 2013), denying opportunities for engaging and challenging tasks that may not be perceived as immediately relevant for achieving expected student outcomes. In our collaboration with the teachers, we sought to accommodate their perceptions of workable activities and assessment priorities, and external stakeholder pressure to improve student learning outcomes as measured by standardised assessment. At the same time we encouraged adaptive innovations arising from possible new practices and environments afforded by the new learning communities.

CREATING AND ANALYSING MULTI-MODAL TEXTS IN ENGLISH CLASSES

CASE STUDIES BACKGROUND

The following two case studies illustrate how effective learning in English in the middle years of school can be enacted in these new open-plan settings, following the principles above. Each case study is a report on an enrichment program designed to develop students' reasoning abilities around text interpretation and construction. Drawing on affordance theory (Gibson, 1979; Greene, 1993), activity theory (Engestrom, 2000), the construct of relational agency (Edwards, 2011), and "sphere of influence" (see Chapter 1), we identify common challenges from each case in terms of teachers and students adapting to the new settings, as well as necessary conditions for successful adaptation. The case studies in this chapter instantiate the new set of skills required of teachers and students in these contexts, as identified in Chapter 2, with a focus on English.

The two case studies are set in Whirrakee College where routines had been established over four years of occupancy in the open-plan settings. In particular, the organisation of students into three tiers, or groups, based on perceived learning needs and abilities, had become a consistent model that was used for differentiating instruction in compulsory subject areas. These groupings represented significant symbolic tools that informed expectations around behavior and influenced student and teacher roles within the activity system of the open-plan setting (Engestrom, 2000). Within each of the differentiated learning groups, micro-activity systems were also evident with students and teachers adhering to particular conventions in terms of seating arrangements and roles, both of which had been devised to cater to the perceived needs of each of the three student groups.

The organisation of students into these groupings reflected a primary affordance (Gibson, 1977; Prain et al., 2014) of the open-plan classroom where a large cohort of students was distributed amongst three teachers in groups of varied size to address different student needs and abilities. As a secondary affordance of the space (Gibson, 1977; Prain et al., 2014) grouping students in this way enabled teachers to share expertise and negotiate roles as each new area of study was introduced. Teachers rotated responsibility for each group after each five-week unit, planning and working together in the open-plan environment. This structure was adopted to provide a clear framework for class organisation and student expectations. The smallest grouping, Build, was designed for students requiring maximum teacher support. The focus for this group was on intensive skill acquisition with highly directed teacher guidance. The Strengthen middle group of students utilised a range of less teacher-supported learning experiences including whole-group or individual direct instruction as required, as well as teacher- and student-directed activities. The Excel group of self-regulating students was expected to work independently, often individually, and to seek advice from their group teacher as a last resort (see Prain et al., 2014). Groupings were considered temporary, with scope for students to move between groups, depending on student outcomes in each unit of work and student perception of the support they needed.

CASE STUDY ONE: YEAR 8 FILM STUDY

Research Design

This case study demonstrates how redesigning a unit of work in an open-plan Year 8 English classroom extended students' ability to engage interpretively with film-texts and developed their capacity to make reasoned claims about film-meanings. The unit was implemented with four groups of middle-to-high ability students (roughly 170 in total), and two teachers, over four weeks, with data being drawn from two of these groups. It involved modifications to an existing film curriculum, requiring only minor changes to the organisational and physical structures of the open-plan setting.

A case study approach (Yin, 2014) was used to identify student and teacher perceptions, spatial affordances and constraints, and disciplinary and reasoning gains. Data were drawn from field-notes, small-group discussions, artefact analysis, one-to-one interviews, and focus groups and involved a sample group of two teachers and eight students who were observed during a four-week unit of work on film. Interviews and focus group questions were structured around key themes including epistemological agency, understanding of reasoning, past curriculum experiences, understanding of film-studies, perceptions of teaching and learning roles, and attitudes to small-group work.

Curriculum Design

The revised curriculum featured a scaffolded sequence of collaborative, multi-modal reasoning activities that emphasised rich forms of participation and the development of higher-order thinking skills. The design of the unit was based on several key theoretical positions:

- First, drawing on dialogic approaches to classroom instruction, it emphasised active, participatory roles for students as text (or film) interpreters (Nystrand et al., 1997; Mercer & Littleton, 2007; Sutherland, 2013);
- Second, it drew on informal reasoning frameworks (Nickerson, 2012) as a valuable means to explore, discern, and scaffold quality interpretations of moving-image texts;
- Third, it emphasised the importance of inducting students into the semiotic resources and mult-imodal vocabulary associated with successful film interpretation (Anderson & Jefferson, 2009; Bateman, 2012; Mills, 2010).

In the context of the Australian Curriculum, the unit emphasised the practices of 'listening, reading and viewing' and involved students in interpretive practices such as the analysis of linguistic and modal choices and the use of evidence to support ideas (ACARA, 2014b). The unit also engaged students in some 'general capabilities' deemed as cross-curricular priorities, including critical thinking and the development of personal and social capability (ACARA, 2014b).

By exploring how this curriculum was enacted within an open-plan Year 8 setting, the case study highlights the affordances and constraints of open-plan learning for similar kinds of curriculum and provides indicators for the design of future quality learning in similar spaces.

Setting

The classes observed occurred in two open-plan rooms, each shared with an additional teacher and student group (approx. 25–30 additional students). The routine organisation of students into three groupings had enabled a differentiated approach to instruction (Prain et al., 2014). The Excel groups involved in this study were large groups of 40–50 students who generally worked independently. Disruptions were infrequent and most students appeared to be procedurally engaged. However, the large group size made whole-class discussions difficult and limited opportunities for peer interaction. The two teachers involved in the case study were interested in enriching the learning of these "top end" students who were "not being stretched and extended enough" (Teacher 2) according to school performance data (Principal comment). These students, whose outcomes reflected a focus on perceived teacher expectations rather than deep learning, were often "resistant to change" (Teacher 1). The revised curriculum presented an opportunity to experiment with different roles and configurations within the space, shifting the emphasis towards more substantive engagement and interaction (see Nystrand & Gamoran, 1991, for a discussion of procedural versus substantive engagement).

At each year level, film studies occurred once a year, and was possibly viewed as a "soft option" (Teacher 1) requiring less rigor than print-based studies, while novel studies assumed a much larger time allotment in the curriculum. Film studies typically focused on a single feature-film, with various activities reflecting the mandated curriculum. Some students appeared to lack a clear understanding of what was required of them. For example, very few students described more than one type of evidence that they could use to support a claim about a film. By contrast, the teachers had clear goals for the film studies unit, with Teacher 2 suggesting that they wanted students "to be skilled at knowing how they're being influenced to think and then seeing past that" while Teacher 1 said that she would like to "see students being aware of the film techniques and how they are used to influence an audience". In junior secondary English where curricular goals are broad, varied, and frequently contested, it is not unusual to find such inconsistencies between teacher and student perceptions of quality.

Framing

In order to invite student higher-order thinking through application work, students were cast as active enquirers, or 'Film Detectives', responsible for articulating and substantiating their own responses to visual texts by making predictions, forming hypotheses, and using available evidence to support claims about meaning. An introductory class brainstorm encouraged students to think about detective roles, attributes, and responsibilities. Students' responses ("find things out", "investigate", "put clues together", "think outside the box", use "problem solving", and "persistence") yielded a range of opportunities for naming the required thinking dispositions.

Students were then given two stills from unfamiliar films and asked to make claims based on the available visual evidence as well as their own prior knowledge. This task reinforced the students' role as agentic film interpreters and emphasised the necessity of grounding theories and hypotheses in visual detail. Students were also prompted to draw on inferential reasoning strategies, providing warrants to establish the links between semiotic construction of the text and the viewer's experience of meaning (see Wildfeuer, 2014). The observations by student 12 are shown in Figure 6.1.

In this early example of reasoning (Figure 6.1), Student 12 assumes an agentic, interpretive role. Her interpretation of the still is supported by a process of basic reasoning marked by claims and evidence. Evidence is drawn from both visual data and the student's (mostly tacit) prior knowledge. The student's reasoning is also characterised by markers of tentativeness, including modal verbs such as "could" and the phrase "as if". This indicates an appropriate understanding of the inferential nature of visual signification and an awareness of the limitations of the available data.

The foregrounding of this task as a reasoning exercise helped this student to develop confidence in the interpretive role. The selection of stills from films thought to be unfamiliar to the students and their teachers encouraged students to develop claims, rather than guessing 'right answers' or resorting to teacher authority. Early limiting of the available data to visual, static material, enabled students to focus on the reasoning process and the use of visual and spatial cues without the complication of temporal sequencing or aural stimuli.

While the process of making meaning from multi-modal texts involves a complex interaction of reading practices and roles (Luke & Freebody, 1999; Serafini, 2012), this unit emphasised directorial intent and semiotic construction as the primary focus. Student attention was directed towards the deliberate, constructed nature of films, addressing teachers' concerns that students "don't realise that in every aspect of a film there's been a choice made by someone. Whether it's the sets or the costume or the dialogue or the angle of the camera, all of it is a deliberate decision by someone trying to create a certain image or present a certain argument" (Teacher 2). The teachers perceived this understanding as important for students' capacity to read films from a critical literacy perspective. The students' responses in interviews both during and post unit confirmed the teachers' perceptions by reaffirming the significance of their discovery that, in film, "everything's there for a reason" (Student 12).

CREATING AND ANALYSING MULTI-MODAL TEXTS IN ENGLISH CLASSES

Claim about Film	Evidence
This man is the sort of person who is protecting something or running from something and acts suspicious.	He has his hand resting on the back of the seat next to him. You do not normally see people doing that unless they are going to turn around to look behind them. However, there is the fact of not knowing if that is even a seat next to him. It could be like a suitcase or something else other than a seat. The man could have his hand on it because he wants to protect it. He could also be reaching into a bag or something. Also because he is a suspicious person he could be reaching into a bag to pull out something, e.g. a gun? I also think that this man is acting suspicious because he is not even wearing his seatbelt.
This man could be wealthy.	He is wearing nice, expensive looking clothes. His gloves look like leather and his jacket looks expensive. As the car is unidentifiable, and . . . looks like an expensive car. The car's seats are leather and so is the steering wheel. The outside of the car looks shiny, so it is either new or washed so frequently it doesn't get dirty.
It is about determination because of how focused this man looks.	The man looks like he is gripping the wheel tightly and . . . His face is quite blank; his eyes are quite focused on the road, as they are quite open. His mouth is just straight; as if he is so focused he is not paying attention.

Figure 6.1. Student 12's reasoning about meaning from an unfamiliar film still

Collaborative Reasoning

Students in these high-ability groups appeared comfortable as independent learners. However, the spatial and interactional routines that dominated their day-to-day experience of English provided limited opportunities to experience

105

multiple perspectives or viewpoints. The inclusion of collaborative, problem-based activities in the curriculum was seen as a potentially powerful means for developing students' reasoning skills and encouraging greater interpretive agency (Mercer, 2008; Reznitskaya et al., 2009). By encountering and negotiating differences, it was thought that students would be encouraged to actively and meaningfully participate in the reasoning process. It was expected that students would explore a range of moves associated with informal reasoning: taking a position, seeking clarification, providing evidence, challenging others' ideas, asking critical questions and exploring alternative possibilities (see Reznitskaya et al., 2009).

Small-group discussions provided an ideal way to engage students as active participants in exploring film meanings. However, teachers perceived the open space as constraining such activity due to: (a) potential for diminished control over participant student behaviour, and (b) concerns about potential noise distractions for other students and teachers working in the space. Up-scaled learning communities can prompt a conservative approach to perceived high- and low-risk activities, especially where there is a strong division of labour around teacher activity, and strongly demarcated spheres of influence for participants (Engestrom, 2000).

Students worked in collaborative groups of three to four to make decisions about film meanings and support their claims with detailed evidence drawn from the visual and aural elements of the film. Shifting their furniture into the group configurations differed from their usual routine, but students were quick to comply and benefited from the experience of working in consistent groups where they could develop their skills together.

The following segment of small-group talk is taken from a group of three that developed their skills collectively as they explored the film's semiosis (see Figure 6.2). Although their talk tended to be cumulative rather than exploratory (Mercer, 1996; Mercer et al., 1999; Mercer, 2008), this group's discussion developed naturally to the point where they began to draw instinctively on the language of film to support their claims. The students had been asked to make a claim about the ideas presented in the opening scene of the film *Invictus*, directed by Clint Eastwood, drawing on visual and aural evidence to show how this idea was communicated to the viewer. Here, the students are developing a case to support their claim that the opening scene shows that "South Africa is a racially divided nation".

In this segment, students are beginning to use film terminology, referring to soundtrack, cinematography, and editing to explore the presentation of a specific idea. Furthermore, while individually, students tend to focus on singular modes drawn from visual, aural, spatial, or temporal data, collectively they build a multi-modal case. Small-group reasoning of this kind prompts an expanded understanding of how films make meaning, inducting students into interpretive practices more difficult to establish in isolation.

By the end of the unit, students felt that the group-work had been highly beneficial, suggesting that it encouraged them to be "open-minded" and helped them to consider

> S14: In the soundtrack you could hear the kids, like, on the...
>
> S13: ...thing calling out Mandela's name...
>
> S18: Yeah.
>
> S14: Yeah, you could hear them on that side and then, like, on the other side you could hear them, like, saying that Mandela...
>
> S13: They didn't really care.
>
> S14: No, they were more, like, disturbed, like you could see that they were disturbed by...stuff...
>
> S13: And the guy called him a "terrorist", the coach called him a "terrorist".
>
> S14: Yeah, and when there was the panorama thing of both schools and what [S18] said before, like, you could see the white s walking on one side, on the other side, of the path.
>
> S18: Yeah, on the other side of the road, yep (overlapping speech).
>
> S14: That was cine-ma-to-graphy.
>
> S18: Yep.

Figure 6.2. Collaborative discussion – Opening scene Invictus

ideas that they would not have thought of themselves. The teachers also recognised the value of these discussions, citing them as one of the ways in which students had gained confidence in their abilities as text interpreters.

Individual Reasoning

Traditional essay writing was mandated at this school as practice for future assessment. Accordingly, students were asked to demonstrate their individual reasoning through the development of a traditional print essay. The essay was completed during class-time, during a double block of 100 minutes. In keeping with the reasoning orientation of the unit and the emphasis on interpretive agency and accountability, a relatively open-ended topic was devised: "What is the main message of *Invictus* and how do the filmmakers get this message across?" Teachers noted the "high quality" of student essays, characterised by appropriate use of film terminology and substantiated claims about meaning. Teachers attributed this success to the scaffolding and sequencing of activities, as well as the disciplined focus on particular skills and reasoning strategies.

The following examples from three student essays illustrate their quality reasoning. These students had worked together on the collaborative activities arriving at a consensus decision about the main message of the film (i.e., 'bringing people together'). However, their essays were completed individually.

Building on structural scaffolding modeled by their teacher, the students developed their essays around an analysis of several scenes selected on the basis of the perceived relevance to their identified central message of 'bringing people together'. The students thus showed a temporal understanding of how meanings are developed in film through the editing of scenes and episodes. More advanced reasoning was evident when students explicitly framed these temporal sequences as evidence of directorial intent, introduced by phrases such as "this is shown by...." (Student 14), or "the filmmaker uses..." (Student 14). Some students relied on tacit assumptions about the relationship between their scene selection and their chosen theme or when their reasoning followed only the internal causality of the narrative. This simplified, and less contextualised, version of reasoning is evident, for example, when Student 17 states that "Mandela wears his Springboks' jersey out to the Rugby World Cup to try and make people realise that the blacks and the whites can all join together".

Students had been instructed to include a range of examples drawn from the cinematography, editing, soundtrack, and mise-en-scène to illustrate how their identified message had been conveyed in each scene through a combination of modes. In their essays students showed a firm grasp of the language of film and its use to obtain particular effects by consistently drawing on film terminology to identify the use of close-up shots, mid-shots, panning, zooming in/out, high and low angles, cuts, costumes, body language, music, sound effects and silence. Most students were able to integrate their accounts of how these modes worked together under broad, summative statements such as: "the filmmaker uses the four different film techniques to help display this message of unity between the nations in this scene" (Student 14). Such statements were typically followed by a progressive and particular elaboration. For example, "cinematography is used...when...it focuses on the boy celebrating with a close-up shot and then it pans out and around a little bit to show the police officers also celebrating" (Student 18).

The most sophisticated multi-modal reasoning was evident when students explicitly accounted for directorial decisions and linked them to identified themes or ideas. Some students repeatedly referred to what "we see" or "hear", orienting their analysis appropriately in the interaction between visual and aural signifiers and the experience of the viewer/listener. Initially, the teachers had commented that it was "difficult to get [students] to incorporate the elements of film" and to understand "how they're being manipulated through those [elements] into their responses"

[Teacher 2]. However, by the end of the unit the students were handling both of these tasks very well.

Summary

Students found the film tasks challenging but exciting. During interviews and written reflections, many described a 'light-bulb' moment in their understanding of the constructed nature of films. Students gained access to the roles and language associated with successful film interpretation by participating in small-group, collaborative tasks that required them to anchor their analysis of film techniques to an argument about the director's intended message. Their experiences were embodied in comparing interpretations and verbalising arguments using a relatively new film vocabulary. Approaching the task in this way, ensured that students perceived the analysis of particular film techniques as a valuable tool that would enable them to support, justify, and purposefully evaluate their own and others' claims about film meanings. As Teacher 2 observed, "you're sort of empowering them to believe that they can do it". These positive outcomes were enabled by the teachers' willingness to experiment with different configurations of students within the space, parting from well-established routines in order to explore the potential of more flexible and diverse approaches to interaction and learning within their classrooms.

CASE STUDY TWO: YEAR 7 BOOK TRAILER

The case study comprised approximately 105 Excel Year 7 students at Whirrakee College who were guided by the researcher as an in-field teacher, to explicitly practise reasoning skills. The students worked in small groups (3–4 students) to construct a multi-modal book trailer based on a previously studied novel. Each small group planned, produced and judged one another's artefacts, generating criteria for quality shaped by their interactions with various multi-modal texts and literacies. The aim of this learning sequence was to develop students' collaborative and individual reasoning skills as they experimented with, and reflected upon, integrating different modes of representation in their book trailers. In this context, a book trailer is an interactive artefact, which integrates various modes to present its intention as a persuasive text. The purpose of a book trailer is to convince and persuade viewers to want to read and learn more about the book being represented through the simultaneous layering of multiple modes of information. In this way, the act of developing a book trailer requires active application and experimentation with multi-literacies.

By implementing a unit that incorporated and adapted some of the features of out-of-school literacies used by adolescents (such as creativity and production of a text, asynchronous online group communication, accessibility to an extensive range of programs, applications and tools afforded through the internet and students' netbooks, and finally, multi-modality), it was anticipated that students would be more inclined to interact and engage with the learning tasks on a higher level. The study monitored not only the motivation and engagement of the students throughout the implementation of the learning sequence, but also the students' developing techno-literacies and skills in navigating and negotiating with modes of technology as vehicles for language, communication, and multi-modal reasoning.

The Setting and Staff

The researcher and teachers implemented the unit with three different Year 7 Excel groups in August 2013, October 2013 and September 2014. The principal and leading staff wanted to extend and challenge their Excel students who are generally competent, high capacity, independent learners. However, although the data of the research study was collected from the Excel students, Strengthen and Build students also completed the book trailer learning sequence. Teachers adapted the unit to suit the needs and capabilities of their students (for example, Build students created their book trailers in pairs and Strengthen students individually, being closely supported by the teacher). One English lesson catered for approximately 75 students in these three separate groups with one teacher allocated to each.

The Excel groups comprised approximately 35 students. Students chose their own groups from those who had studied the same novel earlier in the year. Consequently, groups varied in gender composition and degree of friendship. Four students volunteered to participate in a focus group for each trial. The composition of the focus groups was: trial one, all female, trial two, all male and trial three, all female.

A close and collaborative teacher/researcher relationship was imperative to planning and implementing a unit of this nature in order to understand one another's pedagogical perspectives. Observing Year 7 lessons for 18 months prior to unit implementation enabled the researcher to work closely with the Year 7 English curriculum coordinator to develop a blended literacy unit that incorporated opportunities to work collaboratively and use reasoning and higher- order cognitive capacities, without offsetting the current English curriculum and structure of English learning tasks at the school.

Methodology

Due to the structure and demands of the research design, a mixed methods case study approach was adopted (Yin, 2014). Evidence included: examination of pre and post testing with students and teachers, observations of lessons, collection and analysis of relevant artefacts produced by students, collection of relevant teacher artefacts and documents and subsequent discussion with teachers about future implementation. Data collection centred on the specific themes of student and teacher perspective, multi-modality and multi-literacies, curriculum fit, engagement in middle years, collaborative learning in open-plan settings, and collaborative and individual reasoning opportunities.

Researcher's Role

In the first two trials the researcher adopted a co-teacher role. This was productive as strong connections were developed between the participants and the researcher. However, it also constrained the research because investigation of student reasoning, multi-modal manipulation, and experimentation (as tools to assist with student objectives and collaborative learning) required deeper exploration and quality evidence to support the study's aims and mixed methods approach. In the third trial these issues were addressed by the researcher stepping back from classroom teaching in order to focus on how students applied reasoning skills (decision-making, persuasive argumentation, trial and error, rehearsal, and justification) individually with the resources around them, as a group member assigned roles within a group, and as a group (on a macro level) with a common goal. The researcher briefed teachers and students on reasoning and made explicit the terminology associated with reasoning skills. The teachers used their prior experience to explore concepts of collaborative and multi-modal reasoning with the students.

PROGRAM STRUCTURE

Identifying Specifications and Success Indicators

The learning tasks gave students the opportunity to experiment with and develop their own techno-literacies through applying multi-modal reasoning in a group environment. It was planned that the sequence would take 90 minute sessions over a five-week period. However, interruptions shortened the number of sessions students had to complete the task.

Although the unit combined whole-group, group and sub-group activities, because the unit was designed as a collaborative multi-modal reasoning task, students mostly worked in groups of three or four. The three teachers first showed book trailers of varying quality to the whole group (Build, Strengthen, and Excel). Students critiqued the trailers identifying features that prompted interest in the text. This activity inspired students' interest in and understanding of book trailers. Furthermore, students began to understand the aspects and features of design that would enhance the quality of a book trailer. By the third iteration of the unit, students in the focus group were especially interested in developing a 'professional' product. Through a researcher-facilitated discussion of the attributes and characteristics of a book trailer (that incorporated multiple modes of presentation and an audience) deemed to be professional, students reached a consensual understanding of the 'success indicators' of an effective and high quality book trailer. In focus group interviews students showed their desire and understanding of how to achieve a professional result:

> I wanted to make it look professional. I watched a lot of movie trailers on Youtube, and I wanted to make it look like professionals had made it... In movie or book trailers the thing that makes you want to watch it a lot and like

go to the movie, is whether it's really dramatic or suspenseful. The music and everything make it sound and feel really exciting. [Student 3, Group 1, Trial 3]

I would feel more proud if I thought it actually looks professional. If you have the right sort of camera that isn't blurry, and sound - like actual background music - that would make it look better. Because you see in movies, the trailers sound a lot better and we are trying to aim for that. [Student 2, Group 1, Trial 3]

Students were provided with a teacher-generated list of specifications that included success indicators generated by students in introductory discussions. The book trailer needed to:

- include title of the novel and author's name in the trailer;
- have sound effects (can be originally composed);
- have one quote from the novel and one critic's review;
- have one element of live footage (includes acting and dialogue);
- have one element of originally composed music;
- have consistent transitions and at least one visual effect;
- have voice over.

This list gave all students the opportunity to further understand the interrelation between success indicators and specifications. In particular, Excel groups were further challenged and afforded opportunities for group discussion, decision-making and reasoning and to experiment with different programs, applications and modes of technology. Their book trailers demanded the application of higher-order learning (through participating in collaborative and multi-modal reasoning) rather than the standard audio visual presentation of text and images on the screen with background music (a common lower-order task in middle years classrooms).

Student Roles

Each student undertook two of eight set Director and Editor roles. These roles were allocated to each group member by the group after discussion and negotiation. The allocation of roles ensured that all students actively participated in group reasoning and decision-making while minimising opportunities for domination by some members. Director roles consisted of *dialogue* (scriptwriting, acting and text), *sound* (all audio components), *visual* (all visual and graphic components) and *editing* (collating all elements to create a final product). Editor roles included *goals* (responsibility for documenting the group aims at the beginning of each lesson and whether they were achieved by the end of the lesson), *USB* (ensuring that all digital book trailer files and documents were successfully copied and saved onto the group USB and handed back to the teacher at the completion of each lesson), *secretary* (records and notes of the main points from discussions and decisions made from each lesson and why these were made), and *research assistant* (responsibility for

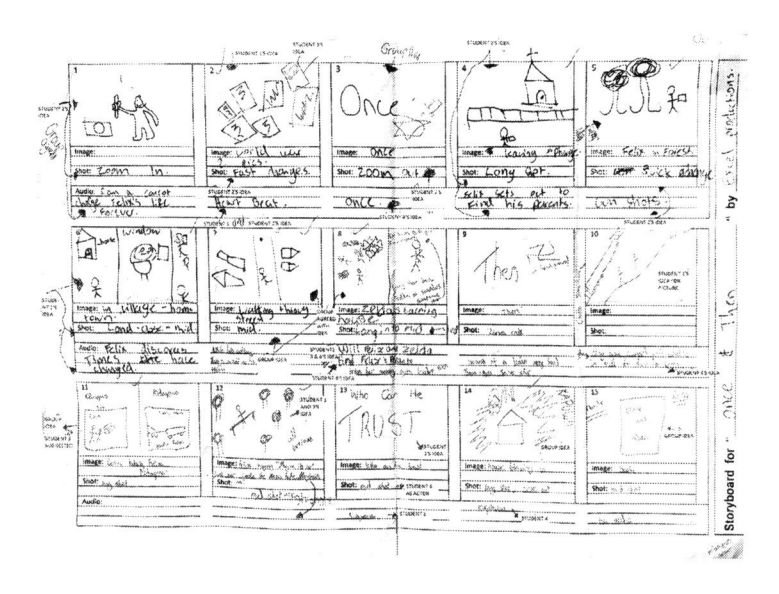

CREATING AND ANALYSING MULTI-MODAL TEXTS IN ENGLISH CLASSES

Figure 6.3. Collaborative storyboard of all-male group with accompanying reasoning annotations

records of communication between group members working on the trailer). Having specific areas of responsibility made each student accountable, and engendered a sense of ownership and pride in the final group product.

Storyboards

To ensure that all group members took an active role in planning and preparation of the trailer, each student developed an individual storyboard (either digitally or a print copy) on their book. All members then presented their storyboard, and justified their ideas to the group. A group storyboard was then developed, incorporating the various ideas of group members and new ideas afforded through collaborative talk and reasoning (Littleton & Mercer, 2010). In constructing the storyboard, the various modes of technology and literacy practices (Street, 1996) that would address the specifications, success indicators, and assessment rubric were considered. These included camera angles, location scouting, developing a script and dialogue, costume design, graphic text, font and background colours, background music, and sound effects.

Collaborative, Multi-Modal Reasoning

Collaborative and cooperative discussion and argument contribute to the quality of student learning (Mercer, 2008). This unit encouraged the development of multi-

113

modal reasoning; reasoning that draws on a variety of technological and embodied media. The students exercised various reasoning skills (such as decision-making) through interaction with technological devices as well as physical tools and artefacts (including their bodies). During the learning sequence, the students demonstrated linguistic reasoning through discussion and dialogue; creative and visual reasoning through trial and error in using tools and visualisation of an outcome; and reasoning by manipulative abduction (Magnani, 2009) through using their bodies to act out scenes, and experiment with actions and technologies.

In the following interview extract, one student reflected on the task-design decisions made in her group. Her reasoning is evident when she justifies and explains design choices, along with trial and error, creative experimentation, and visualisation of the look of the final product based on specifications and success indicators.

> We made many important choices throughout this unit. I'm going to specify some of our main choices and why. To benefit our trailer the group chose to use some footage from the Mrs Frisby movie. We used this because it captured the story really well and it was entertaining to watch. We used a clock ticking to

Figure 6.4. Screen shots of a book trailer presented by an all-female group

represent the race against time to save a sick mouse in the story. Real footage of mice was used to make the story more believable. 'Maxine' and I decided to get in some lab coats and film a scene depicting us experimenting on mice. We did this to show our view of scientists in the story. We used a heartbeat sound effect. This was used to emphasis [sic] tension and worry. We wanted to slowly build up the anticipation at the start of our trailer. One of the main softwares we used [sic] SaveTube, which saves high quality music. SaveTube was used to save most of our music. Our group used many different types of software. Some choices were harder than others but we finally agreed with forming our trailer. (Student 3, Trial 1 Group 5)

Learning Outcomes

Analysis of focus group responses and student surveys indicated that most students found the unit a novel and enjoyable learning experience. Students sustained their motivation and engagement because of the freedom offered and personal accountability to provide a high-quality product.

I really enjoyed it, I liked sitting without teacher guidance, creating our own piece of work and being able to choose what goes in. (Anonymous Post Unit Survey, Trial 2)

It was good to have the freedom to go at our own pace and as an individual group…it was good to conference with the other groups for extra advice and we thought it was a fabulous idea to see where the other groups were. We enjoyed not being told each week where we exactly had to be up to. We enjoyed this because it made us more independent and organised and we knew we had to work hard in class each lesson so we don't fall behind. (Group 8, Trial 2 Group Presentation)

Students liked working in small groups with most preferring to work with friends. While friendship groups resulted in a collaborative, cumulative approach to decision-making, it was observed that non-friendship groups engaged in more negotiation of differences in decision-making and thus more frequently practised such reasoning processes as appeals to evidence to support or rebut claims. It is possible that the individualisation of assessment in English also poses a challenge for promoting an ethos of mutual support among students.

Affordances of the Open-Plan Learning Space

Students in the Excel group were usually seated at two-chair capacity tables in straight lines of approximately five desks. The teacher would typically sit at a 'help desk' at the front of the classroom. For this unit students were encouraged to move furniture for easier collaboration and group-work and by the third lesson were doing so independently of teacher direction. Group-work was also quite foreign to these Year 7 students but they often continued group learning during and after each lesson, seeking out opportunities for collaborative reasoning. Perceiving the affordances of the learning space to promote student learning can result in altered spheres of influence for teachers and students, as students take responsibility for organising their own learning.

The learning space was used effectively throughout the unit and productively constrained various aspects of student learning (see Figure 6.5 for images of informal grouping). Students commented that the teacher was readily accessible to them. The space supported collaborative, multi-modal reasoning as students were near peers completing the same creative task and practicing similar techno-literacies. Readily available powerpoints for student laptop computers enabled mobility and easier sharing of crucial knowledge and information among group members. Teachers were easily able to conduct conferencing sessions enabling deeper thinking and reasoning experiences. The differentiated nature of the task meant that noise was not an issue, though students used headphones when playing loud music to avoid disturbing others. Glare from large, uncurtained windows was easily managed with furniture movement. Furthermore, the large windows enabled the teacher to supervise students who utilised outside space to film and record footage for their product.

Figure 6.5. Informal grouping in the open-plan setting

Key Points

- Students and teachers need to understand that they have to justify and explain their decisions and thinking in class. Teachers need to value reasoning within the middle years English curriculum and feel confident with technology and its affordances.
- Awareness and understanding of multi-modal, collaborative reasoning and how it promotes opportunities for extension and higher-order thinking must be made explicit to both teachers and students.
- Students need more ownership of curriculum learning tasks and to be exposed to group-work in a middle years learning context. Learning tasks need to enable students to develop criteria and success indicators for full understanding
- All tools and technology media must be working and fully accessible to students. Teachers need to encourage students to use and experiment with technology in different ways using multi-literacies and through new mediums as they see fit.
- Students need to be constantly encouraged to justify and explain their thinking as individuals, and as a group collective throughout the unit experience.

IMPLICATIONS FOR TEACHING AND LEARNING ENGLISH IN UP-SCALED LEARNING COMMUNITIES

In order to develop reasoning skills in English, middle school students need multiple and differently-contextualised opportunities for guided practice. The open-plan settings have the potential to constrain or enable reasoning practices. They offer scope for varying audience size markedly, and thus altering the purposes and character of participant interactions. Reasoning can be practised individually, in pairs, in small and larger groups, and in performances and presentations to a whole learning community of up to 105 students (for example the brainstorming of success indicators with the Excel, Build, and Strengthen groups in one up-scaled learning community). Both case studies point to the necessity of varying scale and purpose of groupings over time.

The case studies concur on conditions that enable effective learning about multi-modal reasoning in English in these settings. Students need guided support to participate in purposeful inquiry that entails creative and critical thinking, but also allows students some degree of adaptive flexibility, freedom of choice, experimentation, and orchestrated spontaneity. Teacher and student take-up of the affordances of the increased space of the settings can support innovative approaches, where students practise reasoning about texts, both as individuals and in groups. Our case studies also show how it is possible to address teacher concerns about managing large groups in open spaces through continued development and refinement of focused small-group activities.

REFERENCES

Anderson, M., & Jefferson, M. (2009). *Teaching the screen: Film education for generation next*. Crows Nest, Australia: Allen & Unwin.

Australian Curriculum and Assessment Reporting Authority (ACARA). (2014). *English curriculum*. Retrieved from http://www.australiancurriculum.edu.au/english/curriculum/f-10?layout=1

Australian Curriculum and Assessment Reporting Authority (ACARA). (2014). *General capabilities in the Australian curriculum*. Retrieved from: http://www.australiancurriculum.edu.au/generalcapabilities/overview/general-capabilities-in-the-australian-curriculum

Barr, A., Gillard, J., Firth, V., Scrymgour, M., Welford, R., Lomax-Smith, J., Bartlett, D., Pike, B., & Constable, E. (2008). *Melbourne declaration on educational goals for young Australians*. Carlton, Victoria, Australia: Ministerial Council on Education, Employment, Training and Youth Affairs. Retrieved from http://eric.ed.gov/?id=ED534449

Bateman, J., & Schmidt, K.-H. (2012). *Multimodal film analysis: How films mean*. New York, NY: Routledge.

Beavis, C. (2013). Literary English and the challenge of multimodality. *Changing English: Studies in Culture & Education, 20*(3), 241–252. doi:10.1080/1358684X.2013.816527

Cazden, C., Cope, B., Fairclough, N., Gee, J., Kalantzis, M., Kress, G., ... Nakata, M. (1996). A pedagogy of multiliteracies: Designing social futures. *Harvard Educational Review, 66*(1), 60–92.

Dewey, J. (1902). The school as social center. *The Elementary School Teacher, 3*(2), 73–86.

Edwards, A. (2011). Building common knowledge at the boundaries between professional practices: Relational agency and relational expertise in systems of distributed expertise. *International Journal of Educational Research, 50*(1), 33–39. doi:10.1016/j.ijer.2011.04.007

Edwards, D. (2010). *Prescribing literacies: A critical discourse analaysis of Australian literacy policies* [PhD thesis]. Melbourne, Victoria: La Trobe University.

Edwards, D., & Potts, A. (2008). What is literacy? Thirty years of Australian literacy debates (1975–2005). *Paedagogica Historica: International Journal of the History of Education, 44*(1–2), 123–135. doi:10.1080/00309230701865496

Engeström, Y. (2000). Activity theory as a framework for analaysing and redesigning work. *Ergonomics, 43*(7), 960–974. doi:10.1080/001401300409143

Freebody, P., Barton, G., & Chan, E. (2014). Literacy education. In C. Leung & B. V. Street (Eds.), *The Routledge companion to English studies* (pp. 419–434). New York, NY: Routledge.

Gibson, J. J. (1977). The theory of affordances. In R. Shaw & J. Bransford (Eds.). *Perceiving, acting, and knowing: Toward an ecological psychology* (pp. 67–82). Hillsdale, NJ: Erlbaum.

Golsby-Smith, S. (2013). Singing from the same songsheet: The flexible thinker and the curriculum in the 21st century. *English in Education, 47*(1), 66–78. doi:10.1111/eie.12000

Goodwyn, A. (2012). One size fits all: The increasing standardisation of English teachers' work in England. *English Teaching: Practice and Critique, 11*(4), 36–53. Retrieved from http://education.waikato.ac.nz/research/files/etpc/files/2012v11n4art3.pdf

Goodwyn, A., Reid, L., & Durrant, C. (Eds.). (2013). *International perspectives on teaching English in a globalised world*. New York, NY: Routledge.

Green, B. (2008). English, rhetoric, democracy; Or, renewing English in Australia. *English in Australia, 43*(3), 35–44.

Greene, S. (1993). The role of task in the development of academic thinking through reading and writing in a college history course. *Research in the Teaching of English, 27*(1), 46–75.

Hillocks, G. (2010). "EJ" in focus: Teaching argument for critical thinking and writing: An introduction. *English Journal, 99*(6), 24–32. Retrieved from http://www.jstor.org/discover/10.2307/20787661?uid=3737536&uid=2&uid=4&sid=21106496826893

Kress, G. (2006). Reimagining English: Curriculum, identity and productive futures. In B. Doecke, M. Howie, & W. Sawyer (Eds.), *Only connect: English teaching, schooling and community* (pp. 31–41). Kent Town, SA: Wakefield Press with the Aust. Assoc. for the Teaching of English.

Kuhn, D. (2009). Do students need to be taught how to reason? *Educational Research Review, 4*(1), 1–6. doi:10.1016/j.edurev.2008.11.001

Lemke, J. L. (1993). *Talking science: Language, learning and values.* New Jersey, NJ: Ablex Publishing Corporation.

Littleton, K., & Mercer, N. (2010). The significance of educational dialogues between primary school children. In K. Littleton & C. Howe (Eds.), *Educational dialogues: Understanding and promoting productive interaction* (pp. 271–288). Milton Park, Oxon: Routledge.

Luke, A., & Freebody, P. (1999). A map of possible practices: Further notes on the four resources model. *Practically Primary* 4(2), 5–8. Retrieved from http://www.readingonline.org/research/lukefreebody.html

Magnani, L. (2009). *Abductive cognition: The epistemological and eco-cognitive dimensions of hypothetical reasoning* (Vol. 3). Berlin, Germany: Springer-Verlag. doi:10.1007/978-3-642-03631-6

Mercer, N. (1996). The quality of talk in children's collaborative activity in the classroom. *Learning and Instruction, 6*(4), 359–377. doi:10.1016/s0959-4752(96)00021-7

Mercer, N. (2008). Talk and the development of reasoning and understanding. *Human Development, 51,* 90–100. doi:10.1159/000113158

Mercer, N., & Littleton, K. (2007). *Dialogue and the development of children's thinking: A sociocultural approach.* London, UK: Routledge.

Mercer, N., Wegerif, R., & Dawes, L. (1999). Children's talk and the development of reasoning in the classroom. *British Educational Research Journal, 25*(1), 95–111.

Mills, K. A. (2010). Shrek meets Vygotsky: Rethinking adolescents' multimodal literacy practices in schools. *Journal of Adolescent & Adult Literacy, 54*(1), 35–45. doi:10.1598/JAAL.54.1.4

Morgan, A. M., Comber, B., Freebody, P., & Nixon, H. (2014). *Literacy in the middle years: Learning from collaborative classroom research.* Newtown, New South Wales, Australia: Primary English Teaching Association.

Nay-Brock, P. K. (1984). The role of ignorance in the shaping of an English curriculum: An example from the history of English in NSW. *English in Australia, 67,* 18–25. Retrieved from http://eric.ed.gov/?id=EJ304007

Nickerson, R. S. (2012). Modes and models of informal reasoning: A commentary. In J. F. Voss, D. N. Perkins, & J. W. Segal (Eds.), *Informal reasoning and education* (pp. 291–309). New York, NY: Routledge.

Nystrand, M., & Gamoran, A. (1991). Instructional discourse, student engagement, and literature achievement. *Research in the teaching of English, 25*(3), 261–290.

Nystrand, M., Gamoran, A., Kachur, R., & Prendergast, C. (1997). *Opening dialogue: Understanding the dynamics of language and learning in the English classroom.* New York, NY: Teachers College Press.

Osborne, J. (2010). Arguing to learn in science: The role of collaborative, critical discourse. *Science, 328*(5977), 463–466. doi:10.1126/science.1183944

Peel, R., Patterson, A. H., & Gerlach, J. M. (Eds.). (2000). *Questions of English: Ethics, aesthetics, rhetoric, and the formation of the subject in England, Australia, and the United States.* New York, NY: Psychology Press

Pendergast, D., & Main, K. (2013). The middle years of schooling association's representations of young adolescents. Particularising the adolescent. *Social Alternatives, 32*(2), 25–30.

Prain, V., Cox, P., Deed, C., Dorman, J., Edwards, D., Farrelly, C., Keeffe, M., ... Yager, Z. (2014). *Adapting to teaching and learning in open-plan schools.* Rotterdam, The Netherlands: Sense Publishers.

Prensky, M. (2001). Digital natives, digital immigrants part 1. *On the Horizon, 9*(5), 1–6. doi:10.1108/10748120110424816

Rex, L. A., Thomas, E. E., & Engel, S. (2010). Applying Toulmin: Teaching logical reasoning and argumentative writing. *English Journal, 99*(6), 56–62. Retrieved from http://www.jstor.org/stable/20787669

Reznitskaya, A., Kuo, L. J., Clark, A. M., Miller, B., Jadallah, M., Anderson, R. C., & Nguyen-Jahiel, K. (2009). Collaborative reasoning: A dialogic approach to group discussions. *Cambridge Journal of Education, 39*(1), 29–48. doi:10.1080/03057640802701952

Schleicher, A. (2013). *The case for 21st-century learning.* OECD. Retrieved from http://www.oecd.org/general/thecasefor21st-centurylearning.htm

Serafini, F. (2012). Expanding the four resources model: Reading visual and multi-modal texts. *Pedagogies: An International Journal, 7*(2), 150–164. doi:10.1080/1554480X.2012.656347

Street, B. (1996). Academic literacies. In D. Baer, C. Fox, & J. Clay (Eds.), *Challenging ways of knowing in maths, science and English* (pp. 101–134). Lewes, England: Falmer Press.

Sutherland, J. (2015). Going 'meta': Using a metadiscoursal approach to develop secondary students' dialogic talk in small groups. *Research Papers in Education, 30*(1), 44–69. doi:10.1080/02671522.2013.850528

Turner, G. (2007). Cultural literacies, critical literacies, and the English school curriculum in Australia. *International Journal of Cultural Studies, 10*(1), 105–114. doi:10.1177/1367877907073905

Warren, J. E. (2010). Taming the warrant in Toulmin's model of argument. *English Journal, 99*(6), 41–46. Retrieved from http://www.jstor.org/discover/10.2307/20787665?uid=3737536&uid=2&uid=4&sid=21106496826893

Wildfeuer, J. (2014). *Film discourse interpretation: Towards a new paradigm for multimodal film analysis.* New York, NY: Routledge.

Yin, R. (2008). *Case study research: Design and methods.* Thousand Oaks, CA: Sage.

PETER COX, BRUCE WALDRIP AND VAUGHAN PRAIN

7. PERSONALISING MATHEMATICS FOR LOW SES STUDENTS IN SCHOOLS WITH OPEN-PLAN SETTINGS

REDESIGNING MATHEMATICS LEARNING IN SCHOOL

When recently surveyed about the most useful part of their current mathematics program, three Year 9 students at Ironbark College commented:

> I find the individual program great because we all get to work at our own pace and our own level.

> Working at the level I am at, not just working on whatever we should be at.

> The pre-test because I know what level I'm on and what I need to practise.

Mathematics educators now broadly agree about key dimensions of quality mathematics programs and experiences (Schoenfeld, 2014), but achieving these practices in schools with high concentrations of low SES students remains a challenge in many countries (Black, 2007; Greeno & Collins, 2008). In this chapter we first review current understandings of what enables quality learning in mathematics, as a basis for reporting on the impacts of personalised learning approaches to this subject in three of the BEP colleges: Whirrakee, Ironbark and Melaleuca. We claim that the open-plan settings operated as a catalyst for curricular reform in mathematics, leading to improved student performance and enhanced student attitudes to this subject.

Quality in Mathematics Learning

There is now broad agreement about what enables quality learning in mathematics. As identified by Schoenfeld (2014), effective mathematics programs have five key dimensions around: (1) curricular coherence of the subject, (2) cognitive demand of tasks, (3), student access to mathematical content, (4) opportunities for student agency, authority and identity, and (5) effective use of assessment. Curricular coherence refers to the extent to which discussion in mathematics is focused, and connects procedures, concepts and contexts, so that students learn key mathematical content and practices, and develop mathematical habits of mind.

Cognitive demand is about balancing challenge and consolidation of learning (Stein, Engle, Smith, & Hughes, 2008). Access to content is about ensuring all students are engaged in mathematical core concepts and processes (Oakes, Joseph, & Muir, 2003). Opportunities for student agency, authority and identity occur when students conjecture, pose arguments, build on one another's suggestions, and see themselves as able in mathematics (Engle, Langer-Osuna, & McKinney de Royston, 2014). Effective assessment provides the opportunity to monitor student understanding and to provide timely planning that addresses immediate student needs and offers ways to progress in performance (Black & Wiliam, 2009). We claim that these conditions are met in the three programs outlined in this chapter, and address widely acknowledged problems in schools with high concentrations of low SES students.

Overcoming Well-Recognised Barriers

Extensive research has identified persistent challenges in engaging low SES middle years students (Years 5–9) in the school curriculum generally, and in mathematics in particular (Black, 2007; Greeno & Collins, 2008; Lokan, Greenwood, & Cresswell, 2001; Luke et al., 2003; Sirin, 2005; Vale et al., 2010). Claimed causes for poor performance include: (a) negative contextual influences of low family SES on student aspirations (Sirin, 2005); (b) negative contextual influences of schools with large concentrations of low SES students (Auwarter & Aruguete, 2008; Perry & McConney, 2011); (c) inflexible curricula, lack of links to the community, and lack of variety and responsiveness in teaching strategies (Alfassi, 2004; Black, 2007; Luke et al., 2003), and (d) lack of quality resources and qualified mathematics teachers in low SES schools (Greenberg et al., 2004; Hill, Rowan, & Ball, 2005; Mogari et al., 2009; Wenglinsky, 1998). Numerous research studies link teachers' domain specific academic qualifications to student achievement. Teachers need rich mathematical content knowledge and deep understanding of mathematical concepts to teach mathematics effectively (Brown & Borko, 1992; Collias, Pajak, & Rigden, 2000; Darling-Hammond, 2000; Greenberg et al., 2004; Mewborn, 2001; Mogari et al., 2009; Wenglinsky, 2002). Mewborn (2001) confirmed that although conceptual knowledge is vital for mathematics teachers, it "doesn't ensure that teachers are able to teach it in ways that enable students to develop…deep conceptual understanding". Teachers also need pedagogical content knowledge (PCK) for effective mathematics teaching. That is, the ability to translate content understanding into teaching and learning experiences. Baumert and colleagues (2010) argued that PCK contributes more to student gains than does content knowledge. Hill, Rowan, and Ball (2005) also called for more research into the teaching practice of knowledgeable teachers to understand those aspects of mathematical knowledge that matter for teaching. Targeted professional development has also been found to impact positively on students' achievement (Kennedy, 1998). Ideally, an expert figure provides corrective feedback and suggestions to teachers (Onwu & Mogari, 2004; Mogari et al., 2009; DEECD, 2010).

These challenges were met in the three BEP schools through the following extended strategies: (1) professional learning support for mathematics teachers through external coaches and extensive work on developing a multi-level curriculum (see Prain et al., 2014); (2) block-timetabling of teacher teams to design, enact and review this curriculum and provide timely targeted feedback to students at all levels of the program, and (3) development of high expectations of students in engaging with mathematics learning.

Our Research Aims and Methods

We aimed to identify the effects of this curricular reform on teacher perspectives and student performance and attitudes towards mathematics. We used a case study approach, incorporating quantitative and qualitative data collection and analyses (Merriam, 1998; Tashakkori & Teddlie, 2010; Yin, 2008). Quantitative data included national assessment scores in mathematics for Years 7 and 9 over five years (2008–2012), analysed against benchmarking of expected performance of Australian schools of similar SES at the relevant levels across these years (see Table 7.1). The researchers analysed these data for patterns in the results over time. In Australian secondary schools, student performance at Years 7 and 9 is measured in mathematics and literacy against all other schools in Australia by tests known as the National Assessment Program-Literacy and Numeracy (NAPLAN). NAPLAN is a simple form of data with a 'one size fits all' approach to assessing and measuring students' abilities and progress. The results place students on a scale that compares them to all other Australian students of their year level and with schools calculated to be of similar Index of Community Socio-Educational Advantage (ICSEA) values. In Australia, like the data gathered for PISA, the students' SES is based on data collected at the local level on parents' or carers' income, education and occupation. The school's ICSEA values are calculated on the basis of these student data. In addition, Australian data incorporates a school's metropolitan, regional or remote status and the proportion of indigenous student enrolments. Quantitative data also included a survey of 784 students in Years 7 and 9 on their perceptions of the usefulness of teaching and learning strategies in their mathematics program (see Table 7.2). Responses were scored on a four-point scale where a score of 4.0 represented very useful and 1.0 represented not useful. Themes in the responses from 'most useful' to 'least useful' were identified by the researchers.

A research officer collected qualitative data through one-hour interviews with the school principals, the mathematics coordinators and eight mathematics teachers. These data sources were analysed individually and collectively by the three researchers to address issues of reliability in interpretation. The methods of qualitative data analyses followed principles outlined for qualitative case study research, focusing on identification of patterns in participant responses (Denzin & Lincoln, 2008; Merriam, 1998; Yin, 2008), leading to the development of themes in the light of relevant literature. These themes were identified individually by the researchers, and subsequently refined through group discussion and consensus.

Context of the Study

The AusVELS (AusVELS.vcaa.vic.edu.au) curriculum outlines what is essential for Victorian students to learn during their time at school. This curriculum provides a set of common state-wide standards based on the Australian national curriculum which schools use to plan student learning programs, assess student progress, and report to parents. Each school developed a program where, based on a pre-test topic or task, students were placed into topic-based ability groups with individual work programs set for each student including a goal for the end of unit AusVELS level that they should reach. The visual summary of each school's mathematics program is provided in Figure 7.1. At each school the open-plan settings enabled the development of the models described. The structural changes to the school timetable were also afforded by the open-plan settings and allowed for multiple mathematics classes to be scheduled at the same time in the same space. This change allowed the mathematics teachers at each school to work as a team to aggregate their efforts and to provide a much more targeted curriculum for the students, where the teachers were able to manipulate student groupings, and to tailor a program that could effectively cater for a wide range of students.

Ironbark College

The program consists of a sequence of learning experiences for each mathematics topic, with the same program across all four sub-schools (Figure 7.1). All the mathematics teachers planned together, but taught in teams of three. Prior to a pre-test to determine each student's AusVELS level in the topic, a brief refresher "workshop" was provided to remind the students of what they had studied in their previous year.

Based on the pre-test, students were placed into three topic-based ability groups with individual work programs set for each student including a goal for the end of unit AusVELS level that they should reach. Following a differentiated sequence of work on the mathematics topic the students all sat a post-test. The corrected post-tests were used to provide feedback to individual students and the class on their progress and to recognise and celebrate individual performances. The post-test was not simply used as a summative assessment, and there was provision for students

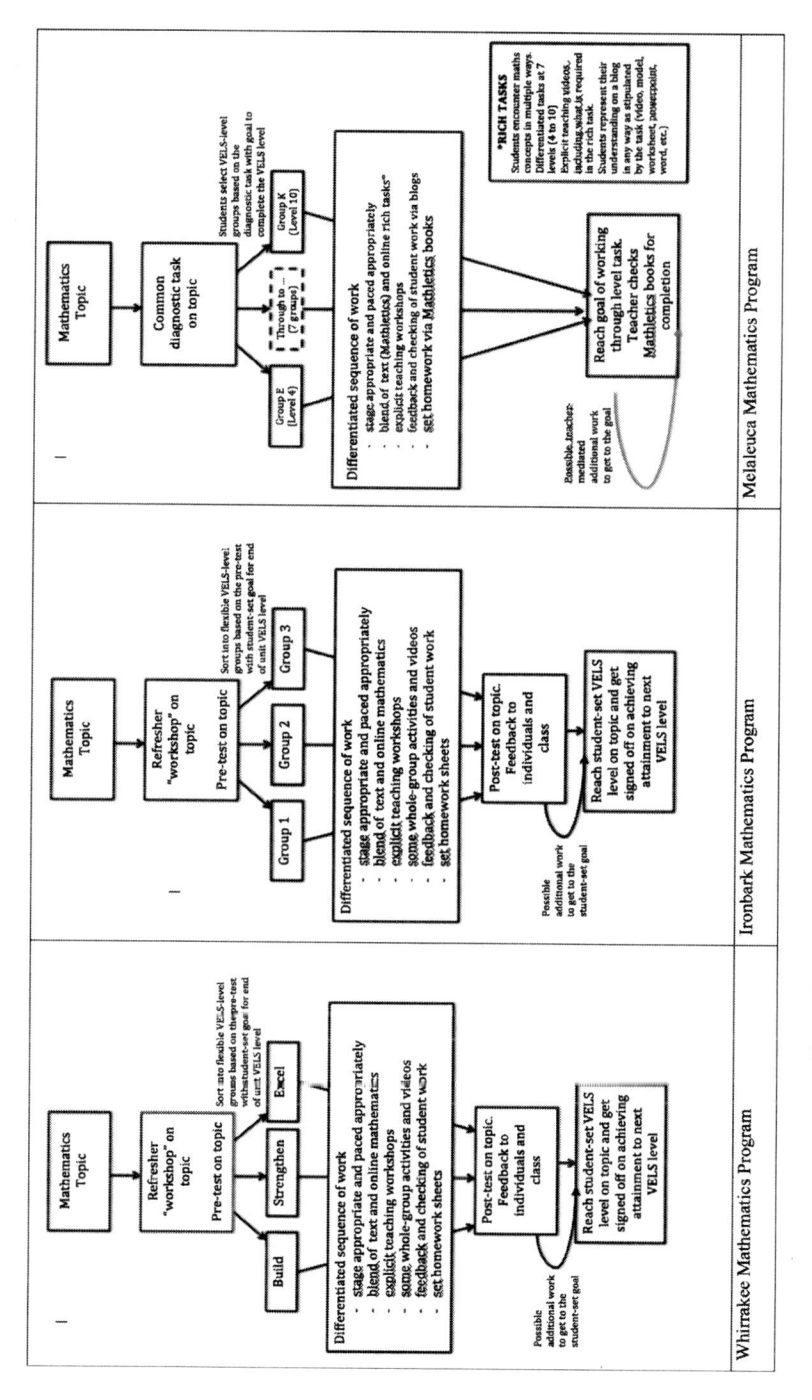

PERSONALISING MATHEMATICS FOR LOW SES STUDENTS

Figure 7.1. Description of mathematics program model in the three schools

to complete additional work to demonstrate that they had reached their personal AusVELS-level goal.

Whirrakee College

As shown in Figure 7.1, Whirrakee's model is very similar to Ironbark's. We focus in this school on the learning model employed within Pods (consisting of three classes of approximately 75 students and three teachers). The model has three distinct groups of students working separately within the one open-learning space, although whole Pod teaching also occurs when relevant. Based on the results from the pre-test for a mathematics topic, students are divided into three groups, the Build, Strengthen, and Excel groups. These groups vary in size due to the nature of the teacher work within each. The Build group is small, approximately 14 students, and takes the students who are below the expected level in this mathematics topic. This small group size allows the teacher to work intensively with the students at one large table to provide a differentiated program based on their skills. The teacher employs concrete examples, modelling, explicit instruction and scaffolding with continuous feedback throughout the learning task. The Excel group of most capable students is the largest with up to 35 students, where the teacher negotiates the task with individuals and allows the learners to self-monitor their learning and to work independently. Where necessary, explicit instruction or whole group discussion can be employed. The Strengthen middle group consists of 26 students and is run more like a differentiated "mainstream" class with a blend of scaffolding, explicit instruction and structure to develop independent learning routines.

Melaleuca College

This program is designed around seven themes to create enhanced mathematical learning: learners create understanding through involvement in rich tasks; learners decide how they represent their understanding; learners identify what they know and need to learn; teaching is done at 'point of need' through workshops; technology is used authentically; the new learning spaces are used flexibly; and teachers work as a team to plan and deliver the program. The program was trialled in 2013 and extended to all Years 7 to Years 9 classes in 2014. This program occupies approximately 60% of student time and provides the context and purpose through which students explore each mathematics topic. Running parallel to the rich tasks is the more traditional program that provides students with the mathematical concepts and practice that needs to be applied to complete the rich task. Each rich task is designed to be open, and have no "right answer". Students need to be creative and make choices in how they provide evidence of completion of the task. This encourages students to "engage in multiple representations of the concept and show how they link together.

As shown in Figure 7.1 the tasks are differentiated on a continuum from Level 4 (Grade 4) through to Level 10 (Year 10). These are represented to the students not as year levels but as letters from E through to K. Students choose their appropriate level by completing a common introductory diagnostic task that is completed by between two and four classes at a time in the flexible learning spaces. The task is pitched "at level" so, for example, Year 8 students complete this diagnostic task set at Level 8. Based on their ability to complete this diagnostic task, students then choose the level of rich task based on what feels right for them. This is a process that is very consistently managed:

> The language used with the students is consistent – students understand that if a task is too easy, that is, if it can be done without any assistance, it is the "wrong task". Similarly, if the task requires students to obtain assistance every few minutes, it is also the "wrong task". Students are encouraged to identify the "right task" based on the need to "stretch" their thinking and require occasional assistance. The vast majority of students choose the right task – those that don't can still be directed by the teacher to the right task. (Mathematics Co-ordinator, 2013)

As teachers are working as a team, each teacher then takes responsibility for a range of tasks (and students) from Group E through to Group K. The teachers support the students working on their tasks and may "roam the open space, identifying students working on the task for which they are responsible and supporting their learning". At times they will "call their students together to give instruction or address a misconception, or clarify what evidence is needed to complete the task". This flexible use of teachers and space means that at times students are free to work anywhere in the open-plan learning spaces.

At Melaleuca College the greatest innovation is the use of technology to augment teacher instruction through videos and for students to upload their representations of evidence of completion of the rich task on their own blog. The website provides the site to house the course that can be accessed directly or by scanning QR codes that are located on large cards pinned up around the open-learning space. This site includes all the rich task material and has instructional videos for each task including explicit teaching of the mathematics concepts. This enables students to "access the videos if they wish to skip ahead; need assistance at home; need to catch up after absence; or need to revisit the material in class". The blogs allow teachers to monitor student progress, and allow students to store their representations in a place that can be accessed from school, or home and via any mobile technology. This enables much greater sharing of student work then the traditional exercise book or folder. Student work placed on the blog can be shared with teachers, peers and parents using any mobile device and is securely filed for later reference. We consider that that this storage and retrieval function is an important feature for low SES students.

STUDY FINDINGS

We report our findings in two sections: (1) analysis of quantitative data on the performances of the colleges in numeracy over the life of the research project, and student survey results, and (2) analysis of teacher and student perceptions of the effects of the differentiated mathematics curriculum.

QUANTITATIVE FINDINGS

One of the graphs presented in Chapter 1 in relation to numeracy, is reproduced below in Figure 7.2. This graph plots each school's ranking among "similar schools", where a ranking of 1 indicates that the school is the top performing school among "similar schools" and a ranking of 0 indicates the school is the lowest performing school among "similar schools". This ranking has been calculated in the following way: for a school ranked R out of N "similar schools" the ranking, r, is calculated by $r = (N-R)/(N-1)$. For example, in 2012, Ironbark's Year 9 NAPLAN (Numeracy) average score was ranked 3/21 "similar schools" and so its ranking, $r = (21-3)/(21-1)$.

This graph and its underlying statistics were the catalyst for this chapter's investigation into student perceptions of the effectiveness of the components of the mathematics programs that had been introduced in three of the four schools.

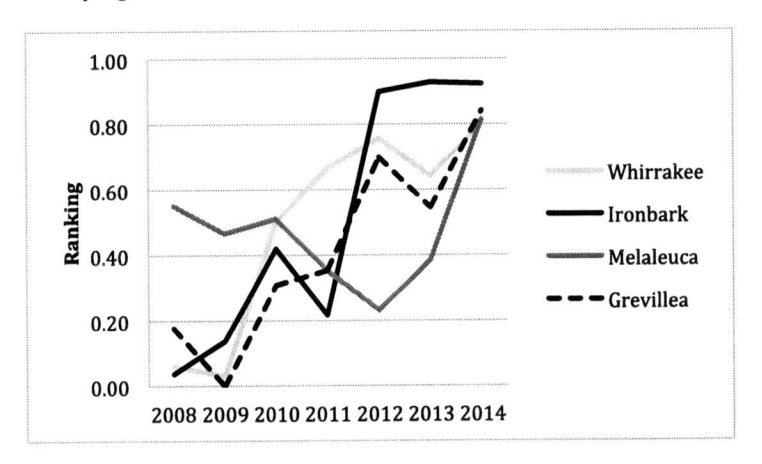

Figure 7.2. School ranking among "similar schools" for year 9 numeracy, 2008–2014

This study investigated student's perceptions in three BEP colleges. They were selected because of their 2013 NAPLAN rankings as shown in Figure 7.2. The two highest-ranking colleges (Whirrakee and Ironbark) were selected as they had increased their rankings earlier and more substantially than the other BEP schools. The third college selected was Melaleuca because it had the lowest ranking among like schools and had introduced a program to address this deficit in NAPLAN results. Melaleuca has dramatically increased its ranking relative to like schools in the 2014 NAPLAN data which indicates that its mathematics program is worthy of documentation. This study had to be limited to three school mathematics programs because of time and resources constraints, and the authors acknowledge that based on the 2014 data now available Grevillea would also have been worthy to be documented. However, the decisions on documenting three different school mathematics programs in this chapter was made in 2013 using the available 2013 NAPLAN data, and so Grevillea was not studied.

This documentation and comparison of the three mathematics programs was based on their program models. The researchers sought to obtain student perceptions of the relative benefits of each element of these programs to their mathematics learning. Students were surveyed using an online Survey Monkey survey. The breakdown of the numbers of students surveyed is provided in Table 7.1.

Table 7.1. Number of students surveyed at each of the three schools in this study

School	Year Level	Female	Male	Total
Whirrakee	Year 7	89	79	168
	Year 9	101	97	198
	Total	190	176	366
Ironbark	Year 7	64	61	125
	Year 9	37	53	90
	Total	101	114	215
Melaleuca	Year 7	60	47	107
	Year 9	54	42	96
	Total	114	89	203

The students were asked to rate the components of their mathematics programs in the following way. On a four-point scale (Not useful (1), Sometimes useful (2), Useful (3), Very useful (4)), students indicated how useful they had found the different components. Each school had different models, but each element of their programs was matched against equivalent elements in the other schools. The list of components matched across the three schools with one school having an additional component. These components and the minor variations at each school are presented in Table 7.2.

Table 7.2. Components of each schools' mathematics program

Component number	Statement for each component (W=Whirrakee, I=Ironbark, M=Melaleuca)
1	Learning intentions and success criteria showing me the what, why and how of each lesson (W, M) Learning intentions showing me the what, why and how of each lesson (I)
2	Pre test to find out my AusVELS level (W) Pre test to find out my AusVELS level (for Year 7) OR Starting topics from where I got up to in Year 8 (for Year 9) (I) Diagnostic task to find the level I need to work at (M)
3	Individual maths program based on my AusVELS level (W, I) Individual Mathletics program based on my AusVELS level (M)
4	Working in a group of students at the same AusVELS level (W, I, M)
5	Teacher workshops on different skills in B, S, E groups (W) Teacher workshops on different skills (I, M)
6	The teacher teaching me when I need it, individually or in my group (W, I, M)
7	Other students helping me (W, I, M)
8	Helping other students (W, I, M)
9	Using my netbook computer (W, I) Using my device to review videos and post Blogs (M)
10	Using other technologies (iPad, iPod, mobile device, etc.) (W, I, M)
11	Completing tasks to demonstrate my understanding (W) Completing hurdles to demonstrate my understanding (I) Completing task descriptions to demonstrate my understanding (M)
12	Completing checkpoints (assessment sheet) and getting the teacher's feedback (W) Completing assessment sheets and getting the teacher's feedback (I) Completing Mathletics booklets and getting the teacher's feedback (M)
13	Post test (test at the end of the topic) (W, I, M)
14	Opportunities to resubmit those parts of my work I have not understood (W, M) Opportunities to redo those parts of my work I have not understood (I)
15	Use of Mathsmate book/Mathletics (W)

Results from each of the three school surveys are presented in Table 7.3.

Table 7.3. Overall average Likert score for each component and the overall percentage of useful and very useful for each of the three schools

Component Number	Whirrakee (n=366) Av. Rating	Whirrakee (n=366) %U&VU	Ironbark (n=215) Av. Rating	Ironbark (n=215) %U&VU	Melaleuca (n=203) Av. Rating	Melaleuca (n=203) %U&VU
1	2.36	41.5	2.31	37.2	2.42	44.3
2	2.72	58.5	2.76	60.9	2.64	58.1
3	2.79	60.7	2.85	65.6	2.61	55.2
4	2.99	66.7	2.87	66.5	2.73	61.6
5	2.88	65.3	2.73	59.1	2.50	48.8
6	3.25	81.1	2.97	67.9	2.87	64.5
7	2.91	66.9	2.57	48.8	2.78	63.5
8	2.79	62.8	2.58	49.3	2.62	58.1
9	3.15	74.6	2.83	59.5	2.56	54.2
10	2.71	51.9	2.78	55.3	2.89	66.5
11	2.94	74.6	2.53	47.4	2.47	50.7
12	2.92	67.8	2.67	58.1	2.60	53.7
13	2.82	62.0	2.79	60.0	2.41	39.9
14	2.92	64.2	2.73	51.2	2.54	49.8
15	2.34	41.0	–	–	–	–

Through a disaggregation of these data it has been found that these themes are consistent for Year 7 and Year 9 students, male and female students, and for low- and high-achieving students at each school.

To highlight the most and least preferred components of the mathematics programs at each school in Table 7.4 (and to be consistent with Table 7.3), the three highest ranked components, and lowest two ranked components, have been shaded. The darker shading indicates the top three ranked components and the lighter shading indicates the lowest two ranked components for each school. For all three schools component 6 (The teacher teaching me when I need it, individually or in my group) is one of the top three preferred components when disaggregated and ranked by year level, gender and ability group.

This shading makes clear the major student preferred components, where component 4 (*Working in a group of students at the same AusVELS level*) and component 6 (*The teacher teaching me when I need it, individually or in my group*) are two of the top three preferred components across the three schools. These results from the student surveys at each school is evidence that differentiation has been successfully achieved, and combined with the evidence from the NAPLAN

P. COX ET AL.

Table 7.4. Overall rank (by average Likert scores) for each component, disaggregated by year level (7 or 9), gender, and ability, for each of the three schools

Component No.	Whirrakee (n=366) Rank by							Ironbark (n=215) Rank by							Melaleuca (n=203) Rank by						
	Year Level		Gender		Ability			Year Level		Gender		Ability			Year Level		Gender		Ability		
	7	9	f	m	l	h		7	9	f	m	l	h		7	9	f	m	l	h
1	15	14	14	15	15	14		14	14	14	14	14	14		13	12	14	11	1	14
2	6	13	13	10	11	12		2	12	4	9	11	2		6	7	5	6	12	5
3	9	12	10	12	12	10		5	3	2	5	5	3		10	5	8	7	7	8
4	3	7	3	3	3	3		8	1	7	2	3	5		5	3	4	4	2	4
5	5	9	9	6	6	6		10	7	8	6	6	7		12	9	10	13	13	9
6	1	1	1	1	1	1		1	2	1	1	1	4		2	1	1	2	3	1
7	11	3	7	5	5	9		12	9	11	12	7	13		3	4	2	5	4	3
8	12	8	11	7	9	11		11	13	12	11	12	10		9	6	6	8	8	7
9	2	2	2	2	2	2		3	5	5	4	2	9		4	14	12	3	5	11
10	13	10	12	13	4	13		9	4	3	7	4	11		1	2	3	1	1	2
11	8	4	6	4	8	4		13	11	13	13	13	12		11	13	11	12	11	12
12	7	6	5	8	10	8		7	10	10	8	10	8		7	8	7	10	10	6
13	4	11	8	11	13	7		6	6	9	3	8	1		14	11	13	14	14	13
14	10	5	4	9	7	5		4	8	6	10	9	6		8	10	9	9	9	10
15	14	15	15	14	14	15														

132

graph suggests that the models of mathematics teaching has been very successful in differentiating the mathematics curriculum and for lifting the performance of low socioeconomic students relative to their like schools.

The lighter shading in Table 7.4 indicates the lowest two ranked components for each school. In all three schools component 1 (Learning intentions and success criteria showing me the what, why and how of each lesson) was one of the lowest two preferred components. This result may reflect teacher uncertainty about how to characterise this aspect of mathematics classes, and the relative novelty of this approach, leading to student failure to perceive these aspects as deeply meaningful.

QUALITATIVE FINDINGS

Principal and Teacher Perspectives

Interview comments of teachers and principals support positive learning outcomes from the implementation of new mathematics curricula in the open-plan settings. According to Teacher A, one of the main enablers of the open-plan spaces is being "able to break the students into small groups and have them working in like ability areas". The open-plan learning spaces allowed students to function as a whole group with three teachers for preparation for the units or whole-group appropriate stimulus videos. The open-plan learning spaces also encouraged teachers to work together for planning and team-teaching. As noted by Teacher A, "Each teacher is given an AusVELS level to concentrate on to make sure the curriculum is relevant and accurate…Teachers also have a homework sheet to develop and they share that". Both Teacher A and Teacher B enjoyed collaborating with colleagues:

> It just gives you the opportunity to share. There's greater flexibility in what you can do and deliver, bouncing ideas, sharing curriculum, sharing ideas, helping one another out, collegiality, building a rapport with other staff members. I've only been here two years and I feel that my transition to this school has been a lot easier because I have been working closely with other teachers than I was at my previous school where I was working in isolation. (Teacher B)

Teacher B also "loves… having the choice and the flexibility of being able to move things around. Teacher X and I can change our students over [from one class to another] and I can still see my students if I need to. Teacher X and I communicate during the class." The visibility of open-pan spaces encourages a sense of community among teachers and students. Students have the advantage of variety in the flexible groupings of teachers and students they work with. "Because of our grouping, students work with people they wouldn't normally mix with or even their friends from another group that they don't work with normally" (Teacher B). The low density of open-plan learning spaces allows unused space to be used for spontaneous restructure of groupings. The mathematics coordinator has been "honestly quite surprised at the positive effect" the open-plan learning spaces have had on teaching and learning. "Students are being exposed to a wider range of teaching styles, teaching abilities, as well as other students and the way they learn. As peers they are learning a lot more from each other as well."

The principals, mathematics coordinators, and teachers reported positive changes in student and teacher practices and attitudes as a result of the innovation. Student motivation and desire to learn improved, evident in increased homework, more self-directed learning, students working above the expected AusVELS levels, and more positive attitude-to-school survey results. There was also increased cooperation amongst teachers who were operating at higher conceptual levels and planning together. One principal believed that the students were "trying harder while the mathematics coordinator claimed that the school had "a more supportive environment for the student". In commenting on teacher change, she said "a lot of people felt quite uncomfortable at the beginning. But seeing the students and their behaviour and their engagement helped the staff to see that it was working really well". The mathematics co-ordinator at Melaleuca believed that the program has "increased engagement in mathematics across all learning styles and abilities, and increased the capacity of students to work independently, take responsibility for their learning, use technology appropriately, and think creatively".

Student Perspectives

Students were also invited to comment, in open-ended questions, on which parts they found the most and least useful (Tables 7.5, 7.6 and 7.7). Their positive comments on the most useful program features align with the teachers' perspectives. Themes and schools where there were ten or fewer comments were excluded from the table. Comments on the most useful parts of the program (Whirrakee, 327 comments; Ironbark, 148 comments; Melaleuca, 151 comments) again confirm that the students understood and appreciated differentiation of their program to meet their individual needs.

The student responses from all three schools indicate that the design of each school's mathematics program had its own differing strengths. However, at this point it is worth noting that these qualitative open-ended student responses have provided a triangulation of the quantitative data presented in Tables 7.3 and 7.4. The ranking of each component differs in the analysis of the qualitative and qualitative data sets, but the two common components present in the top three ranked components for all three schools from Table 7.3 (components 4 and 6) are present in each school's table based on the students' open-ended responses. This strengthens the argument that these two components are major design features that students perceive to be the most useful and are the ones that indicate that differentiation of student mathematics programs has been a result of implementing these programs.

Table 7.5. Summary of comments on the most useful program strategies (Whirrakee)

Most useful parts of program	Example of individual comments
3. Individual maths program based on my AusVELS level [42% of comments: (W#1)]	I think doing the pre test is one of the most useful things. This is because we then get to fill out a planner, which tells us which we need to work on. This also means that we are doing work that is at our own level. (W#37) I really enjoyed having my own personal learning program. It has allowed me to focus my learning on the areas that I struggle with, or need to improve within that given topic. As a result, I find that I can strive for higher results and organise / study more effectively come post-topic tests. (W#217)
4. Working in a group of students at the same AusVELS level [33% of comments: (W#2)]	the most useful parts of the program to help me learn maths is working in bse groups because I am doing work that is my own work level. (W#39) The most useful parts of the program to help you learn maths is when we are put into excel, strengthen and build, because they are at the same level as you. (W#56)
6. The teacher teaching me when I need it, individually or in my group [28% of comments: (W#3)]	Having one on one time with the teacher to talk about what I need to learn and not everyone else. (W#12) The most useful parts of the program is when I am working with my teacher when I am confused about a certain part of the task, and having him fully help me get a better understanding of it. (W#294)
15. Use of Mathsmate book/ Mathletics [14% of comments: (W#4)]	The most useful program is using the mathsworld 7 pdf program to complete the planner sheets. (W#78) Math mate because its a good start to every lesson to refresh your brain. (W#351)
11. Completing tasks to demonstrate my understanding [8% of comments: (W#5)]	... Also the planner that we do is also helpful because it helps us to know what we have to do to understand what we are doing. (W#32) Probably using the planner to demonstrate what I've learnt through out the unit. (W#229)

Table 7.6. Summary of comments on the most useful program strategies (Ironbark)

Most useful parts of program	*Example of individual comments*
3. Individual maths program based on my AusVELS level [36% of comments: (I#1)]	were [sic] all at our own individual levels and can work at our own pace and we don't repeat what we already know (I#137)
	Having a sheet so you know what your working on individually and keeps your work organised. It is a goal to complete. (I#184)
6. The teacher teaching me when I need it, individually or in my group [22% of comments: (I#2)]	Having the teacher explain the topic the way you understand and helping out when I don't understand. (I#211)
	One on one with the teachers, Working on the board (working out questions with the teacher on the whiteboard) (I#180)
4. Working in a group of students at the same AusVELS level [19% of comments: (I#3)]	That we are in the same group and being at the same AusVELS groups as other people, not mixed up groups. (I#68)
	I like how we are in our own Vels groups, it works better (I#127)
5. Teacher workshops on different skills [16% of comments: (I#4)]	Workshops by teachers that explain how to do things. (I#177)
	Teacher doing the workshops at the start of the class. (I#191)
12. Completing assessment sheets and getting the teacher's feedback [11% of comments: (I#5)]	Having a sheet so you know what your working on individually and keeps your work organised. It is a goal to complete. (I#184)
	The most useful parts include the sheets with all the things you need to do in the level, and using netbooks. (I#98)

Table 7.7. Summary of comments on the most useful program strategies (Melaleuca)

Most useful parts of program	Examples of individual comments
6. The teacher teaching me when I need it, individually or in my group [36% of comments: (M#1)]	The teachers teaching us when we need it. (M#65) When the teachers come over individually to help me learn. (M#250)
12. Completing assessment sheets and getting the teacher's feedback [26% of comments: (M#2)]	The mathletics booklets, feedback is useful because it shows what level I can work with in math. (M#7) Mathletics booklets help to back up and cement what you have been learning. (M#256)
11. Completing task descriptions to demonstrate my understanding [23% of comments: (M#3)]	I think that the Rich Task was quite useful because you can choose the level that you want to learn at. (M#48) The general maths teaching and tasks set up by our teachers seem to work well, they are easy to engage in and the teachers do a good job in keeping us occupied. (M#293)
3. Individual maths program based on my AusVELS level [17% of comments: (M#4)]	It is at my own level. I can understand the work I am given in the mathletics booklet. I can also work at my own pace without getting rushed to complete tasks. (M#217) I like that everyone gets to work at their level not the level they are expected to be at because everyone's different. (M#265)
9. Using my device to review videos and post Blogs [11% of comments: (M#5)]	Being able to go onto the site and re watch the video so you can understand it in a better way. (M#219) [with the device] you can watch the video as many times as you want if you don't understand. (M#229)
4. Working in a group of students at the same AusVELS level [9% of comments: (M#6)]	The groups with other people at your level. (M#8) Being put into groups with people who understand at the same level as me. (M#27)

DISCUSSION AND CONCLUDING REMARKS

Improving low SES students' performance in mathematics has been conceptualised in the literature as a predominantly curricular and teacher expertise challenge (Black, 2007; Greenberg et al., 2004; Luke et al., 2003) with strong socio-psychological dimensions around the need for students to connect with school and post-school aspirations (Yeager & Walton, 2011). Our findings confirm the need for high expectations of learners, and extended teacher contact with students to improve mathematics performance (Lewis, 2000; Mogari et al., 2009; Tomlinson, 2005). There is also the need to establish supportive structures to underpin student learning and thus improve student self-efficacy and aspiration (Bandura, 1986, 1994, 1997; Blackwell, Trzsniewski, & Dweck, 2007; Cohen et al., 2006; Walton & Cohen, 2007, 2011; Yeager & Walton, 2011). Students in this study were encouraged to set goals and recognise their progress and achievement in this subject to overcome the challenge of negative contextual factors (Sirin, 2005), with some evidence of the development of positive attitudes.

In addressing these aspects of mathematics learning, students were experiencing quality learning as claimed by Schoenfeld (2014). The quantitative and qualitative results presented in Tables 7.3 to 7.7 provide evidence of this claim from a student perspective. Curricular coherence is provided through a focus on student learning intentions, individualised mathematics programs, and teacher workshops on specific skills; cognitive demand of tasks is provided through pre-testing, individualised programs, students working in groups at the same level, and teacher workshops; student access to mathematical content is provided through pre-testing, targeted timely teacher coaching, completion of tasks that demonstrate understanding, completion checkpoints, and successful use of resources such as textbooks; opportunities for student agency, authority, and identity are provided though the components already mentioned, but also through peer assistance as both adviser and recipient, and opportunities to resubmit work; and effective use of assessment is provided through a combination of many of these components.

Our case study also draws attention to the potential for broader structural changes to the physical context of mathematics learning to support these curricular goals. The opportunities for teachers to team, to conceptualise, enact and evaluate processes to support student learning in mathematics are not currently systemic, as noted by Horn (2010), Domina and Soldana (2011) and others. While the heightened visibility of teachers to one another and the potential for flexible space use in this setting were not the dominant factors in student learning gains, these conditions complemented other key elements, including strong school leadership to address student academic attainment, expert curricular support, and effective use of mandated testing programs as a resource for focusing student motivation and achievement, and sustained teacher commitment to student success. These conditions are clearly not easily up-scaled to address the needs of larger low SES mathematics student cohorts in many countries, but they point to the need for significant investment to address this persistent significant challenge in changing learning outcomes in this subject.

This study also points to the potential value of using standardised testing regimes, common to many countries, as one practical diagnostic resource, among many, for analysing and improving low SES student performance in high stakes subjects. As in many countries, standardised testing regimes are trenchantly criticised for their reductive effects on curricular content and methods, and their putative self-fulfilling outcomes in relation to student SES (for critique and analyses of NAPLAN outcomes, see Leder, 2012). However, in this case study, these results enabled both teachers and students to pinpoint levels of student achievement as a basis for tailoring curricular experiences and progressions to meet the developmental needs of individuals in mathematics.

Despite these positive aspects, the students' mathematics performance gains were relatively modest against standardised progression expectations. This points to the significant long-term challenge of improving low SES student engagement and sustainable success in this subject. There were attitudinal gains for both students and teachers, but there is clearly scope, and need, for more academic gains. On the basis of the students' NAPLAN performance in 2014, the principal and teachers had further aims for the mathematics program, including: (1) increased specific and clear feedback about progress to students and parents; (2) the use of common assessment sheets and moderation to ensure consistency across the faculty; (3) a focus on key concepts linking students' mathematical understandings in different units, increasing conceptual understandings; (4) further improvement in attainment across the whole school in mathematics; and (5) more students enrolling in higher level mathematics beyond Year 10.

In the gains made so far, and in the projected refinements, a common feature has been the focus on setting up and adhering to enabling structures and protocols that create a shared positive culture for staff and students. This is evident in expectations around teacher and student roles and behaviour in living the mathematics curriculum as a set of flexible routines that serve individual student learning. The new open-plan settings have supported teacher teamwork and provided a potential impetus for re-imagining how students' learning experiences in mathematics and other subjects could be achieved. The collaborative design and enactment of the program in each school supported gains in teacher pedagogical and content knowledge in this field. However, such student and teacher learning also depends to a large extent on establishing and sustaining the quality and timeliness of the enacted curriculum.

REFERENCES

Alfassi, M. (2004). Reading to learn: Effects of combined strategy instruction on high school students. *Journal of Educational Research, 97*(4), 171–184. doi:10.3200/JOER.97.4.171-185

Auwarter, A., & Aruguete, M. (2008). Effects of student gender and socioeconomic status on teacher perceptions. *Journal of Educational Research, 101*(4), 242–246. doi:10.3200/JOER.101.4.243-246

Bandura, A. (1986). *Social foundations of thought and action.* Englewood Cliffs, NJ: Prentice-Hall.
Bandura, A. (1994). Self-efficacy. In V. S. Ramachaudran (Ed.), *Encyclopaedia of human behaviour* (Vol. 4, pp. 71–81). New York, NY: Academic Press. (Reprinted in H. Friedman (Ed.). (1998). *Encyclopaedia of mental health.* San Diego, CA: Academic Press)
Bandura, A. (1997). *Self-efficacy: The exercise of control.* New York, NY: W.H. Freeman.
Baumert, J., Kunter, M., Blum, W., Brunner, M., Voss, T., Jordan, A., ... Tsai, Y. (2010). Teachers' mathematical knowledge, cognitive activation in the classroom, and student progress. *American Educational Research Journal, 47*(1), 133–180. doi:10.3102/0002831209345157
Black, P., & Wiliam, D. (2009). Developing the theory of formative assessment. *Educational Assessment, Evaluation and Accountability, 21*(1), 5–31. doi:10.1007/s11092-008-9068-5
Black, R. (2007). *Crossing the bridge: Overcoming entrenched disadvantage through student-centred learning.* Melbourne, Australia: Education Foundation Australia.
Blackwell, L. A., Trzesniewski, K. H., & Dweck, C. S. (2007). Theories of intelligence and achievement across the junior high school transition: A longitudinal study and an intervention. *Child Development, 78*(1), 246–263. doi:10.1111/j.1467-8624.2007.00995.x
Brown, C., & Borko, H. (1992). Becoming a mathematics teacher. In D. Grouws (Ed.), *Handbook of research on mathematics learning and teaching* (pp. 209–239). New York, NY: MacMillan.
Cohen, G. L., Garcia, J., Apfel, N., & Master, A. (2006). Reducing the racial achievement gap: A social-psychological intervention. *Science, 313*(5791), 1307–1310. doi:10.1126/science.1128317
Collias, K., Pajak, E., & Rigden, D. (2000). *One cannot teach what one does not know: Training teachers in the United States who know their subjects and know how to teach their subjects.* Retrieved from http://www.c-b-e.org/PDF/OneCannotTeach.pdf
Darling-Hammond, L. (2000). Teacher quality and student achievement: A review of state policy evidence. *Education Policy Analysis Archives, 8*(1), 1–44.
Denzin, N., & Lincoln, Y. (2008). *Collecting and interpreting qualitative materials.* Thousand Oaks, CA: Sage.
Domina, T., & Saldana, J. (2011). Does raising the bar level the playing field? Mathematics curricular intensification and inequality in American high schools, 1982–2004. *American Educational Research Journal. 49*(4), 685–708. Retrieved from http://aer.sagepub.com/content/early/2011/11/12/0002831211426347
Engle, R. A., Langer-Osuna, J. M., & McKinney de Royston, M. (2014). Toward a model of influence in persuasive discussions: Negotiating quality, authority, privilege, and access within a student-led argument. *Journal of the Learning Sciences, 23*(2), 245–268.
Greenberg, E., Rhodes, D., Ye, X., & Stancavage, F. (2004). *Prepared to teach: Teach preparation and student achievement in eighth-grade mathematics.* Paper presented at American Education Research Association 2004 Annual Meeting, 12–16 April. San Diego, California.
Greeno, J., & Collins, A. (2008). Commentary on the final report of the national mathematics advisory panel. *Educational Researcher, 37*(9), 618–623. doi:10.3102/0013189X08327997
Hill, H. C., Rowan, B., & Ball, D. L. (2005). Effects of teachers' mathematical knowledge for teaching on student achievement. *American Educational Research Journal, 42*(2), 371–406. doi:10.3102/00028312042002371
Horn, I. (2010). Teaching replays, teaching rehearsals, and re-visions of practice: Learning from colleagues in a mathematics teacher community. *Teachers College Record, 112*(1), 225–259.
Kennedy, M. (1998). *Form and substance in teacher in service education* (Research Monograph No.13). Madison, WI: National Institute for Science Education. Retrieved from http://www.losmedanos.edu/deved/documents/KennedyeffectsofPD.pdf
Leder, G. (2012). *Mathematics for all? The case for and against national testing.* Paper presented at the 12th International Congress on Mathematics Education, July 8–15, Seoul, Korea.
Lewis, A. C. (2000). A tale of two reform strategies. *Phi Delta Kappan, 81*(10), K6–K18.
Lokan, J., Greenwood, L., & Cresswell, J. (2001). *15-up and counting, reading, writing, reasoning: How literate are Australian students? The PISA 2000 survey of students' reading, mathematical and scientific literacy skills.* Melbourne, Australia: Australian Council for Educational Research Ltd.

Luke, A., Elkins, J., Weir, K., Land, R., Carrington, V., Dole, S., ... Stevens, L. (2003). *Beyond the middle: A report about literacy and numeracy development of target group students in the middle years of schooling* (Vols. 2). Brisbane, Australia: J. S. McMillan Printing Group.

Merriam, S. B. (1998). *Qualitative research and case study applications in education.* San Francisco, CA: Gossey-Bass Inc.

Mewborn, D. (2001). Teacher's content knowledge, teacher education and their effects on the preparation of elementary teachers in the United States. *Mathematics Education Research Journal, 3,* 28–36.

Mogari, D., Kriek, J., Stols, G., & Iheanachor, O. U. (2009). Lesotho's students' achievement in Mathematics and their teachers' background and professional development. *Pythagoras, 70,* 3–15. Retrieved from http://amesa.org.za/amesap_n70_a1.pdf

Oakes, J., Joseph, R., & Muir, K. (2001). Access and achievements in mathematics and science. In J. A. Banks & C. A. McGee Banks (Eds.), *Handbook of research on multicultural education* (pp. 69–90). San Francisco, CA: Jossey-Bass.

Onwu, G. O. M., & Mogari, D. (2004). Professional development for outcomes-based education curriculum implementation: The case of Univemalashi, South Africa. *Journal of Education for Teaching, 30*(2), 161–177.

Perry, L., & McConney, A. (2010). Does the SES of the school matter? An examination of socioeconomic status and student achievement using PISA 2003. *Teachers College Record, 112*(4), 1137–1162. Retrieved from http://www.tcrecord.org

Schofield, J. W. (2010). International evidence on ability grouping with curriculum differentiation and the achievement gap in secondary schools. *Teachers College Record, 112*(5), 1492–1528. Retrieved from http://www.tcrecord.org

Sirin, S. R. (2005). Socioeconomic status and academic achievement: A meta-analytic review of research. *Review of Educational Research, 75*(3), 417–453. Retrieved from http://steinhardt.nyu.edu/scmsAdmin/media/users/lec321/Sirin_Articles/Sirin_2005.pdf

Stein, M., Engle, R., Smith, M., & Hughes, E. (2008). Orchestrating productive mathematical discussions: Five practices for helping teachers move beyond show and tell. *Mathematical Thinking and Learning, 10,* 313–340.

Tashakkori, A., & Teddlie, C. (2010). *Mixed methods in social & behavioural research.* Los Angeles, CA: Sage.

Tomlinson, C. (2005). Grading and differentiation: Paradox or good practice. *Theory into Practice, 44*(3), 262–269. doi:10.1207/s15430421tip4403_11

Vale, C., Davies, A., Weaven, M., Hooley, N., Davidson, K., & Loton, D. (2010). Leadership to improve mathematics outcomes in low SES schools and school networks. *Mathematics Teacher Education and Development, 12*(2), 47–71.

Walton, G. M., & Cohen, G. L. (2007). A question of belonging: Race, social fit, and achievement. *Journal of Personality and Social Psychology, 92*(1), 82–96. doi:10.1037/0022-3514.92.1.82

Wenglinsky, H. (1998). Finance equalization and within-school equity: The relationship between education spending and the social distribution of achievement. *Educational Evaluation and Policy Analysis, 20*(4), 269–283. doi:10.3102/01623737020004269

Yeager, D., & Walton, G. (2011). Social-psychological interventions in education: They're not magic. *Review of Educational Research, 81*(2), 267–302. doi:10.3102/0034654311405999

Yin, R. (2008). *Case study research: Design and methods.* Thousand Oaks, CA: Sage.

VAUGHAN PRAIN, BRUCE WALDRIP AND VALERIE LOVEJOY

8. "THEY CAN'T JUST GOOGLE THE CORRECT ANSWER"

Personalising Science Learning in an Open-Plan Secondary School

CHANGING SCHOOL SCIENCE LEARNING

Natalie, a Year 8 student, responding to a scientist's blogged suggestion that her diagram of her invented spider-bat might need bigger ears (to explain its super-keen hearing and effective survival tactics), blogged back:

> Thanks Dr Dave. I'm glad you like the idea for my Spider-Bat and I will definitely try and fix those ears and I agree that my critter does seem a little defenceless. I will make sure to think about some ways in which my Spider-Bat can avoid being lunch!! Thanks again.

Enhancing students' interest in and learning from school science experiences has remained a challenge for decades in many countries (DeWitt, Osborne, Archer, Dillon, Willis, & Wong, 2013; Duit, 2007; Tytler, 2007). This challenge is variously attributed to: (a) too much didactic teaching that casts students as reluctant bystanders tasked with memorising expert claims, (Duit & Treagust, 1998; Osborne & Dillon, 2008; Lyons, 2006); (b), a disconnect between official science curricula and students' everyday worlds and interests (Aikenhead, 1996); and (c) lack of teacher familiarity with current scientific agendas, discoveries and methods (Chubb, 2014). Proposed and enacted solutions include: changes to the content, purposes and physical settings for learning (Duschl, 2008; Sadler, 2004; Tytler, 2007); integration with other subjects (Freeman, Marginson, & Tytler, 2015); more links with practising scientists (Chubb, 2014); more use of virtual resources (Linn, Davis, & Bell, 2013); and increased explicit focus on opportunities for students to use these and other resources as reasoning tools for learning in this subject (Lehrer & Schuable, 2006; Tytler, Prain, Hubber, & Waldrip, 2013).

In this chapter we briefly review an emerging consensus about quality learning in science as a basis for framing our account of attempts to personalise learning in Year 8 science in one of the BEP schools. We report on the teaching of two 9-week Year 8 science topics, Adaptation, and Science Inquiry), in the second half of 2014. The first topic, called "The Future is Wild", represents a relatively common approach in Australian schools, whereas the second was innovative, not only for this school but for Year 8 science in Australia. We report on each topic to show: (a) how the teachers adapted the topics to the open-plan settings and team-teaching; and (b) to indicate the ways in which the teachers sought to enact the goals for quality learning in school science as outlined above. Finally, we present a case study of Year 10 students' reasoning through representations to learn in science from another school.

CHARACTERISING QUALITY IN SCHOOL SCIENCE EDUCATION

Science education researchers now broadly agree that quality learning entails students understanding, enacting and valuing how scientists produce, justify, judge, and share knowledge in this field (Duschl, 2008; Moje, 2007). In this way, as discussed in Chapter 1, quality learning in science needs to engage students deeply, and provide experiences that parallel how scientists produce and disseminate knowledge claims. From this perspective, quality learning entails a complex blend of propositional, procedural, and communicative knowledge and skills as well as dispositional commitment to the value to self and others of learning how this knowledge is made, shared, and revised. In understanding these processes, students learn how to integrate practical inquiry with visual, linguistic, and mathematical modes to reason about causal changes to phenomena, where an engaging, meaningful curriculum motivates them to participate in a sequence of activities and reasoning practices that achieve theses outcomes (Duschl, 2008; Lemke, 2015; Osborne, 2012).

Rather than learning mainly to memorise past expert claims in this field, students also need to have first-hand experience of the challenges and pleasures in making persuasive claims in this subject. When encouraged to explain and justify these claims using different forms of representation, including diagrams, drawings, models, and verbal explanations, students can learn how to reason about scientific topics, advance their content knowledge, and practise the subject-specific ways to represent scientific processes and findings (Ainsworth, Prain, & Tytler, 2011; Liu, Won, & Treagust, 2014; Tytler et al., 2013). As noted by Haste (2004), Lindahl (2007), and Schreiner and Sjoberg (2007), students also need to understand the creative side of scientific reasoning, enabling identity work in this subject to be appealing and valued. By approaching science in this way, students are likely to find science immediately engaging and a source of stimulating challenges. Students are also more likely to view science as meaningful if they can apply scientific methods and findings productively to everyday problems and challenges that relate directly to their lives (Tytler, 2007).

From our perspective (Tytler, Prain, Hubber, & Waldrip, 2013), quality learning in science occurs when students actively construct representational claims, rather than being mainly exposed to canonical representations. Their own constructions focus their attention on the affordances of modes and their uses, productively constrain their thinking, and channel attention to selective key features of phenomena. This engagement with the problem space prepares them to appreciate canonical solutions later introduced by the teacher (Bransford & Schwartz, 1999). Following Vygotsky (1981) and Cazden (1981), we recognise that students' learning capacities are often in advance of their explicit understandings, and therefore they benefit from multiple opportunities to attempt representational tasks before they have achieved full competence in them. Quality learning entails epistemological understandings of the nature of models and representations and their selective purposes. This meta-representational knowledge arises from explicit discussion of representations, and feeds back into their selection and refinement processes.

QUALITY IN PRACTICE

Needless to say, achieving this range of goals and outcomes across 13 years of schooling represents a significant challenge. However, one Year 8 science class at Melaleuca College addressed many of these goals. Drawing on the spatial affordances of a large open-plan area, three teachers planned and team-taught two topics in the second semester of 2014 (*the Future is Wild*, a unit about adaptation, and *Mythbusters*, a practical unit on science inquiry methods) with 70 students using whole-class and group-work approaches. See below for a description of the content and detailed approach taken in each topic. The space was viewed as enabling an enactment of Lave and Wenger's (1991, p. 12) "community of practice" where students were guided to construct knowledge and where their ideas were scrutinised, critiqued, given feedback, refined, and presented to a community of "scientists" that is, their peers. The students were expected to share understandings within small groups, explore and enhance the robustness of their perspectives, and seek to validate, justify, and elaborate their understandings through different representations to their teachers and peers, including blogs and demonstrations. In this way, the teachers sought to avoid a heavily didactic, teacher-dominated process of instruction, and to give students considerable control over choices of topics and the representational resources through which scientific claims were made. Students were also encouraged to connect these choices and topics to their own lives or interests. To enhance the currency and reality of the topics, some interested students were linked with practising scientists in a 'global science' forum. These scientists provided virtual and same-time expert feedback on students' emerging work, questions, and findings by responding to the students' blogs and in follow up Skype conversations (The Global School, 2015). The students were also encouraged to access a variety of virtual resources to support and guide their inquiry, but not to provide a shortcut to ready-made answers. As Bob, one of the teachers noted, the intention of the inquiry process was to set the students achievable new challenges where they could use the internet as a resource or a confirmation of their inquiry findings, but "they can't just Google the correct answer" because of the focus of undertaken inquiries.

The Future is Wild

The Future is Wild unit aimed to cover biological sciences and earth and space sciences content strands of the AusVELS Science curriculum, The students were to consider life on earth at one of three time periods in the future: 5,000,000 years, 100,000,000 years, or 500,000,000 years. Within those time periods they had four choices of environment to study, combining climate and vegetation (hot, cold, desert, forest). For their chosen time period and environment type they had to:

1. describe the physical and adaptive characteristics of three or four actual organisms from the chosen time period;
2. explain why these organisms existed and where they belonged in the food chain;
3. design their own organism, explain how its physical characteristics would allow it to adapt to the chosen environment, how it would interact with other organisms, and where it would fit in the food chain.

The teachers recognised that their student cohort had a spread of tested literacy and numeracy abilities ranging across seven year levels (Years 4–10). The robust

Level E	Represent the life cycle of your organism
	Represent how your organism interacts with the environment
Level F	Design your organism with structural and behavioural features that helps it survive
Level G	Describe the physical conditions of your organism that help or hinder its survival
	Describe the geological and extreme weather conditions that have affected your organism's environment
Level H	Classify your organism as if it were alive today
	Construct a food web that includes your organism and the other organisms present in your ecosystem. Include labels for producers, consumers and decomposers.
	Describe the seasons in your environment
	Describe a water cycle in your environment
Level I	Represent and label three kinds of cells in your organism
	Represent the internal structure of your organism. Describe how it digests and reproduces.
	Describe the rocks in your environment. How were they formed?
Level J	Describe your animal's systems, with a flow diagram to show how all these work together in your animal
	Describe the population of your organism. What affects its population?
	Describe, using plate tectonics, how your environment has changed since today
Level K	Describe the water, carbon, nitrogen and phosphorus cycles in the biosphere of your environment
	Represent the DNA, genes and chromosomes of your animal
	Describe how genes are passed on from the parents of your animal to its child. How did your animal evolve? And from what? Describe the process.

Figure 8.1. Curricular guide for the topic of adaptation

curriculum accommodated this spread, providing a positive learning experience for all students, by incorporating curricular goals that spanned seven levels for each topic (see Figure 8.1 for the topic of Adaptation). All students started at level E (Grade 4), but quickly moved over the course of the unit to at least level I, representing expected progress at Year 8 level.

Bob explained that beginning at the same level was appropriate as students had experienced limited, discontinuous exposure to science in primary school making it difficult to diagnose an entry level. Furthermore, "science, unlike mathematics, does not have a clear hierarchy of conceptual understanding". The teachers wanted all students to have a sense of "the big ideas" in science and a larger developmental sense of topics rather than being constrained to thinking about a narrow single-year level perspective on science content. Concepts like the life cycle could be made more or less challenging according to the needs of the students by varying the complexity and familiarity of the organism being studied. With students all beginning at the same stage, they could observe rates of progress among peers, and motivate one another. The additional two levels (J and K) provided extension work to Year 10 level for more able students.

Students watched a general introductory video about adaptation (The Future is Wild, 2015) before choosing their time period. Once selected, they had a further choice of four environments within that period. They watched an initial video on their environment that introduced them to organisms that may exist within the environment, their adaptive characteristics, and interaction with other organisms. They also watched instructional videos at the point when they were ready to learn about a particular aspect of their study. Students were able to bring their own portable devices and use their QR Code Scanners to connect instantly to the videos (QR codes were on the wall for every video) so they could work at their own pace and access the next step when ready. The teachers' intention was that in engaging in rich tasks, students should use a range of technologies to exercise problem-solving ability, creativity and to take responsibility or ownership for their learning. The students uploaded evidence of their understandings on their personal blog sites, with a choice of ways to represent their understandings including posters, photographs, models, drawings, or 3D printing. Fifteen students volunteered to be part of a global science community where they were further enriched by interacting with practising scientists. The scientists' feedback on the student blogs was sometimes followed up by a Skype conversation between scientist and student. Bob found it "mind-blowing to see a marine biologist in Townsville having a genuine non-teacher mediated discussion with a student who was designing a marine animal".

Three teachers (Bob, Steve, and Sue) worked with a combined class of 70 students. The 70-minute lessons usually started with one teacher providing an introduction, orientation and restatement of goals at the start of the lesson. This whole group session might entail introducing a virtual or actual resource to refresh students' memories and enthuse them, setting up the learning goals for the day or week, giving students general feedback on progress, introducing a new section of the topic, or recapping on intended student progress. Students were expected to raise and answer questions at this time.

Following the introduction, students generally moved into small groups to work on their topic, making use of the whole space available, with a range of seating options. Though not stipulated, students found it beneficial to work with others completing the same level. Some students worked at tables in groups of three or four while others worked alone. Some groups worked at computer terminals in the middle of the open-plan space, while others worked outside. Though working collaboratively, students designed their individual organisms, outlined their organism's life-cycle based on life cycles of animals today, created food chains and webs that showed how their organisms interacted with other organisms present in their ecosystem, and identified their animal as consumers, producers and decomposers.

In the course of the lesson, the three teachers circulated to provide feedback and support for individual students, or, where deemed appropriate, provide a practical session or focused discussion for a group of students at a particular level. Bob considered that team-teaching was a "no-brainer" given the open-plan classroom and timetable structure. Team-teaching, according to Bob, allowed teachers to "utilise their particular strengths to better address the diverse needs and interests of their students". Bob tended to work with the more advanced students and conducted workshops for them as they began a new level. For example, he conducted a workshop on habitat and the forces that shape it for eight students beginning level G. He deliberately kept the workshops brief to avoid defaulting to a transmissive style of teaching. Steve assisted those students in the middle range and Sue, a trained primary teacher, worked with the students previously identified as having literacy difficulties. However, this organisation was flexible to respond to student needs, and the teachers were keen for students to understand that they had access to all three teachers during and outside class-time.

Lesson conclusions usually entailed students being gathered together for a short summary session of 10 to 15 minutes. Sometimes teachers praised particular students for working diligently, or the content of an individual student's work was discussed as exemplary. Students were praised for independent problem-solving as well as seeking help, and were also reminded of possible sites for further research. Sometimes the teachers restated the rationale for the multi-year-level curriculum as "the new way we do science at this school". This curriculum was seen as a chance for students to know exactly what level they had achieved or could achieve, to meet year-level expectations by the end of units, and also to progress at their own pace. All three teachers participated in these discussions.

In reviewing this unit, the teachers thought that the use of a 'story shell' to frame the topic was worthwhile. It enabled the curriculum to be differentiated without a perception that students were streamed on ability as all students worked on the same topic but at various levels of complexity. The topic initially "grabbed students' imaginations and fired their creativity". When interviewed about this subject, students expressed a desire for more practical hands-on experiments revealing that this unit challenged their expectations about the format of science lessons. The teachers are considering ways in which aspects of the unit could be explored as experiments in a laboratory environment. Bob was delighted at the quantity of evidence of learning on the student blogs from this unit. However, he was disappointed that students had not taken sufficient advantage of the many options suggested for representing their understandings. Ironically, the students complained that there "was too much drawing" in the unit, yet they had "taken the path of least resistance", to upload photographs of their labelled freehand drawings and writing on their blogs as evidence of their learning. Bob thought this could be addressed by providing visual examples of the options and referring students to previous students' blogs for inspiration.

Mythbusters

The *Mythbusters* unit provided different challenges for teachers and students. The unit presented the students with the opportunity to explore a much more open-ended task. Students were expected to devise, enact, and critique their own scientific inquiry around a question in biology, chemistry, physics, or psychology, with students given many prompt topics in each field. For example, prompt questions in psychology included the following: Can you tell what something is just by touching it? Can you tell where sound comes from when you are blindfolded? Can things be identified by just their smell? Does the human tongue have definite areas for certain tastes? The program was organised in a similar way to the Adaptation unit, with students made aware of the prescribed learning outcomes from the AusVELS science curriculum from levels E to K. The students were given a rubric that specified these outcomes developmentally in relation to demonstrated skills in questioning and predicting, planning and conducting, processing and analysing, and evaluating and communicating, as well as a set of guide questions for their inquiry. The students were also able to access sample reports to guide their own investigations. The teachers provided feedback through topic approval, guidance with resources, and ongoing support for each phase of the student's inquiry. The open-plan settings were used in the same way as in the Adaptation unit, with video material (*Mythbusters*, 2015) used to engage and guide students, and teachers team-taught as in the previous unit. However, in this unit, teachers assisted individual students at their point of need. "With *Mythbusters* there was so much diversity right from the get go." Bob noticed the atmosphere of industry and harmony in the classroom. "The classroom was really humming. Some students were working outside, Steve was assisting students with experiments in the laboratory, Sue was helping students to write their reports and I was assisting students with psychology experiments". Bob thinks the key to successful team teaching is to "make the call according to each team's particular dynamic. You need to use that specialisation to meet the diverse needs and interests of the students".

The student survey conducted at the end of the unit revealed a high degree of satisfaction with the degree of choice, the freedom to choose and work on individual tasks, and to work in different spaces. However, the teachers were not entirely satisfied with the quality of the evidence of learning and understanding provided by most students. Bob thought the unit showed up the gaps in basic scientific understandings about laboratory equipment and safety, drawing accurate diagrams, and writing up results in a scientific report. These have since been addressed in a new preparatory chemistry unit, *Marooned*, which in future will lay the groundwork in basic scientific knowledge before the open-ended unit *Mythbusters* is attempted. More checks and balances were also needed to ensure that students were completing tasks in a timely manner.

One of the great successes of the unit was the quality of the scientist-student blog interactions. We report here briefly on the inquiries of two students, Sarah and Nerissa. Sarah undertook a "corrosive combinations lab report", and Nerissa studied the electric voltage generated by potatoes. We consider that these interactions heightened student interest through their novelty and expert input, and by enriching the quality (and challenge) of the investigations.

Sarah: Corrosive Combinations Laboratory Report

In her experiment, Sarah aimed to identify the efficiency of corrosive properties in soft drinks, using five beakers "with four different types of soft drink and one with water as the control to have something to compare to". In reporting on the process she claimed that "next you get 10 nails of the same size; five steel and five stainless steel. Put one type of nail in each jar. Leave these jars for 7–14 days. Once taken out, weigh all nails on a scale which goes down to 0.00g. Calculate the additional weight. This will show corrosion on the metals". Renée Webster, a fuel chemist, posted the following reaction on Sarah's blog:

> Your experiment sounds good but I have a couple of questions for you: 1. I think you probably planned to do this but just forgot to write it down, are you going to weigh the nails before as well as after? 2. What is the property of the soft drinks that you think might affect the corrosion? Is there any way you can test or measure this before you start? I'm interested in your statement that chemistry experiments only have to be done once- what makes you think this? Looking forward to your answers.

Sarah responded:

> I did weigh the nails before, throughout and at the end of the test but forgot to include that in this post. I am not sure what properties of the soft drink would cause the corrosion and I am not really sure how I could find that out. I believed that doing the experiment once would be enough when I begun but

now I see that with multiple tests, I would get a better and more accurate result. Thanks for having a look at my blog, Sarah.

Renée responded:

Hi Sarah, your final report looks really good. The multimedia you included really helps to understand your experiment and your data collection was thorough. I was interested that you mentioned a decrease in volume of the soft drinks and attributed it to the corrosion reaction. Do you think there could have been evaporation as well? Could you test this variable I wonder? Good work, Renée.

Nerissa: Electric Voltage Given Off by Potatoes

Nerissa's original hypothesis at the start of her experiment was that larger potatoes will "give off" more electrical energy than smaller ones. "The potatoes with a larger mass have a greater area in which to store energy, therefore they will give off more electrical energy. The potatoes all up won't give off a lot of energy, but I might be surprised".

Renée responded:

Hi Nerissa, I like your experiment idea. Sometimes in my job I work with fuel made from plants so I like to see another way to bring energy and living things together! I'm a bit confused about the first part of your experimental plan; "10 potatoes of 4 different masses". Are you cutting the potatoes so they weigh the same, or you've just managed to carefully select whole potatoes of the same weight? Also I wonder if you are using the same variety of potato or different ones? Looking forward to your answers, Renée.

Nerissa blogged back:

I'm going to cut down the potatoes until they are the same mass, the potatoes will all be white potatoes of the same variety.

Nerissa reported on her approach to the investigation, and Renee responded:

I have one more question, I hope you don't mind. How did you decide to put the electrodes 2 cm apart? Do you think a smaller/larger distance would affect the voltage? Not necessarily something you want to test in this experiment, I am just curious.

After recording the voltage of 10 peeled potatoes Nerissa concluded that "the larger potatoes only had a slight voltage difference from the smaller potatoes, the juiciness of the potatoes affected the volts more than the size did" (Figure 8.2).

Potato Volts

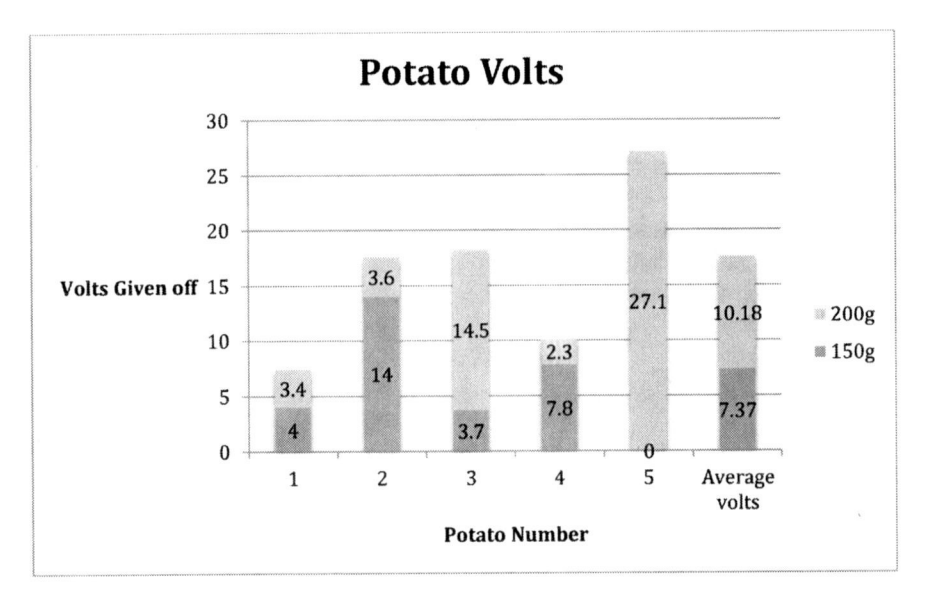

(Bar chart showing Volts Given off vs Potato Number, with 200g and 150g series)

Potato Number	150g	200g
1	4	3.4
2	14	3.6
3	3.7	14.5
4	7.8	2.3
5	0	27.1
Average volts	7.37	10.18

Figure 8.2. Nerissa's graph comparing potato size and volts

Renée blogged back:

Hi Rachel, super work on your experiment, and how exciting to get a nice result that was different to your hypothesis! Did you judge the moisture content just with your sight and touch? Do you think there's a way that you could maybe measure the juiciness of the potato? Well done on the planning of your project too, this definitely would have helped you get good data. Renée

Another scientist, Tim Moore, an electrical engineer, also responded to Nerissa's results:

Hi Nerissa, it's always interesting to see a stand-out result! Did this potato seem to be juicier than the others you tested? If it's producing a higher voltage it might be because it has more of the active elements in the juice that cause the voltage to occur, or possibly the juiciness just allows the electricity to flow a bit more easily. There could also have been juice on the volt-meter prongs. If the potato has dried out already don't worry too much – this is something you can keep an eye on from now on. And if you're not already, give the volt-meter prongs a wipe-down between each potato, so one potato doesn't give voltage to another! If you'd like to talk about it on Skype we can set up a session during your class time – let me know what times you'll be around if you want to talk it through! Tim

In her final discussion of her experiment, Nerissa noted that "to improve the data collected I could have monitored the juiciness of the potato and timed how long since I peeled the potato. To improve the accuracy of the whole experiment I could have double-tested each potato in different areas of the potato".

These blog exchanges indicated that the scientists engaged with the students as informed scientific inquirers, expressing serious interest in their investigations. They did not provide ready-made answers but used their feedback as an opportunity to ask questions that encouraged the students to extend their thinking on the topic, to consider a new method of investigation, a new or alternative hypothesis, or a possible alternative solution. Some students, according to Bob, were over-awed by this communication, but as we can see from these examples, others were able to respond to the feedback in a way that revealed they were utilising it to further their reasoning.

Approximately 20% of the class voluntarily participated in the global science forum in both units. Bob hopes to extend this participation as he believes it provides "an authentic audience for the students' work". He finds students are inspired and grow in their interest in science and understanding by participating in authentic interactions in a serious scientific forum. Students also realise that their teachers are not confined to those adults physically present in the classroom and gain confidence to extend their virtual networks. These exchanges and student reasoning highlight the value of: (a) students choosing their own topics for investigation, and having access to timely multiple providers of expertise; (b) teachers encouraging the use of ICTs to facilitate this access; and (c) a structured but flexible personalised curriculum that accommodates these aspects.

PERSONALISING SCIENCE THROUGH STUDENT REASONING OPPORTUNITIES

> Two years later, other teachers tell me that they can tell which students I had taught in this project. They are now better team workers and better problem solvers. (Teacher)

In making and justifying scientific claims through constructing and explaining multi-modal representations, students also have opportunities to personalise their understanding of topics (see Tytler et al., 2013). This focus on collaborative consultation, as noted by Kuhn (2015), encourages both personal and collective meaning-making around claims, warrants and evidence, where the teacher can challenge and guide student reasoning. Here we report briefly on two further examples of these shared reasoning processes in a Year 10 science class at Waratah College, a companion school in our study. These students had undertaken this science unit because of a school requirement that they must complete a minimum number of science units. The class was conducted in an open-plan setting, but in this case with one teacher working with a group of 25 students.

Atomic Structure and Electron Shells: Isotopes and Half-lives

While undertaking a study of atomic structure and electron shells, after the teacher had explored students' current understandings of why dental patients wear an apron for X-rays, she introduced the concept of isotopes, and guided further discussion about nuclear reactions and differences between elements. Depending on their perceived relevance by the teacher, the students' initial ideas were sought and explored. After a review of individual students' written accounts of isotopes, some students recalled a previous discussion about the concept of half-life. The class was asked to demonstrate their understanding of models of half-life using M&Ms (a coloured confection marked with the letter M on one side). Some students placed their M&Ms in a linear fashion, alternating marked and unmarked sides. A few students chose to tip the M&Ms onto their tables and removed any M&Ms that did not have the lettering facing upwards (see Figure 8.3).

Figure 8.3. Students sorting labeled from non-labeled M&Ms

They repeated this activity with the remaining M&Ms and plotted the results. The other students, after some discussion linked to previous experiences where they had seen half-life graphs, adopted a variation of this approach to describing half-lives. Finally, students compared the general shape of their graphs from this activity with published half-life graphs to determine how these different graphs supported the concept of half-life and the differences between the graphs. In addition, they talked about how the shape of the graph could differ if the isotope had a longer or shorter half-life. The teacher had accustomed this group of students to explain their ideas, challenge one another, and justify their own claims and understandings. For these students, it was natural to complete the class with discussion about the part that

"THEY CAN'T JUST GOOGLE THE CORRECT ANSWER"

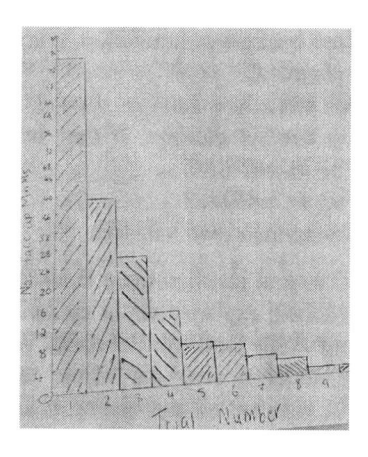

Figure 8.4. Student half-life graph

chance had played in the process. In this way, students built explanatory shared accounts that connected past and current experiences:

Teacher: Will your rate of decay ever become zero?
Student: Yes. Because you will have none left.
Teacher: Can you show me why?
Student: If 24 decay, we have 28 left. If 13 decay, we have 15 left. If 8 decay, we have 7 left.... eventually one decays and we have none left.
Teacher: Is this what happens in real life?

The resultant discussion explored the concept of large numbers of atoms decaying. The group eventually came to the conclusion that the rate of decay would decrease so much that it might be difficult to detect:

Teacher: What patterns did you find in your graph?
Carl: Mine was fairly even.
Eva: Mine wasn't. It wasn't even because it involved chance.
Megan: Mine halved every time.
Ben: That's different from what we got.
Teacher: What would happen in real life?

Pause

Teacher: What could affect half-lives and how they decay?
Ben: The temperature. It can't decay if it is frozen.
Carl: In areas where it is frozen, there is no radioactivity decay.
Gwen: But there is always background radiation.
Teacher: You mean that in Antarctica that there is no radio-active decay?

155

Carl:	There is always background radiation. It is found everywhere. It is just another chemical.
Teacher:	How does this affect how isotopes decay?
Steve:	It mixes with another element. If they have different half-lives, what would be its half-life?
Gwen:	Would it affect its half-life?
Ben:	They would keep their own half-life.

Students discussed their ideas and justified them from their observations and past experiences. They modified their explanations as evidence was provided and they showed how their ideas were viable for the initial claim. While classroom discussion was dominated by some students, over the whole lesson almost all students participated. Some students, who lacked confidence at the beginning, were quieter at the introduction of a new concept and became more involved as the lessons progressed until a new concept was introduced where this hesitancy was again apparent.

Motion and Forces

To introduce this topic, students were asked to summarise their journey to school in writing (mode of transport, distance covered, time taken), compare notes, and then translate their understanding into a graph of either distance or speed over time, with

Figure 8.5. Student timing balloon movement on fishing line

some examples shared on a whiteboard. Other students physically labelled places of constant speed, as well as increasing or decreasing speed on the graph, and had to justify their decisions. The teacher further tested their understanding of motion by having students construct a distance-time graph of a video of Usain Bolt running a foot-race, with students asked to focus on changes of speed. The resulting discussion talked about speed, constant speed, velocity and acceleration.

The class was then asked to reconstruct their understanding of motion. Some groups attempted to show this by attaching an inflated balloon to a straw that had a long fishing line running through the straw, taking measurements that would allow them to accurately plot a motion graph showing time separately from distance or speed. The imperfections resulting from the motion were discussed as students compared graphs with the observed motion in the Usain Bolt video. The students mostly measured the distance the balloon travelled until it reached the end of the fishing line and how long it took to travel this distance. One group tried to measure the acceleration of the balloon. When they presented their views, other students questioned their account, drawing their attention to the difficulties in measuring acceleration, especially over a relatively short distance. This discussion led to the students realising that the suggested time taken for the inflated balloon to travel the distance was difficult to measure because the time taken to travel the distance was only slightly less than a person's reaction time. The class was asked how they could address this challenge by first writing reasons, demonstrating their suggestions, and then modifying their suggested improvement. The class was constantly asked to consider how their individual understandings reflected what they were observing or what they were currently claiming.

These students not only made claims through supportive collaboration, they looked for evidence to support or challenge their claims, constructed an explanation, tested their assertions, and linked their views to both past learning and new situations. This collaboration was aimed at developing a higher quality response than if they had worked alone (Littleton, 2011). Students needed to probe one another's thinking so that their responses were more considered. The resulting dialogue allowed them to clarify understandings in a non-threatening way. In student interviews, they remarked that, at times, discussion with fellow students resulted in a better understanding than teacher-directed learning did. They constantly asked questions that challenged the robustness of each other's claims:

> Listening to other students helps me understand better, not just listening to the teacher's explanation is good. It helps you to understand in a language you know. (Student 5)

Students asked many more questions than they had previously using traditional teaching techniques. The class was not dominated by a few students and had relatively few students asking minimal questions. In this type of class, the teacher's role was to ask questions that tested and extended current student understanding rather than to supply answers. These teacher questions were rarely closed or simple response items. The teachers, who used wait-time to understand students' thinking and reasoning, felt rewarded by increased student engagement, interest, and participation in the learning. The students' views were supported by the teachers' comments:

Interviewer: What has changed during this last term of teaching?

Teacher: I was more careful about what students said. I used more of what they already knew. For instance, choose eight elements from the periodic table and tell me what you know about them.

The answers in the exams were more on track with more detail than there had been before. Some of the answers compared to other years were much more insightful. There was more detail in their drawings.

It resulted in a confidence boost with students. They became more confident to become involved in class discussion and activities. They learnt more than they generally did. This year there were much more 'why', 'how come?' or 'hang on, if we did this..." questions. The student questioning was a lot more insightful.

They can explain and justify their thinking, whether they were right or wrong.

The willing students came up to the board and had a try. The girls particularly gained confidence. Their friends would prompt assistance. Everyone is expected to have a go.

Giving the students time to do something is more important than rushing through the material.

Building explanatory reasoning and argumentation skills has drawn considerable attention from science education researchers in recent years (Osborne, 2010). Understanding and justifying causal links are significant demands in deep scientific understanding, but can be enabled by students developing, justifying and sharing representational claims (Tytler et al., 2013). When the teacher focuses on students' thinking and reasoning with a series of representational challenges, the teacher can examine the robustness of these claims to support quality conceptual learning (Waldrip, Prain, & Carolan, 2010; Prain & Waldrip, 2006).

CONCLUDING REMARKS

Our case studies point to key affordances of open-plan settings that can enhance students' interest and learning in science. These settings can act as a catalyst to enable and prompt teachers to devise a rich developmental science curriculum that:

(a) enables tasks to be differentiated to address diverse student capabilities and interests; (b) can be team-taught drawing on the particular expertise and interest of teachers in the team, and (c) enables students to connect science learning with their everyday worlds. The first two case studies demonstrate how a heavily didactic approach to teaching can be avoided by restructuring classes to optimise student group and individual work and timely teacher coaching opportunities as required. In this program the students had access to current scientific agendas, discoveries, and methods through virtual meaningful contact with practising scientists via skype and blogging. In these ways the program's design incorporated features recommended in the literature as likely to engage science learners. The third case study indicates that the settings do not preclude a more traditional organisation of learning, where one teacher worked over time with a group of students deploying a range of reasoning tools for learning in this subject.

As noted by Bob, the teachers did not view the Melaleuca science program as providing exemplary learning experiences in all aspects, but rather the outcomes pointed to workable strategies to personalise science learning for this group of students with a team of teachers. There were still challenges around setting high expectations for all students, and encouraging them to use a wider, more challenging range of representations to make advanced claims in science topics. Students also need to learn how to negotiate and customise learning goals and practise co- and self-regulated learning experiences. To move from reluctant bystanders in this subject, students need opportunities to develop their capabilities and confidence as contributors to a collective learning community.

Our case studies indicate that student learning and engagement can be personalised in science when teaching and learning experiences are based on a series of representational challenges, where:

- students generate representations to actively explore and make claims about phenomena;
- teachers and students ask questions that seek clarification about the robustness of student ideas in a supportive environment;
- there is an interplay between teacher-introduced and student-generated representations where students are challenged and supported to refine, extend, and coordinate their understandings;
- adequate links are made to student interest, current learning, and past learning in a manner that facilitates this process as a continuum rather than an isolated discussion; and
- students' input is not seen as replicating past teaching but as a reasoning process that is robust, relevant, and challenging to their context.

REFERENCES

Aikenhead, G. (1996). Border crossing into the subculture of science. *Studies in Science Education*, 27(1), 1–52 [Published online 2008]. doi:10.1080/03057269608560077

Ainsworth, S., Prain, V., & Tytler, R. (2011). Drawing to learn in science. *Science, 333*(6046), 1096–1097. doi:10.1126/science.1204153

Bransford, J., & Schwartz, D. (1999). Rethinking transfer: A simple proposal with multiple implications. *Review of Research in Education, 24*, 61–100. Retrieved from http://www.jstor.org/stable/1167267

Cazden, C. (1981). Performance before competence: Assistance to child discourse in the zone of proximal development. *Quarterly Newsletter of the Laboratory of Comparative Human Cognition, 3*(1), 5–8.

Chubb, I. (2014). Australia needs a strategy. *Science, 345*(6200), 985. doi:10.1126/science.1259741

De Witt, J., Osborne, J., Archer, L., Dillon, J., Willis, B., & Wong, B. (2013). Young children's aspirations in science: The unequivocal, the uncertain and the unthinkable. *International Journal of Science Education, 35*(6), 1037–1063.

Duit, R. (2007). *STCSE – Bibliography: Students' and teachers' conceptions and science education*. Kiel, Germany: IPN-Leibniz Institute for Science Education. Retrieved from http://www.ipn.uni-kiel.de/aktuell/stcse/stcse.html

Duit, R., & Treagust, D. F. (1998). Learning in science – From behaviourism towards social constructivism and beyond. In B. J. Fraser & K. Tobin (Eds.), *International handbook of science education, part 1* (pp. 3–25). Dordrecht, The Netherlands: Kluwer Academic Publishers.

Duschl, R. (2008). Science education in three-part harmony: Balancing conceptual, epistemic and social learning goals. *Review of Research in Education, 32*(1), 268–291. doi:10.3102/0091732X07309371

Freeman, B., Marginson, S., & Tytler, R. (Eds.). (2015). *The age of STEM: Policy and practice in science, technology, engineering and mathematics across the world*. Oxon, England: Routledge.

Haste, H. (2004). *Science in my future: A study of the values and beliefs in relation to science and technology amongst 11–21 year olds*. London, UK: Nestlé Social Research Programme.

Kuhn, D. (2015). Thinking together and alone. *Educational Researcher, 44*(1), 46–53. doi:10.3102/0013189X15569530

Lave, J., & Wenger, E. (1991). *Situated learning: Legitimate peripheral participation*. Cambridge, England: Cambridge University Press.

Lehrer, R., & Schauble, L. (2006). Cultivating model-based reasoning in science education. In K. Sawyer (Ed.), *The Cambridge handbook of the learning sciences* (pp. 371–387). New York, NY: Cambridge University Press.

Lemke, J. L. (2015). *Demonstrating the value of informal learning*. Retrieved from http://www.jaylemke.com/

Linn, M. Davis, E., & Bell, P. (2013). *Internet environments for science education*. Oxon, UK: Routledge.

Littleton, K., & Mercer, N. (2010). The significance of educational dialogues between primary school children. In K. Littleton & C. Howe (Eds.), *Educational dialogues: Understanding and promoting productive interaction* (pp. 271–288). Milton Park, Oxon: Routledge.

Liu, Y., Won, M., & Treagust, D. F. (2014). Secondary biology teachers' use of different types of diagrams for different purposes. In B. Eilam & J. K. Gilbert (Eds.), *Science teachers' use of visual representations* (pp. 103–121). Switzerland, Europe: Springer. doi:10.1007/978-3-319-06526-7_5

Lyons, T. (2006). Different countries, same science classes: Students' experiences of school science in their own words. *International Journal of Science Education, 28*(6), 591–613. doi:10.1080/09500690500339621

Osborne, J., & Dillon, J. (2008). *Science education in Europe: Critical reflections*. London, UK: Nuffield Foundation.

Sadler, T. (2004). Informal reasoning regarding socioscientific issues: A critical review of research. *Journal of Research in Science Teaching, 41*(5), 513–536. doi:10.1002/tea.20009

Schreiner, C., & Sjøberg, S. (2007). Science education and youth's identity construction—two incompatible projects? In D. Corrigan, J. Dillon, & R. Gunstone (Eds.), *The re-emergence of values in the science curriculum* (pp. 231–247). Rotterdam, The Netherlands: Sense Publishers.

The Future is Wild. (2015). Retrieved from http://www.thefutureiswild.com

The Global School. (2015). Retrieved from http://theglobalschool.net/science/

Tytler, R. (2007). *Reimagining science education: Engaging students in Australia's future*. ACER. Retrieved from http://research.acer.edu.au/aer/3

Tytler, R., Prain, V., Hubber, P., & Waldrip, B. (Eds.). (2013). *Constructing representations to learn in science*. Rotterdam, The Netherlands: Sense Publishers.

Vygotsky, L. (1981/1986). In A. Kozulin (Ed.), *Thought and language* (Rev. ed.). Cambridge, MA: MIT Press.

Waldrip, B., & Prain, V. (2006). Changing representations to learn primary science concepts. *Teaching Science, 52*(4), 17–21. Retrieved from http://www.asta.edu.au/resources/teachingscience

Waldrip, B., Prain, V., & Carolan, J. (2010). Using multi-modal representations to improve learning in junior secondary science. *Research in Science Education, 40*(1), 65–80. doi:10.1007/s11165-009-9157-6

MARY KEEFFE AND VALERIE LOVEJOY

9. PERSONALISED LEARNING AND DIFFERENTIATION IN STUDIO ARTS

Juggling Prescriptive Curriculum and Artistic Nurture

Arts educators now broadly agree that quality school learning experiences in this field should address both intrinsic and extrinsic goals, leading to multiple outcomes (Clapp & Edwards, 2013; Seidel, 2013; Smith, 2014). Intrinsic goals relate to students developing and valuing a personalised aesthetic capability or creative artistic intelligence (including understandings, dispositions and skills) through studio-like activities and through guided appreciation of past art products and history. Extrinsic goals and outcomes refer to the potential and actual application of this learning to problem-solving and learning in other subjects and contexts (Ewing, 2010; Gallagher, 2005; Kagan, 2009), and to broader community building and participation (Seidel, 2009). Kagan (2009) suggests the arts contribute strongly to learning because they regularly combine the major tools the mind uses to acquire, store and communicate knowledge: motor skills, perceptual representation, and language. Learning by doing or learning by making and engaging with the specificity of material processes are key factors in knowledge acquisition and production (Barrett & Bolt, 2013; Groff, 2013).

Arts studies today encompass far more than the traditional media of painting, drawing and sculpture. Contemporary artworks tend to focus on the production of experiences that alter understanding, encourage thinking and feeling through objects and the development of spatial intelligence. Personalised learning in this context means students experience programs that draw on a wide range of arts media to build on their strengths, interests and abilities, empowering them to become more confident and decisive in developing, monitoring and realising these cognitive goals.

This approach to personalised learning assumes that students can learn through processes that focus explicitly on their own cognitive, metacognitive and affective attributes as learners (Meyer, Haywood, Sachdev, & Faraday, 2008). Through this understanding, each student gains more insight into how to become autonomous in making decisions about learning and develop a level of learner resilience to overcome learning difficulties and solve problems within the field. The role of the teacher in personalised learning is to motivate, and guide students and make these learning skills explicit for learners. The teacher actively interprets learners' needs (a dialogic and a relational process) with expertise in the content area to differentiate the curriculum and extend student learning (through evidential learning outcomes). In this way, studio arts might seem a subject that is easily personalised compared to mathematics, in that students are choosing an elective they have interest in, and are expected to follow individual preferences in subject choice and media.

However, teachers have an active responsibility in a quality program to promote learner confidence and self-awareness by assisting students to set goals, build skills, practise, develop deeper insights, explore, take risks, face challenges and realise success. In many ways this is an intensely personal dialogue that is made more complex and rewarding as peers, groups and colleagues all grow and support each other within learning experiences. Teachers in our case study approached the diverse strengths, interests and abilities of each student, and their teacher partners, as resources within a relational approach to differentiation. They balanced the tensions that exist between the personal understandings and negotiations they share with their students and their professional knowledge of the curriculum. They structured the learning process through a relational lens to differentiate the curriculum to suit the diverse abilities of all students. They contrived learning experiences to promote motivation, learner self-awareness and peer support and they accessed their content area expertise to facilitate creative and inspiring learning activities.

In this chapter we explore how collaborative relationships and dialogue informed the differentiated curriculum in a studio arts context. First we identify the basic tenets of personalised learning and examine how they relate to the differentiated curriculum. Next we propose various approaches to the differentiated curriculum to emphasise how a complex understanding of each learner's needs impinges on the choice of learning activities. Throughout our analysis of the differentiated curriculum we emphasise the role of dialogue and relational agency to maximise learning outcomes in studio arts.

PERSONALISED LEARNING AND THE DIFFERENTIATED CURRICULUM

Personalised learning, as noted in Chapter 1, entails recurring themes and tensions between learners' needs, prescriptive curriculum, and differentiation:

- Learning is focused on the educational needs, interests and abilities of each student;
- Student autonomy is developed so that students understand themselves as learners;
- Students are actively involved with learning contexts and make informed decisions about their learning;
- Learning processes are modified to suit learner strengths, interests and abilities;
- Curriculum is interpreted in learning activities that challenge students within a range of capacities from basic skills practice to critical inquiry and deep learning;
- Students are active within a global learning environment where they can seek and manage multiple information resources;

- Students are fluent with information technologies that facilitate process and product in learning outcomes;
- Relationships between teachers and students are dialogically based as shared problem solvers, co-producers of knowledge and co-regulators of the learning experience;
- Teacher professional capacity is comprehensive in both discipline expertise and understanding the diverse qualities of learners.

Critiques of personalised learning promote concerns about a vague teaching method (Sebba, Brown, Steward, Galton, & James, 2007) that will only suit those who are already favoured in the education system, students from privileged backgrounds who know how to 'play the game' of school success (Campbell, Robinson, Neelands, Hewston, & Mazzoli, 2007). There is also a concern that performative assessments such as statewide benchmarks restrict more creative approaches to individualised curriculum (McTighe & Brown, 2005) and that delivery of an authentically differentiated curriculum is an unrealistic premise (Macbeath, 2004).

An important argument relevant to this chapter is that the content focused and measurable outcomes defined in educational standards today are significantly different from relational experiences of personalised learning and that each requires complementary pedagogical approaches: one is evidence-based and the other dialogic (Beach & Dovemark, 2009). We found that teachers in this case study promoted evidence-based learning through a dialogically informed understanding of the students in their class. The tensions between expected standardised "measurable" learning outcomes and relationships in the class were mediated through a structured and dialogic approach to differentiation.

THEMES IN DIFFERENTIATION

The affordances and challenges mentioned above have resulted in a range of approaches to personalised learning where the differentiated curriculum is an integral component. Some familiar differentiation strategies include: streaming into ability/interest groupings (Forgasz, 2010); Tomlinson's model for differentiation (Tomlinson, Brimijoin, & Narvaez, 2008); discipline based differentiation (Singer, Nielsen, & Schweingruber, 2012); developmental and stage based learning (Bandura, 2001); Universal Design for Learning (Hall, Meyer, & Rose, 2012); constructivist or inquiry approaches (Piaget, Dewey, Vygotsky, Friere and others) and a thinking skills curriculum (De Bono, 1987; Eggen & Kauchak, 1988). While each model of differentiation will have its own limitations and strengths, the choice of differentiation strategies depend on the teacher's preference, the context and the student's educational needs, so that eclectic approaches to differentiation are often implemented in the same classroom. If differentiation is to be such an individualised process, then it is important to understand how various differentiation strategies complement or conflict with each other in a classroom where students have diverse abilities.

In this case study, the teachers selected strategies from each of these approaches to create an eclectic educational experience for students with a range of abilities and motivations for studying art. Consistent with discipline-specific approaches the teachers want students to understand a range of skills and techniques so they can apply this knowledge to various problems as they arise in their projects. They created opportunities for the students to position their projects and new learnings in a global community of art and artists from which they can draw inspiration and a passionate connection to life-long artistic appreciation. A range of collaborative negotiations to establish short- and long-term goals informed all aspects of how and why learning was personalised and the curriculum differentiated.

A familiar and convenient method of differentiation involves streaming, ability grouping or tracking (Forgasz, 2010). The permanent and hierarchical nature of many streaming practices led Schofield (2010) and others to question whether ability groupings were a strong pedagogical and social response to diverse learner groups and also to suggest that early labelling had a detrimental effect on learning expectations and aspirations. Schofield found that peer achievement and ability groupings were correlational, in that higher ability groupings led to an improvement in learning while lower ability groups tended to reduce learning outcomes. To bypass this problem of label destiny, groupings in the studio arts context were based on workshops relating to various purposes: a specific skill, task or topic; shared interests; skills of peers; colours/numbers or other nondiscriminatory clusters; projects; and research. The range of short-term groupings addressed issues that related to pedagogy, prescribed content/skills, motivation and ability.

> The workshops usually come out of a need. So if there's a need for some kids to learn how to do shading with drawing then we might bring them all together. (Teacher, studio arts)

Carol Ann Tomlinson (2001) proposed a model of differentiation that included modifying content, process, product and assessment. In Tomlinson's model the 'what' of learning is kept fairly consistent (the regular curriculum, for example) with some changes made according to each student's abilities. Teachers are encouraged to identify what is core or essential and what may be preferable or extension knowledge in each discipline or topic. The studio arts teachers provide structure to promote higher-level thinking or problem-solving for the more able artists by encouraging more ambitious projects and reflection. Students who had difficulty with basic concepts were encouraged to maintain interest and motivation with graduated success and challenging activities. In the studio arts program the teachers created a passionate approach to art and a network of supports so that students sustained initiative and self-motivation in their own learning projects.

Developmental approaches to discipline specific skills and abilities propose that a student who lacks basic skills is unlikely to progress to a higher level of achievement in that discipline. Singer, Nielsen, and Schweingruber (2012) argue that a coherent understanding of principles that underpin a field will lead to expertise in application, problem-solving, research and the future integrity of the discipline. Clearly such an approach makes sense in learning trajectories in mathematics, but is less obviously the case in an experiential subject like studio arts, where chance discoveries and generative "accidents" can play a part in learning, mastery and motivation. The challenge for teachers in planning the differentiated curriculum is to create and manage learning activities that address curriculum outcomes and sustain and develop students with diverse abilities and interests. In the following case study, student attainment of artistic skills and content knowledge are accepted as two of the real challenges teachers face in preparing students for further study in art. In addition, the teachers also understand that modeling their own passion for the subject area inspires the development of resilience and independence in learners.

STUDIO ARTS – THE CONTEXT

The studio arts class took place in a well-lit large open area (70+ square metres) in a space designated for teaching science and studio arts. This design was based on the assumption that these two subjects share a focus on visual/spatial reasoning and can benefit from inquiry synergies (Ainsworth, Prain, & Tytler, 2011). The College had recognised the potential for linking these two subjects, and ran a two-day whole-school science/arts expo in 2014, where science provided the content for a variety of creative works, including wall murals on astronomy, drawing classes on the movement of insects, jewelry design based on molecular structure, and the chemistry of soap-making. In this way, learning in arts was viewed as enabling more effective learning in other subjects (Ewing, 2010; Gallagher, 2005; Kagan, 2009). In this chapter, we focus particularly on student acquisition of studio arts skills, but also recognise broader applications of these skills across other subjects.

The model for differentiation of these skills in the studio arts classroom was based on a dialogic approach where learning goals were negotiated and learning experiences shared within the structured framework of curriculum customisation. Two teachers shared a double class of 50 students from Years 9 and 10. The class comprised boys and girls of varying levels of ability, from beginning art students to more talented and experienced young artists. The site enabled an extended focus on how the students and teachers created and shared a personalised learning space, negotiated learning goals, embedded ICT, and structured learning outcomes for a large group of students with diverse abilities and interests. The students kept a visual art diary as a record of progress on projects, notes, images and sketching. This personal record provided a focus for conversations and insight into each student's strengths, interests and abilities. Each student negotiated his/her own art project at the beginning of the term. A range of projects were conducted during the semester.

The researchers visited the art studio site for a 90 minute lesson each week for 14 weeks. They conducted interviews with the teachers, students and school administration. Data from each session were coded and discussed to provide a focus for each week's observations and interviews. Anne Edwards theory of relational agency (see Chapter 1 discussion of Edwards, 2011, 2012) informed the analysis of the dialogic approach to differentiation, particularly as we investigated professional relationships between teacher partners, teachers and students and peers. Themes recur in the data related to both dialogic and evidence-based learning processes and outcomes:

- Dialogic processes included: relational agency and differentiation; teacher teamwork; teacher and student relations; consultation with peers and experts; negotiated learning plans; peer support; teacher critical reflections; decision making; and
- Evidential processes included: structuring of outputs, choice and flexibility for the differentiated curriculum; portfolios; art diaries; projects; intensive group work.

The students were responsible for their own decision-making from the first weeks of the term. A personal diary of artistic interests helped to inform their expression, the choice of medium and the outcome. The student selected projects included: oil, pastel and water colour paintings, photography, etching, a balsa wood replica of the Brooklyn Bridge, architectural design, pen and ink drawings and prints. Each project had a personal and purposeful significance for the student as they explored expression and skill.

STRUCTURE, CHOICE AND FLEXIBILITY FOR THE DIFFERENTIATED CURRICULUM

The students finalised their learning plans by week three when they were locked into art project choices for the semester:

> The VELS (Victorian Essential Learnings) for the arts are all about creating, making, exploring and responding so we cover those beautifully with the Individual Learning Plans. The students are creating and making all the way through. They are exploring and responding with their arts appreciation work and the other one we do is managing personal learning. They do that through their written individual learning plans and being able to self-motivate and direct themselves through the classes. So reporting is quite easy. (Teacher, studio arts)

The curriculum is structured according to the strengths, interests and abilities of each student as well as the assessment requirements for progression to an art program at senior secondary college. These considerations inform the learning plans unique to the learning outcomes determined by each student. Some students choose the elective for their own interest or for the completion of a particular project rather than further study. For example, one student was interested in a career in architecture and aimed to complete a scale model of a house that he had designed. Another student claimed the art class provided her with the emotional space she needed to stay calm in all other classes:

At the start of each term, we go through a possibilities exercise with the students. Whether a student may be interested in painting, drawing, photography or whatever their passion is, we talk to them about their choices. Then we give them a few sessions to do a bit of research themselves. They have a look in their netbooks, they do some drawing, they have a look through art books until they can focus in on what they really want to learn for the term. (Teacher, studio arts)

From the first day, the students began an art diary to research artistic interests and propose art projects. Later, the art diaries were assessed as a summary of understandings of theory, research and practice:

Figure 9.1. Page from student visual arts diary

"Occasion of Wonder" is the name I gave to this painting I did. The idea for the painting came from an image in a Mike Stilkey painting that I couldn't find the name of. In his it was a picture of a man painted on book covers glued to a canvas. I decided I would paint the background to look like books. Coming up with names to put on them was the hard part. I used acrylic paint and then used a gloss on the black areas such as his hair and clothes. With choosing the book colours I just thought of real old books I've seen and I just did those. This painting was asked by my teachers to go In the Raw Arts exhibition. Unfortunately I didn't win but at least I had a lot of people complimenting it without knowing I was there listening. I was one of eleven people who got invited to put it in a second exhibition. But unfortunately I was away. (Transcript of text on page)

Students then progressed one major work or three smaller art works for assessment. More experienced artists could choose a major work while other students gained experience from investigating a variety of approaches. This resulted in a range of activities being conducted in the room at the one time and some of these included: oil painting, drawing, photography, model making, cartoons, dot paintings, decoupage, pastels and water colours. Students found the degree of choice enhanced their motivation and willingness to experiment. In the following discussion with a researcher, the student expressed the desire to perfect his skill with pen and ink as well as his interest in trying new media:

Figure 9.2. Student pen and ink drawing

Researcher:	You like drawing with pen and ink obviously?
Student:	Yeah, yeah, mostly because you know if you screw up on it you kind of like, you can't go back on it without turning a line into something else. Yeah, I didn't actually screw up on that one, I was just like I'll give it a bit more.
Researcher:	I'm interested in that. Why is it that you like that you can't go back on it?
Student:	I sort of want to say that it demands perfection but that sounds kind of weird like you can't screw up at all and I kind of like that and also you get a good look if you do sketchy lines, so it makes it look a bit more …sketchy. [struggles to come up with a word and after hesitation settles for sketchy]
Researcher:	Do you think your skills have developed over the last term?
Student:	Yes I used to just draw with …grey lead and I used to work on doing something really well and I just started using pen and I like how it turns out.
Researcher:	So you've used pen to challenge yourself to get to a higher standard because there are no second chances?
Student:	Yeah, whereas with grey lead you can rub it out and try again six times. It just makes the paper look grey.
Researcher:	What are you going to try this term?
Student:	Maybe try with pastels to see if that's okay because I'm terrible with those so let's hope I can get better with them. so they don't look like a three year old's 'Daddy I love you' drawing.

Small group sessions called mini-workshops were held when common themes such as shading or composition were explored and when full class discussions were required to explain theoretical or administrative components of the program.

Once the learning plans were developed the routine for each class rarely changed. The teachers marked the roll then the students took out their projects and began working on them. The teachers moved around the class and offered advice or help to resolve difficulties. This often involved in-depth discussions of possibilities or purposeful moments of praise and encouragement. The student who was developing the model for his house design was having trouble with the truss line on the roof as it extended over the patio. The wings on the fairy "look[ed] strange". The decoupage needed gluing to a fine structure. And the wedding album deserved a decorative cover. Students delighted in discovering that "giving it a go" could give results that exceeded their expectations and earn them praise from teachers:

Researcher:	Tell me about this piece
Student:	It's based on a painting by Egon Schiele, I think it's called 'Russian Soldier' and I really liked it so I thought I'd try and give it a go. It's really different obviously.

Researcher: What do you like about your painting? Is it coming out well for you?
Student: I just like the colours and I like how the colour...on the bottom half I wasn't going to colour the shirt in because it isn't in his but I just liked the effect of the look of it as like having the head and a tiny bit of the shirt.
Researcher: What sort of feedback are you getting from the teachers?
Student: Really good feedback. They like me trying different things.

Figure 9.3. Student painting based on Egon Schiele

Students respected the time the teachers spent with others and tried to resolve difficulties independently or in discussion with their peers. There was no evidence of obstruction or boredom. Each teaching moment created a context where the teachers reinforced the value for all students of learning in the art class:

You have got to be on the ball. You've got to totally know where the students are at and how to keep them motivated. There are students that you know are going to get on with it and they are great. You check on them, give them advice and you really pick their brain about what they're doing. There are others that need a lot more of your attention, those that are new to the arts. That's probably the biggest challenge. You've got to be really organised. I don't ever have a problem with it but it can be a bit difficult for some teachers to teach this way. It is actually learning to let go a bit and allow the students to have a bit of control. It doesn't mean that the class is chaotic, it's not by any means, but it's very, very busy. And the students are really into what they're doing. For some teachers giving that control over to the students is difficult. (Teacher, studio arts)

The teachers emphasised that letting go of content control did not reduce their responsibility to maximise learning outcomes. The facilitative teaching approach of discussing progress and solving problems with each student as they worked on their projects, was enhanced by structured mini workshops. In the workshops, students were given more direct instruction in relevant skills or content. For example, all students who were doing drawing have a mini workshop related to light and shading. The workshop lasted for about 20 minutes and the students were able to complete practice exercises with the teacher before moving back to their own projects. The students claimed the mini workshops were valuable because problems in their art practice were overcome quickly.

Information access was not limited to the collective wisdom in the classroom. Instead, each interchange had a multiplier effect on the students' capacity to solve problems. Part of the advantage of belonging to a group that purposefully shares structures for practice, achievement or problem-solving is that a sense of solidarity develops that can overcome barriers when necessary. This leads to the understanding that social learning and connectedness deeply influence the quality of personalised learning.

I am not very good at anything in school and this art class gives me my own emotional space. It helps me cope with everything else. Sometimes I do angry art work and other times it is calm and positive. (Student, Year 9)

Students accessed the internet on their laptops for informed inspiration. Researching artists and their particular styles gave their learning global immediacy and created fascination and interest. The 'wow' factor was often shared with their friends or others working in a similar field before the students settled to reference and explore the artists in some depth. This created another cycle of research, information and dialogue for the student. In other cases, the students further personalised their learning by using technology in the artistic process:

Figure 9.4. Student computer aided drawing

Researcher: Tell me about this piece.
Student: I did the same thing with the main drawing. I drew it out on paper first, then scanned it onto the computer. I made different shapes because these two are the same picture just flipped around. These are some lyrics from my favourite songs in the background. I printed them out and went over them with a tea bag a couple of times.
Researcher: What made you think of the tea bag effect?
Student: I'd seen some other students doing it and I thought I could do it in my own way and make it look really good.

RELATIONAL AGENCY AND DIFFERENTIATION

Positive relationships are the most important enabler for differentiation in the studio arts classroom. The range and variety of relationships are a form of social capital that contribute to the rich texture of the learning experience and ensure students are not isolated in the class. Students can access teacher opinions and advice, they refer to their friends and colleagues in the classroom, they interact with the artistic styles of world experts and, in a more abstract way, they also interact with the learning spaces of the art classroom, the school and the community. The teachers viewed the complex network of interactions within the classroom as a resource where the range of dialogic relations created and maximised student autonomy and independence.

The students accessed resources (teachers, peers, ICT, international experts, trends and issues, magazines, tools, equipment, parents) to solve their artistic problems. Rather than focusing only on artistic technique (content) the teacher's role was to build skills and personal confidence in each student. Some students who lacked confidence in their own abilities had insecure understandings of art and of themselves as learners. While the quality and complexity of the final artefacts differed within the class, the pride and self-awareness that each student demonstrated was consistent. Students with diverse artistic abilities enjoyed the semester art elective, revealed newly developed attributes as learners in art, engaged with self-expression, and became a community of learners in their own class, locally and internationally.

> Sue likes that she has the opportunity to try different media and likes the encouragement she gets in this class. "It makes it easier to do well". She likes learning about "different sorts of art" and wants to be an art teacher one day. (Teacher, studio arts)

Teacher Teamwork

No strategic planning formula guarantees that teachers will team, and in most circumstances the choice is directed by the administrative convenience of workload and timetables. While gender, personalities, experience, skills, interests, risk taking and innovation need as much consideration as the subject area expertise, the reality is that most team teachers will have to complement each other irrespective of their own talents and abilities. A level of professional respect and resilience is required so that teachers working in teams can complement and support each other:

> ... and the mix of the teachers is very important. In art you see a very experienced teacher with a very inexperienced teacher and they have a good personal and professional relationship. They bounce off each other. They get along very well. (Principal)

The art teachers in our case study shared a vision that a differentiated art program could maximise learning opportunities and encourage creative expression for all students. Together, they aimed to negotiate and structure learning activities to cover both theoretical and practical components of the curriculum as well as provide personal support for students to develop their own individual strengths and interests.

> The short-term goals are about student engagement...igniting each student's passion in the arts. That is also a long-term goal because it is something that grows over time. The long-term goals are really about getting the quality of work from the students, for them to find a passion for the arts and to be able to continue on to VCE (Secondary College) studio arts. (Teacher, studio arts)

Like students, the art teachers also had different skills, abilities and expectations, yet were able to aggregate this diversity to enhance student achievement, something they were less likely to attain alone. The scope of the teachers' skills contributed to create new opportunities for learning and creativity. Once a shared vision for the conduct of the program was established, the teachers then had to determine the nature of the personalised learning approach that suited the diversity within the art class and their own teaching styles. They determined that positive and respectful relationships underpin all aspects of personalised learning. Their goal was to create an environment where the learning opportunities are maximised as students learn with, and from each other, their teachers and artistic experts they accessed through the Internet. Students were encouraged to view the distributed and sum knowledge of the group as resources that sustained their interest and created independence in learning.

The change from a closed classroom to a more public open area teaching space provided another dimension to the differentiated curriculum. The teacher no longer had complete control of a defined space with a specific number of students. Instead, they had responsibilities to a teaching partner and a cohort of students who may move from one area to another and join different learning groups. To gain the multiplier effect of shared resources, the teachers needed to function with some level of synchronicity so teachers worked to complement each other in content expertise and relationships with the students. They described a rich and diverse teaching experience due to the range of student projects.

> For me the opportunities are endless. You are able to have really in-depth, rich discussion with the students about what they are doing, to teach them skills on a range of things. In one classroom you could be teaching a student how to paint using shadows and highlights. Five minutes later I could be teaching a student how to develop a cartoon drawing. Another student may want to know what types of artist to look at for her photography. So for myself, it's about bringing together all my knowledge in the arts to be able to engage the students across the board in one class. It's a really enriching way to teach. (Teacher, studio arts)

The facilitative, yet active role, of the teacher underpins the collaborative discussions that set the tone of the classroom. The learning environment is structured to be a calm place where: art problems are opportunities to explore; practice is informed by access to world experts; art trends and innovations are willingly investigated; small group work focuses on learning skills; large projects are shared; and where advice is provided so each student can expand their artistic appreciation. In addition to the diagnostic assessment of each student's abilities and interests, the teacher also has to evaluate the students' willingness to work in a productive way and to stay focused until the completion of each project. To do that, the structures within the classroom created autonomy (learning plans, workshops, equipment, processes) and the relationships between teachers and peers were constructive, encouraging, friendly and respectful.

Teacher and Student Relationships

The beginning of term was a vital time in the studio arts class as it set the tone for relationships, engagement and achievement during the term. An important beginning whole-group activity was a "possibilities exercise" in which a range of options was introduced to the students to ascertain "whether a student is interested in painting, drawing, photography or whatever their passion is. We talk to all the students about what the choices are for them" (Teacher interview). The students followed up with their own research. "They have a look on their netbooks, they do some drawing, they have a look through art books until they can focus in on what they really want to learn for the term." (Teacher interview).

By the end of the second week of term, each student in the studio arts class had completed an individual learning plan which set out their long-term goals, covering such topics as what they intended to create, which artistic style they would emulate, which theme they would explore and which medium they would work with. In addition, students signed an agreement to bring their portfolio to class, to work consistently and independently but to ask for assistance when needed to achieve their objectives. Finally, each student completed a plan for the term's work. As they completed a piece for their portfolio they were required to reflect on "what worked well" and what they would change next time.

The teachers were partners with the students in their learning. They moved from one student to the next to discuss the art problem at hand and consider possibilities for improvement. The recurring themes of negotiation and collaboration characterised the teachers' understandings of the relationships between their content expertise and the students' needs. In the personalised learning classroom, the teachers no longer owned unique access to the knowledge base of the discipline. Instead, students accessed discipline skills and knowledge from many sources, one of which was the teacher. Other ways of accessing the knowledge they needed was through their peers or from searches on the Internet:

> We're seeing a gradual release of control by teachers. When I reflect on my two year journey, I look back and see that I gradually released responsibilities to the students over that period of time. So, as different groups of students have come through, I tinker with my practice and that creates a climate of autonomy for the students. (Teacher, studio arts)

While the students generally worked with a strong sense of commitment, some students still needed more encouragement than others. Beginning artists needed more direct help to focus on their plans and others needed more guidance to stay on task. Access to teacher expertise was managed by the students themselves. For example, one Year 10 student was overheard saying "I don't need to go to the workshop because I'm focused on what I'm doing already" while in the following exchange, students also took the initiative:

Teacher:	Can I help you with this?
Student 2:	No thanks. I don't need your help.
Student 3:	I do. Can you come here and look at this?

The learning environment was busy but relaxed and students hummed and chatted as they planned, painted and created.

Peer-to-Peer Learning

Peer learning is a positive resource in the studio arts differentiated curriculum context. Although the peer–to–peer learning was minimally structured in the studio arts classroom, the level of trust and the diverse abilities within the classroom led to shared knowledge and understandings. Four to six students usually worked on each desk area although some students worked alone by choice or because of the size or nature of their project. Conversations between the students about their art works were encouraged as they helped each other with advice, reflections and supportive encouragement. A level of chat was expected in the classroom yet it was interesting to note that some students were so absorbed in their own work that the distractions from others working close by did not impinge on their engagement at all. It was clear that friendship groups worked well together to remain on task and solve problems.

CONCLUSION

In summary, key factors contributed to the quality of learning in this case study. These included:

- the catalysing effect of the open-plan setting in enabling new practices to be imagined and enacted by the teachers and students;
- the professional expertise of the teachers in devising and enacting dialogic and relational components of a differentiated curriculum, including ongoing negotiations with students about each stage and phase of their artistic growth as well as an insight into their individual strengths, interests and abilities;
- the adaptive capacities of the students to respond productively to an increased expectation of self-directed sustained learning.

By providing structured learning experiences, choice, peer and online learning the teachers and students coped with multiple projects, a diverse range of abilities and various expectations. Our experience with the studio arts case study has shown us that creativity, flexibility and a strong sense of organisational structure are also needed to differentiate the curriculum to provoke challenging learning experiences for all students in the class.

REFERENCES

Ainsworth, S., Prain, V., & Tytler, R. (2011). Drawing to learn in science. *Science, 333*(6046), 1096–1097. doi:10.1126/science.1204153

Bandura, A. (2001). Social cognitive theory: An agentic perspective. *Annual Review of Psychology, 52*(1), 1–26. doi:10.1146/annurev.psych.52.1.1

Barrett, E., & Bolt, B. (Eds.). (2012). *Carnal knowledge: Towards a 'new materialism' through the arts.* London, UK: I. B Tauris & Co.

Beach, D., & Dovemark, M. (2009). Making right choices? An ethnographic account of creativity, performativity and personalised learning policy, concepts and practices. *Oxford Review of Education, 35*(6), 689–704. doi:10.1080/03054980903122267

Campbell, R., Robinson, W., Neelands, J., Hewston, R., & Mazzoli, L. (2007). Personalised learning: Ambiguities in theory and practice. *British Journal of Educational Studies, 55*(2), 135–154. doi:10.1111/j.1467-8527.2007.00370.x

Clapp, E. P., & Edwards, L. A. (2013). Editors' introduction: Expanding our vision for the arts in education. *Harvard Educational Review, 83*(1), 5–14. Retrieved from http://search.proquest.com.ez.library.latrobe.edu.au/docview/1326778673?accountid=12001

De Bono, E. (1987). The direct teaching of thinking as a skill. In M. Heiman & J. Slomianko (Eds.). *Thinking skills instruction: Concepts and technique* (pp. 218–229). West Haven, CT: NEA Professional Library. Retrieved from http://files.eric.ed.gov/fulltext/ed306559.pdf

Edwards, A. (2011). Building common knowledge at the boundaries between professional practices: Relational agency and relational expertise in systems of distributed expertise. *International Journal of Educational Research, 50*(1), 33–39. doi:10.1016/j.ijer.2011.04.007

Edwards, A. (2012). The role of common knowledge in achieving collaboration across practices. *Learning, Culture and Social Interaction, 1*(1), 22–32. doi: /10.1016/j.lcsi.2012.03.003

Eggen, P. D., & Kauchak, D. P. (1988). *Strategies for teachers: Teaching content and thinking skills.* Englewood Cliffs, NJ: Prentice-Hall.

Ewing, R. (2010). *The arts and Australian education: Realising potential.* Camberwell, Australia: Australian Council for Educational Research.

Forgasz, H. (2010). Streaming for mathematics in years 7–10 in Victoria: An issue of equity? *Maths Education Research Journal, 22*(1), 57–90. doi:10.1007/BF03217559

Gallager, S.(2005). *How the body shapes the mind.* Oxford, England: Oxford University Press.

Groff, J. (2013). Expanding our frames of mind for education and the arts. *Harvard Educational Review, 83*(1), 15–39. Retrieved from http://search.proquest.com.ez.library.latrobe.edu.au/docview/1326778752?accountid=12001

Hall, T., Meyer, A., & Rose, D. H. (Eds.). (2012). *Universal design for learning in the classroom: Practical applications.* New York, NY: Guilford Press.

Kagan, J. (2009). *The three cultures: Natural sciences, social sciences, and the humanities in the 21st century.* Cambridge, England: Cambridge University Press.

Macbeath, J. (2004). Democratic learning and school effectiveness. Are they by any chance related? In J. Macbeath & L. Moos (Eds.), *Democratic learning. The challenge to school effectiveness* (pp. 19–51). London, UK: Routledge Falmer.

McTighe, J., & Brown, J. L. (2005). Differentiated instruction and educational standards. *Theory into Practice, 44*(3), 234–244.

Meyer, B., Haywood, N., Sachdev, D., & Faraday, S. (2008). *Independent learning literature review: Learning and skills network.* London, UK: Department for Children, Schools and Families.

Schofield, J. W. (2010). International evidence on ability grouping with curriculum differentiation and the achievement gap in secondary schools. *Teachers College Record, 112*(5), 1492–1528. Retrieved from http://www.tcrecord.org

Sebba, J., Brown, N., Steward, S., Galton, M., & James, M. (2007). *An investigation of personalised learning approaches used in schools.* Nottingham, England: DfES Publications.

Seidel, S. (2013). Foreword: Exploding parameters and an expanded embrace: A proposal for the arts in education in the twenty-first century. *Harvard Educational Review, 83*(1), 1–4. Retrieved from http://search.proquest.com.ez.library.latrobe.edu.au/docview/1326778670?accountid=12001

Singer, S., Nielsen, N., & Schweingruber, H. A. (Eds.). (2012). *Discipline-based education research: Understanding and improving learning in undergraduate science and engineering.* Washington DC: National Academies Press.

Smith, R. A. (2014). *The sense of art: A study in aesthetic education.* New York, NY: Routledge.

Tomlinson, C. (1999). *The differentiated classroom: Responding to the needs of all learners.* Alexandria, VA: Association for Supervision and Curriculum Development.

Tomlinson, C. (2001). *How to differentiate instruction in mixed ability classrooms* (2nd ed.). Alexandria, VA: Association for Supervision and Curriculum Development.

Tomlinson, C. A., Brimijoin, K., & Narvaez, L. (2008). *The differentiated school: Making revolutionary changes in teaching and learning.* Alexandria, VA: Association for Supervision and Curriculum Development.

PETER SELLINGS, BRUCE WALDRIP, VAUGHAN PRAIN
AND VALERIE LOVEJOY

10. USING STUDENT VOICE IN SOCIAL STUDIES/ HUMANITIES TO PERSONALISE LEARNING

ALTERING STUDENTS' ROLES IN LEARNING

Tabitha (student): "We got feedback from people who actually knew what it was like to do this assignment".

Mark (student): [Students] "were more sympathetic towards my work as they had done the work".

Jane (Teacher): "It is a valuable skill for students to have, to be able to judge the value of an item, and to think about what they did, where they can improve, where they went wrong and decisions that they can make next time to make work better".

Promoting student voice in school learning is now broadly advocated to enhance the quality and personalised nature of this learning (Beattie, 2012; Elias, 2010; Mitra & Gross, 2009). In this chapter we report on a program where Year 8 low SES students participated in peer formative assessment in a humanities inquiry-based project, where they chose both the type and context of learning activities, and were taught by three teachers in an open-plan setting. The students assessed their peers' presentations and also self-assessed their work, with some co-regulated support through the use of teacher-provided rubrics. The teachers believed it was a valuable learning opportunity, in that students had a heightened sense of owning their learning and, as we will argue, had a personalised learning experience that developed their capacities as independent self-aware learners.

What counts as quality learning in social studies continues to be contested, with advocacy of an explicit focus on many themes, including ecology, global and local citizenship, racism, sexism, prejudice, critical thinking, inquiry processes and informed action (Ross, 2014). However, educators in this subject broadly agree that quality learning in social studies should entail the development of positive student values and action clarification, with a strong focus on social justice and democratic ideals. In this chapter we focus more on processes that enable effective engagement and learning in this subject rather than curricular content around particular themes. We consider that the processes for learning about democratic ideals should themselves democratise students' learning experiences.

THE CASE FOR STUDENT VOICE

Many students feel alienated from the processes and purposes of assessment (Kuhn, 2015). Based on student feedback, teachers at Wattle College wanted to change students' perception of the assessment process and to make learning more personalised. As Kuhn (2015) suggests, students learn better when they work together to solve a problem that matters to them. Through engagement and practice, students learn to appreciate other students' viewpoints, especially when the learning results in a better solution in a social context (Barron, 2003; Grueniesen, Wyman, & Tomasello, 2014; Wertsch, 1979).

Many researchers advocate increasing student voice to improve learning and engagement (Beattie, 2012; Elias, 2010; Elliott-Johns, Booth, Rowsell, Puig, & Paterson, 2012; Jenkins, 2006; Mitra, 2003; Mitra & Gross, 2009). From this perspective, students should have the option of being heard, collaborate with teachers in choosing learning activities suited to their particular abilities, and provide feedback that teachers can use to guide future instruction/tasks (Elliott-Johns et al., 2012). In this way, students are viewed as 'experts' on what works for them, and teachers can adapt future lessons to address learners' needs and interests (Mitra, 2003). Developing student voice enables students to become active participants in their own learning (Elliott-Johns et al., 2012). Teachers who provide opportunities for students to discuss key concepts and collaborate on learning activities will find that "talk is an invaluable tool for learning and for communicating that learning" (Elliott-Johns et al., 2012, p. 30). Student voice acknowledges students' rights as learners, as enshrined in the United Nations Convention on the Rights of the Child (1989), whose principles include respect for the child's opinion. This respect for the learner's viewpoint recognises both the students' input into learning and that learners need to take greater responsibility for this learning (Mintzes, Wandersee, & Novak, 1999; Sluijsmans & Prins, 2006; Wiliam, 2013).

STUDENT VOICE IN ASSESSMENT

Assessment is broadly understood as the "systematic process for gathering information about student achievement" (Wilson & Bertenthal, 2005, p. 3), but often fails to impact on student learning (Wiliam, 2006a). Researchers note the need for quality feedback to address this disconnect (Bennett, 2011; Biggs, 1998; Black & William, 1998, 2009), where students learn to identify and act on their strengths and weaknesses (Black & William, 1998; Mavrommatis, 1997). Falchikov (2004) stresses the value of students participating in assessment processes, thus voicing their opinions, reflecting critically on their own work, and gaining feedback from multiple perspectives.

Despite an extensive literature on assessment of learning generally, Black and Wiliam (1998) noted that the theoretical basis for assessment, particularly formative assessment, is at best under-developed, with many assumptions about teacher and learner capacities around assessment practices remaining tacit or ill-defined. These accounts assume as unproblematic the specific aspects that should be learnt in class, or what types of feedback enable learning or the direct benefits of feedback. It is also important to examine how students respond to these feedback opportunities, and why this feedback works. In other words, which underpinning explanatory pedagogical theory will explain the success (or failure) of this learning, assuming that all learners benefit equally from exposure to standardised processes? For Black and Wiliam (1998, 2009), these accounts of formative assessment imply considerable agency on the part of students to manage their own learning, and that an enhanced voice in the process will enable students to align effort with their teachers' goals. In this chapter we note the need for considerable co-regulation and support by teachers to develop these learner capacities, especially in low SES students.

Black and Wiliam (2009, p. 9) considered assessment to be formative when evidence of student achievement is:

> elicited, interpreted and used by teachers, learners or their peers, to make decisions about the next steps in instruction that are likely to be better, or better founded, than the decisions they would have taken in the absence of the evidence that was elicited.

This account clearly recognises many elements in the process, and is cautious about what should count as progress towards learning goals, and for whom. Black and Wiliam (2009) claimed various types of activities enable successful formative assessment. These include: teachers sharing success criteria with students; classroom questioning; teachers' written feedback on student work; peer and self assessment by students; and formative use of summative assessment to guide subsequent student test performance. They claimed that the teacher needed to establish what learners knew, what goals needed to be addressed, and what strategies would support achieving these goals. Again, this account of appropriate practices assumes as unproblematic what learners should learn in discipline areas, the individualistic nature of student learning processes, and how student agency and motivation will lead to learning gains. Bennett (2011) argued that new developments focus on conceptualising approaches grounded in specific content if the effects of formative assessment are to be maximised. This chapter illustrates how this can be achieved in the social sciences.

PERSONALISING LEARNING

As noted in Chapter 1, personalising learning entails student choice, individual student responsibility, and customised approaches to knowledge-making, where learning is linked to local and wider community contexts (Beach & Dovemark, 2009; Bevan-Brown, McGee, Ward, & Macintyre, 2011; Brimijoin, 2005; Stockhill, 2011). Childress and Benson (2014) assert the importance of schools making decisions that enable students to take more responsibility for their own learning by tailoring courses to meet individual skills and interests. This type of student responsibility is highlighted by Clarke (2014) as a shift of control in student learning from teachers who have traditionally held much control to the students themselves. Moving responsibility and control fit well with Stockhill's (2011) ideas of key components of a more personalised learning environment (see Table 10.1).

Table 10.1. Key components of a more personalised learning environment

Component	Strategies
Effective teaching & learning	Lessons in learning Mentoring strategies Wider teaching repertoire Interactive, inclusive teaching programmes ICT across the curriculum
Curriculum entitlement and choice	Pupil choice for study Extension and catch up material Flexibility leading to relevant qualifications Creating time for tailoring curriculum
Beyond the classroom	Parental Involvement Learning in community contexts Business partnerships Networks and collaborations
Personalised assessment	Setting personal targets Using assessment as a diagnostic tool Effective feedback to the learners Peer & self-assessment Improved transition and transfer
School as a learning organisation	Leadership focus on learning & teaching Workforce organised appropriately Buildings facilitate personalised learning Clear behaviour and attendance policies

Table 10.1 highlights the importance of a teacher-established culture where students set goals, have a voice in curriculum decisions, and actively participate in their education. This framework also highlights school policies and links with parents and the wider community to make learning more personalised. Consistent with components of a personalised learning curriculum suggested by Sebba, Brown, Steward, Galton, and James (2007), the key features shown in Table 10.1, include self and peer assessment (assessment for learning), curricular flexibility, and strong links to the local and wider community (Sebba et al., 2007). All learners need to find their learning meaningful (Diack, 2004; Prain et al., 2013), but this can also

pose challenges (Brimijoin, 2005; Wiliam, 2006a). High stakes testing often causes a conflict between what teachers believe is best practice and how they address accountability concerns, with teaching to tests often supplanting personalised learning approaches (Brimijoin, 2005). The introduction of personalising learning can improve student performance on high stakes testing, but only if teachers are sufficiently skilled to implement this form of learning in a manner that focuses on the teacher finding out where students are currently at and modifying the teaching and learning to move each student forward (Brimijoin, 2005).

Personalising Learning through Assessment

Personalising learning is enhanced when formative assessment and instructional processes aligns in a manner that allows the instruction to changed based on ongoing assessment of the students. Formative assessment is seen by many as valuable because of its capacity to refocus and guide learners (Baroudi, 2007; Black & Wiliam, 2009; Onion & Javaheri, 2011; Swaffield, 2011; Trauth-Nare & Buck, 2010; Wiliam, 2006b). On this basis, student peer- and self-assessments are viewed as powerful learning tools to personalise learning. Baroudi (2007) suggests that peer assessment develops students' understanding of what constitutes quality work, allowing them to explore not only their own notion of quality, but also other students' ideas. Bourke and Mentis (2013) highlight that self-assessment allows students to explore their own self-identity by reflecting on their performance. This self-assessment process can be influenced by feedback from teachers and peers as well as by personal goal-setting (Bourke & Mentis, 2013; Stockhill, 2011). Student input on formative assessment can be integrated into instruction when students are required to refine representations of a particular concept after small group and classroom discussions to demonstrate emerging understanding (Waldrip & Prain, 2006; Tytler, Peterson, & Prain, 2006). Peer assessment can facilitate refinement of students' views and conceptual understanding through a cycle of discussion, representational activity, focused discussion and feedback, and then re-representing understandings (Waldrip & Prain, 2006).

METHODOLOGY

In researching the effects of peer assessment, we examined the following questions:

1. How can assessment processes be adapted to give students more voice in their learning?
2. What are students' perceptions of the value of assessment processes that include peer and self-assessment?
3. What are teachers' perceptions of the value of enhanced student voice in learning and assessment?

Setting and Preparatory Professional Learning

Over both semesters of 2012, two humanities classes (each with 45–50 students) at Wattle College were team-taught by two teachers in an open-plan setting. One of the teachers taught both classes; hence, there were three teachers involved in this study. In the previous year, 2011, the researchers had worked with one of the three teachers in the areas of differentiating the curriculum through choice and assessing by rubric. The researchers were consulted by the three teachers involved in this study particularly around the area of assessment and how best to get students involved in the assessment of their peers. During classes, the researchers observed the classes, often having discussions with students about their learning. The three teachers involved in this study rewrote aspects of the curriculum in response to the 2011 Wattle College Year 8 student results for the Personalised Learning Environment Questionnaire (PLEQ) conducted as part of the IRL project (for further detail of the PLEQ see Prain et al., 2014, Chapter 2).

Table 10.2. Wattle college year 8 PLEQ engagement and learning data (N = 133)

	Mean	Std. Dev.
Self Directed Learning (Self-management)	3.69	.56
Self Directed Learning (desire for learning)	3.37	.67
Self Directed Learning (self-control)	3.84	.53
Teacher support	3.54	.74
Personal relevance	3.36	.62
Shared control	2.73	.87
Student negotiation	3.17	.87
Emotional Engagement	3.21	.94
Cognitive Engagement	3.57	.67
Behavioural Engagement	3.36	.74
Congruence for Planned Learning	3.57	.69
Authenticity	3.19	.77
Student Consultation	2.91	.78
Transparency	3.38	.74
Academic Efficacy	3.56	.74
Peer Relationships	3.71	.71
Self report on Disruptive Behaviour	2.55	.90
Individualisation	3.10	.75
Opportunity for Personal and Social Development	3.40	.82

The Year 8 students' responses to the PLEQ survey (Table 10.2) influenced the teachers' thinking. In this survey the students responded to a 5 point Likert scale, where 5 equated to strong agreement to statements on each theme.

The survey data indicated that students held strong positive perceptions about self-directed learning, peer relationships and teacher support, but reported lower positive perceptions about shared control, student consultation, individualisation and authenticity. This data set was shared with the year-level teacher team who identified the areas that they believed could be improved. The teachers selected personalising learning, enhancing student input, and giving students more control over their learning by allowing students to make choices as part of the learning process. This was discussed in terms of making learning more authentic, with students given more choice in selecting areas of interest. Each team member was asked to devise an intervention based on these issues.

THE INTERVENTION

United Nations Project

This subject contained three lessons each week with each lesson lasting approximately 75 minutes. The focus of this research, the United Nations project, ran for about four weeks in each semester of 2012, with the last week being assessment week. The United Nations was chosen as the topic because the teachers felt it could be linked easily to the students' "real world" knowledge, making it a more authentic learning experience. The United Nations project had a Humanities theme that required students to analyse selected United Nations projects. The teachers sought to focus on student thinking and reasoning skills and develop subject matter consistent with the state-wide curriculum for the humanities discipline area. They developed a curriculum that gave students choice and the ability to study different areas of interest rather than a common topic. Students could choose which region of the world they wanted to study. [The United Nations task showing the choices available to students is shown in Appendices 1 and 2]. The teachers set rules to ensure that students picked at least one aspect of their topic that demanded higher order thinking skills of analysing, creating or evaluating. The themes were linked by the first topic in which the teachers explicitly taught thinking skills, with activities on de Bono's hats, thinkers' keys and habits of mind being completed by students (de Bono, 1989).

Addressing Student Voice through Peer and Self-Assessment

Student voice was addressed by introducing peer and self-assessment processes that required students to present to a small group and then assess themselves and other students within the peer group. The teachers agreed that "pre-work" on peer to peer feedback was needed before formal peer assessment could be conducted in the class.

This development of feedback was incorporated into earlier work completed by students by adapting activities that were already a part of the course. Both the peer assessment rubrics and the self-assessment rubrics were presented to the students prior to commencing this project so that students understood how they would be assessed. Teachers perceived that using a rubric during the formative assessment process could provide appropriate co-regulation and feedback to students in inquiry classes. As part of this process, students were asked to complete a separate self-assessment rubric where they reflected not only on the finished product but also on the process used to develop the final presentation.

At the conclusion of the United Nations theme, students were asked to present their best three pieces of work to a small group of students. Each student, as part of a small audience, was asked to peer-assess the work through a purpose-designed rubric. [see Appendix 3]. Each presenting student was also asked to complete a teacher-designed self-assessment rubric [see Appendix 4]. After the peer assessment and self-assessment sessions, students were required to submit a final copy of their work. The teachers had not routinely used formative assessment as part of their teaching, but had attended professional development sessions that explained formative assessment practices.

The researchers worked closely with the teachers, providing support and ideas for the implementation of peer assessment and self-assessment in the classroom. The teachers retained control of the content, cooperatively planning the United Nations project as a small group and developing the teaching strategies that they used during the project. To prompt positive feedback to peers during presentations, students were given sentence starters by the teachers, including "I liked the way that." and "The best part of your presentation was." These sentence starters were designed to facilitate students becoming comfortable with how to frame positive feedback. Initially the teachers modelled this feedback to students so that students were clear about the types and purposes of these interactions.

Once students had learned to offer meaningful and constructive feedback, the teachers further developed peer feedback through a computerised activity centred on student goals. Students placed their goals and recorded their progress towards reaching their goals online. Other students then wrote constructive feedback to assist the student to achieve their goals. Students were given less structure in how to give this feedback to see if the quality of their peer feedback was developing further. The teachers closely monitored this feedback, intervening with several students on feedback deemed inappropriate, asking these students reflective questions (e.g., How do you think your feedback will help that student to progress towards completing their goal?) to allow students to deepen reflection.

These feedback sessions culminated in a formal peer assessment activity where the students worked in groups of 4–5 with each group member presenting their three pieces of work on the United Nations to the small group, and then others in the group would complete a formal peer assessment using a rubric. During each presentation, the peer assessors were asked to formulate a question to ask the presenter at the conclusion of the presentation. The rubric was then completed by the student assessors. Students were required to rate each other in three areas (see Appendix 3 for peer assessment rubric), write the questions asked of the presenter, and make extra comments about the presentation. The teachers decided that groups would be randomly constructed and arranged students accordingly. Presenters were asked to keep their presentations to no more than five minutes. Students were asked to complete a self-assessment rubric that examined more than just the finished product.

DATA COLLECTION, ANALYSIS, AND RESULTS

The researchers visited and observed over 40 classes during the semester. Developing students' skills in peer assessment was a key focus. These visits particularly focused on student reactions to feedback given by other students. Student interviews were held with a representative group of students to examine student perceptions about both peer and self-assessment processes. The researchers discussed self-perceived student learning with many students during each class to get a sense of the activities that the students found interesting and to get a sense of how students viewed this class. A targeted group of individual student interviews to represent the range of views within the class was held with a small focus group of students (n = 7). Artefacts from all students such as student work examples and peer assessment sheets were analysed by the researchers to identify how well students had grasped feedback processes and the quality of comments on peer assessment sheets.

The researchers interviewed the teachers involved in the development of the peer and self-assessment rubrics to determine whether the teachers believed that the peer and self-assessment processes enhanced student learning. The teachers were also interviewed about student learning in class with a particular emphasis on the impact of formative assessment on students' learning. Specifically the teachers were asked whether or not they thought that this change in assessment had impacted on learning and engagement. Both interview and observation data were regularly examined for emerging themes and the relative importance of these themes to student learning.

FINDINGS

Teacher and Student Perceptions of Personalised Learning

The students had a personalised learning experience because the activities allowed them to have more say in the way learning took place and in the associated assessment. The teachers had developed a "wide range of learning tasks that gave students the opportunity to make choices based on their interests, the appropriate level of difficulty and a learning style that they felt comfortable with" (Wendy). The teachers stated that some of the students made choices based on their own perceptions of which task seemed easiest, while other students chose tasks that were suited to them. Some students welcomed the chance to choose, while others still needed teacher assistance. Wendy, one of the teachers noted:

> some of the students really challenged themselves with the choices that they made and this seemed to be when they chose on their particular area of interest rather than examining each task and looking at what had to be done to complete it.

She further claimed that "students who chose this way, seemed to have less difficulty completing the tasks; the students who made choices in other ways needed more assistance and sometimes realised that they had not made the best choices", and "some students didn't recognise the level of difficulty of certain learning tasks until after they had chosen them".

Two students required teacher assistance to make their choices. In taking into account students' preferences, teachers recognised the need to expose these students to other forms of learning so that they developed as learners. The task itself seemed to have enough options for all ability levels, with the teachers discussing chosen tasks with individuals and using probing questions to gauge student capability. This process was new to the students as the "subject is very different to other subjects because they were given a choice of tasks" (Cassie). In addition, students felt that this process required them "to think outside the box" (Cassie) and to "pay attention and concentrate hard" (Brett).

Overall the teachers seemed to believe that many of the students had challenged themselves. Tanya noted:

> the system of choice worked well although some students didn't challenge themselves enough; I have used a points system of choice in another subject and may have to think about how I could incorporate such a system in this United Nations project so that all students are challenged.

Both the teachers and students believed that students had reacted positively to this opportunity. The teachers thought that allowing student choice with clear assessment criteria motivated the students and allowed them to perform at a higher level. Tanya noted that "having the rubrics and the tasks up in the classroom allowed students the opportunity to know what they have to do to get a high grade and what they are assessed in. If students don't know how they are being assessed, they can't perform accordingly".

Identification of Key Concepts

The identification of key concepts at the planning stage of any unit of work is important to ensure that all activities allow students to explore concepts (Waldrip, Prain, & Carolan, 2010) and facilitate students to become interested in relevant media events. These researchers suggested that teachers should allow students to represent and re-represent their learning to extend and demonstrate their new learning and their understanding of key concepts. Through the feedback given from the peer assessment process, students were able to demonstrate their learning and gain insight into where they could go with future learning.

The teachers reported that there were several key concepts that they were focussing on when developing this unit of work. Jane commented "when we wrote this unit of work, one of our main goals was to further develop higher order thinking skills among the students". When the United Nations task was examined by the researchers, it was clear that higher order thinking was embedded in the tasks listed as level 1 (see task in Appendix 2). An example of this is the task that requires students to "evaluate the environmental footprint …" This links well to AusVELS in the thinking processes domain which suggests students must have the opportunity to use thinking skills in a more flexible and discretionary domain". For Tanya, "our other main goals were to make our students more globally aware and to give the students the opportunity to manage their own learning".

Development of Thinking Skills

Students reported that the focus on the United Nations gave them a task that engaged them in real world issues including watching current news events. They felt empathy towards other people who were in greater need: "I feel that I know more about the sad things going on in the world" (Lucy). They stated that they had a greater awareness of real global needs and what they could provide for these people. The exploration of this topic caused them to constantly relate their explanations to the responsibilities of global citizenship and to become more critical of what they read. "This class has made me watch the news and has helped me to think more about what is going on in the outside world" (Cassie). They saw it as supporting learning in other curriculum areas and it assisted in them to develop higher levels of critical thinking skills. According to Lucy, "we do work in this class that is more sophisticated in terms of thinking. This class helps me in English when we are asked to analyse newspaper articles".

Because the class was more concerned with developing thinking skills and the topic was a vehicle to facilitate this, students felt that quality of thinking was more important than the ability to find facts. Tasks were well constructed and no matter what options the students chose to investigate, the key concepts became evident as the students were exposed to higher order thinking skills and the responsibilities of humans as global citizens. The teachers felt that it allowed students to develop a broader range of thinking skills. Jane claimed:

> This class gives students the chance to develop thinking skills. It doesn't have a lot of content like most subjects – you don't get the students to learn facts, you allow the students to explore different ways to think which can be quite challenging for both students and teachers.

The teachers felt that the tasks allowed students to develop a more critical account of the topic and an increased awareness of their responsibilities as global citizens explaining that during the previous focus area of water. As noted by Tanya:

> We found that students were unaware of global issues such as the lack of suitable drinking water in underdeveloped countries, giving responses such as but they can just turn on a tap to get fresh drinking water. This lack of awareness was something that the other teacher and I discussed when determining the focus of future learning.

The three teachers cited the importance of students knowing more about the world around them, but recognised that these particular tasks would only "make them more aware of their responsibilities" rather than "giving them a detailed knowledge of what the United Nations is doing in all countries around the world" (Tanya).

Teacher Perceptions of Peer- and Self-Assessment Process

During peer assessment activity, students were asked to listen to a presentation and complete a rubric to assess their peers. All students thought of questions to ask each student presenter, although the teachers deemed some questions superficial. Upon examination, four out of every five assessment sheets had meaningful comments in the comments section (see rubric in Appendix 3) by student assessor that supported choices made in the rubric. A small group of students (n = 4), for a range of reasons such as leaving their work at home and being unable to find their work on their computer, did not present to their group. One of these students claimed "I need to get more organised for next time", indicating that the peer assessment process had also been one she had learnt from.

Students reacted positively to the first feedback task that required them to give feedback on another student's whole class presentation. Initially feedback was a little superficial: "I liked the pictures that you chose for your presentation" (Amanda). However, as students became more familiar with the process and the teachers modelled appropriate feedback, comments became more focused and meaningful: "I thought the reasons that you gave to explain why you chose your information made a lot of sense" (Bill). Giving other students "public" feedback was viewed as successful. The teachers perceived that learning was taking place as part of the whole feedback process. When limited or superficial feedback was given, the teacher was able to further question the student to improve the quality of response. The teachers commented positively about the improvement in students' ability to improve their feedback to peers.

Teachers perceived the second feedback task as less successful. In this activity, students were asked to offer suggestions about how less desirable habits of other students could be overcome and give feedback that discussed a student's progress towards a goal. While the teachers monitored the discussions electronically and gave students feedback about their constructive comments, the electronic forum seemed less successful in getting students to develop skills in giving feedback. This result might have been because students perceived that it was an electronic forum, with one student suggesting that feedback given to others was "the way we always talk online" (Brett), while another student stated "it's only my mate who sees it" (Cassie). This suggested that students saw this electronic feedback as more hidden and inconsequential, and reverted to past online cursory communicative practices.

The teachers thought the peer assessment resulted in students taking more responsibility and reflecting on their own learning as well as being fair. This process allowed the teacher to focus on other aspects as well as addressing the peer assessment results. One teacher, Tanya, perceived that students undertook the peer assessment seriously and provided fair evaluations.

Teachers felt that the students were engaged in a deliberative process, beneficial to enhancing learning. They were surprised at how seriously students undertook peer evaluation, as noted by Jane:

> I was surprised [how well they had got into this peer assessment activity] because usually when you do Peer Assessment, either they give the other students a straight 100 per cent because it is their friend or they go "I hate him" and give them zero. They were really conscientious about it and they really assessed each other properly. This could have been because they weren't with their friends and because of the structure that we used in making them all present and assess in their small group.

Teachers felt that students were very positive about the impact of peer assessment on students' learning and that the students valued the opportunity to become involved in learning how to conduct peer evaluation. Wendy noted that "they were very positive, all of them really liked it. because finally someone of their own age was looking at the work and would finally get it and understand it in a way that we couldn't". Wendy thought that "students were totally into the peer assessment and this was a lesson where there was "no. trying to get out of the assessment". Jane suggested that the students "were fascinated by the ideas that they got to share with one another. Tanya thought that the process helped students to empathise with each other in that "students appreciate what you [the student] have to do to complete the work" and developed a more supportive environment. Tanya also suggested that it was important that the students worked cooperatively in their groups stating that "we wish to create transferrable skills that kids take to other classes and to life in general" and "we must ensure that we teach students how to work cooperatively in groups as they don't actually have the skills when they come into our class". The teachers perceived that these students were less focused on non-class related activities and more engaged in the class material than they were earlier in the year. More than four out of each group of five peer assessment sheets had meaningful comments included on them that were constructive and relevant, indicating that students took the opportunity to learn from each other seriously.

The teachers felt that the peer and self-assessment process was beneficial to learning and that: "peer assessment is something that we should be doing more of" (Wendy). Tanya observed that:

> if the students can assess each other and themselves accurately, it takes the load off us as teachers" in that "it is a valuable skill for students to have, to be able to judge the value of an item, and to think about what they did, where they can improve, where they went wrong and decisions that they can make next time to make work better.

These observations about the peer assessment process resulted in the teachers using peer- and self-assessment in other classes

Student Perceptions of Peer- and Self-Assessment Process

The peer assessment process allowed students to work in teacher-determined groups and facilitated social interaction. It was well-received by students, with student groups listening intently to each other, and carefully completing their peer assessment sheets that asked students to assess a presentation using a rubric, with space allowed for comments. The students reported beneficial perceptions of feedback as they stressed the value of peer views on their work. They felt that it was a fair process, allowed them to see what others had done and they appreciated their peer feedback as valuable and it assisted them in producing a better quality product. As a student observed "this peer assessment was good because we got feedback from people who actually knew what it was like to do this assignment. You teachers only know how you think it should be done" (Tabitha). Another student expressed that peer feedback assisted in developing a better final artefact, suggesting that "getting other people's feedback, not just the teachers' is good. It helps you to know how you could make your work better next time" (Mark). This student's perception was reasonably common. Students agreed that it gave them direction and "ideas for next time". It allowed students to "check their understanding" (in a friendly, supportive environment in which they could clarify) "ideas with other members in the group" (Audrey). The self-assessment process allowed students to reflect on the effort that they put into their own work as well as the feedback that was given by each member of their group, with one student stating that it was "good to think about how you did and rate yourself" (Tabitha).

The Value of Peer- and Self-Assessment

In summary, students and teachers found the feedback meaningful and helpful to student learning because it required students to collaborate and learn from each other in a non-traditional classroom environment. Student small-group presentations and feedback generated student input, resulting in perceived student ownership. In a more comfortable atmosphere, students could check and refine understandings.

DISCUSSION AND CONCLUSION

Our research addressed the challenges and possibilities in addressing key dimensions of personalised learning Stockhill (2011). In setting up formative assessment processes entailing peer assessment and student choice, it is possible to foster personalised learning, provided that the students are coached about appropriate roles. The teachers reported positive outcomes, suggesting that this approach should be used more widely across their school. Most students felt that there were significant benefits from both peer- and self-assessment, with several stating that it was easier to assess peers than to assess themselves. The three teachers reported benefits for students when formative assessment processes were introduced, suggesting that enhanced student input allowed students to be more engaged in their learning. These teachers explained that the students wanted to perform well in front of their peers and worked consistently in class to achieve this goal. Students were very positive about these formative assessment practices, indicating that they should be used more widely. The students reported that they learnt more about areas that they could improve through this process of presenting to a small group and receiving feedback than when assessed solely by their teacher, thus changing their perceptions of, and purposes for, assessment. The open-plan setting was a catalyst to encourage this curricular innovation, where teachers provided mutual support in introducing the focused student group work. The student responses to peer feedback indicate the potential for this kind of formative assessment to promote a close alignment between the goals of teachers and students' understandings of these goals. These signs of alignment, through guided processes of engagement, point to a theory of practice around conditions for effective assessment.

Our study confirms that learning can be made individually meaningful for students and be perceived by them to meet their learning needs, and thus reflect personalising processes and experiences. For this to happen, teachers need to relinquish tight control of the focus and means of learning, but at the same time provide, at least initially, co-regulatory strategies that support students to adopt new roles. Students are encouraged to develop as considered and considerate reasoners, to make thoughtful choices, and take on new extended responsibilities for their own and their peers' learning. Some students, as in this case study, do not expect to participate in evaluating and providing peer feedback as part of their learning, and expect teachers to be solely responsible for assessment. Our case study suggests that these students can be encouraged to reframe their understanding. Some teachers under-estimate students' capabilities and offer at best token roles and choices. Our case study points to conditions that support more positive teacher accounts of student capabilities as instantiated in new practices.

As noted often in the literature, student voice is not a fixed or singular attribute, and the voices of student can flourish or atrophy depending on how teachers frame their own and students' roles in learning. Formative assessment in these open-plan classrooms gave students opportunities to share understandings, reason about, and reflect upon their own and others' learning processes and needs. The peer assessment component of this voice allowed students to hear other students' views, allowing them to further develop their work and improve their learning. This position is consistent with findings from researchers such as Kuhn (2015) and Elliott-Johns et al. (2012) who suggest that increased student voice in classrooms promotes quality student learning.

REFERENCES

Baroudi, Z. (2007). Formative assessment: Definition, elements and role in instructional practice. *Post-Script, 8*(1), 37–48.

Barron, B. (2003). When smart groups fail. *Journal of the Learning Sciences, 12*(3), 307–359. doi:10.1207/S15327809JLS1203_1

Beach, D., & Dovemark, M. (2009) Making right choices? An ethnographic account of creativity, performativity and personalised learning policy, concepts and practices. *Oxford Review of Education, 35*(6), 689–704. doi:10.1080/03054980903122267

Beattie, H. (2012). Amplifying student voice: The missing link in school transformation. *Management in Education, 26*(3), 158–160. doi:10.1177/0892020612445700

Bennett, R. E. (2011). Formative assessment: A critical review. *Assessment in Education: Principles, Policy and Practice, 18*(1), 5–25. doi:10.1080/0969594X.2010.513678

Bevan-Brown, J., McGee, A., Ward, A., & MacIntyre, L. (2011). Personalising learning: A passing fad or a cornerstone of education, *New Zealand Journal of Educational Studies, 46*(2), 75–88.

Black, P., & Wiliam, D. (1998). Assessment and classroom learning. *Assessment in Education, 5*(1), 7–74. doi:10.1080/0969595980050102

Black, P., & Wiliam, D. (2009). Developing the theory of formative assessment. *Educational Assessment, Evaluation and Accountability, 21*(1), 5–31. doi:10.1007/s11092-008-9068-5

Bourke, R., & Mentis, M. (2013). Self-assessment as a process for inclusion. *International Journal of Inclusive Education, 17*(8), 854–868. doi:10.1080/13603116.2011.602288

Brimijoin, K. (2005). Differentiation and high stakes testing: An oxymoron? *Theory into Practice, 44*(3), 254–261. doi:10.1207/s15430421tip4403_10

Childress, S., & Benson, B. (2014). Personalized learning for every student every day. *Phi Delta Kappan, 95*(8), 33–38. doi:10.1177/003172171409500808

Clarke, J. (2014). Adapting secondary schools to personalized learning. *Principal Leadership, 15*(1), 38–42.

Convention on the Rights of the Child, opened for signature. (1989, November 20). 1577 UNTS 3 (Entered into force 2 September 1990).

De Bono, E. (1989). *Six thinking hats*. London, UK: Penguin

Diack, A. (2004). Innovation and personalised learning. *Education Review, 18*(1), 49–56.

Elias, M. (2010). School climate that promotes student voice. *Principal Leadership, 14*(1), 23–27.

Elliott-Johns, S. E., Booth, D., Rowsell, J., Puig, E., & Paterson, J. (2012). Using student voices to guide instruction. *Voices from the Middle, 19*(3), 25–31.

Falchikov, N. (2004). *Improving assessment through student involvement: Practical solutions for higher and further education teaching and learning*. London, UK: Routledge.

Grueneisen, S., Wyman, E., & Tomasello, M. (2015). Children use salience to solve coordination problems. *Developmental Science, 18*(3), 495–501. doi:10.1111/desc.12224

Jenkins, E. W. (2006). The student voice and school science education. *Studies in Science Education, 42*(1), 49–88. doi:10.1080/03057260608560220

Kuhn, D. (2015). Thinking together and alone. *Educational Researcher, 44*(1), 46–53. doi:10.3102/0013189X15569530

Mavrommatis, Y. (1997). Understanding assessment in the classroom: Phases of the assessment process – The assessment episode. *Assessment in Education, 4*(3), 381–399. doi:10.1080/0969594970040305

Mintzes, J. J., Wandersee, J. H., & Novak, J. D. (1999). *Assessing science understanding: A human constructivist view.* San Diego, CA: Academic Press.

Mitra, D. (2003). Student voice in school reform: Reframing student-teacher relationship. *McGill Journal of Education, 38*(2), 289–304. Retrieved from http://bcps.org/offices/oea/pdf/student-voice.pdf

Mitra, D., & Gross, S. (2009). Increasing student voice in high school reform. *Educational Management, Administration & Leadership, 37*(4), 522–543. doi:10.1177/1741143209334577

Onion, A., & Javahari, E. (2011). Self and peer assessment of Mathematical processes. *Mathematics Teaching, 224*, 30–32. Retrieved from http://www.atm.org.uk/write/MediaUploads/Resources/ATM-MT224-30-32.pdf

Prain, V., Cox, P., Deed, C., Dorman, J., Edwards, D., Farrelly, C., Keeffe, M., ... Yager, Z. (2013). Personalised learning: Lessons to be learnt. *British Educational Research Journal, 39*(4), 654–676. doi:10.1080/01411926.2012.669747

Ross, E. W. (Ed.). (2014). *The social studies curriculum: Purposes, problems and possibilities* (4th ed.). Albany, NY: State University of New York Press.

Sebba, J., Brown, N., Steward, S., Galton, M., & James, M. (2007). *An investigation of personalised learning approaches used in schools.* Nottingham, England: DfES Publications.

Sluijsmans, D., & Prins, F. (2006). A conceptual framework for integrating peer assessment in teacher education. *Studies in Educational Evaluation, 32*(1), 6–22. doi:10.1016/j.stueduc.2006.01.005

Stockhill, J. (2011). *Student focussed strategies: Supporting achievement* (Research Associate Full Report). National College for School Leadership. Retrieved from http://www.nationalcollege.org.uk/docinfo?id=151988&filename=student-focused-strategies-full-report.pdf

Swaffield, S. (2011). Getting to the heart of authentic assessment for learning. *Assessment in Education: Principles, Policy & Practice, 18*(4), 433–449. doi:10.1080/0969594X.2011.582838

Trauth-Nare, A., & Buck, G. (2011). Assessment for learning. *The Science Teacher, 78*(1), 34–39.

Tytler, R., Peterson, S., & Prain, V. (2006). Picturing evaporation: Learning science literacy through a particle representation. *Teaching Science, 52*(1), 12–17. Retrieved from http://hdl.handle.net/10536/DRO/DU:30004071

Waldrip, B., & Prain, V. (2006). Changing representations to learn primary science concepts. *Teaching Science, 52*(4), 17–21. Retrieved from http://www.asta.edu.au/resources/teachingscience

Waldrip, B., Prain, V., & Carolan, J. (2010). Using multi-modal representations to improve learning in junior secondary science. *Research in Science Education, 40*(1), 65–80. doi:10.1007/s11165-009-9157-6

Waldrip, B., Cox, P., Deed, C., Dorman, J., Edwards, D., Farrelly, C., ... Yager, Z. (2014). Student perceptions of personalised learning: Validation and development of questionnaire with regional secondary students. *Learning Environments Research, 17*(3), 355–370. doi:10.1007/s10984-014-9163-0

Wertsch, J. V. (1979). From social interaction to higher psychological processes: A clarification and application of Vygotsky's theory. *Human Development, 22*, 1–22. doi:10.1159/000272425

Wiliam, D. (2006a). *Does assessment hinder learning?* Paper presented at ETS Invitational seminar, July 11, 2006, at the Institute of Civil Engineers, London, UK.

Wiliam, D. (2006b). Assessment for learning: Why, what and how. In R. Oldroyd (Ed.), *Excellence in assessment: Assessment for learning* (pp. 2–16). Assessment Network Conference, University of Cambridge. Retrieved from http://www.assessnet.org.uk/e-learning/file.php/1/Resources/Excellence_in_Assessment/Excellence_in_Assessment_-_Issue_1.pdf

Wiliam, D. (2013). Assessment: The bridge between teaching and learning. *Voices from the Middle, 21*(2), 15–20.

APPENDIX ONE: THE UNITED NATIONS TASK

UNITED NATIONS

Using the Thinking Skills covered complete the following task. You have six lessons to research, develop and present your report to a small group of your peers.

Assessment: This will be in two parts, a peer and self-assessment of overall project and time use in class. A rubric will be used as a basis for the assessment.

The United Nations currently has five key areas. The following website-http://www.un.org/en/ is a direct link to the United Nations page which highlights these areas.

- Peace and Security
- Development
- Human Rights
- Humanitarian Affairs
- International Law

Within these areas the United Nations has identified key focus points where action is required in the world. You should select one area to work on for your project.

Task:

1. Choose at least three tasks from the grid provided.
2. You must choose one task from each column and one from each level.

APPENDIX TWO: THE UNITED NATIONS GRID

	Column 1	Column 3	Column 2
Level 1	State conclusions about what the future might hold for your area chosen of the United Nations Focus areas. Include the following topics: transport, communication, employment, housing, food and entertainment. Present your work as a news report, film it and submit it. This should be at least 500 words. Possible keys and hats to use are Brainstorming, What if, prediction and Interpretation picture, alternative, black and yellow.	Write a submission to the United Nations and Government of the relevant country suggesting action needed to instigate positive change in the area. This should be at least 500 words. Possible keys and hats to use are prediction, what if, alternative and yellow.	Evaluate the environmental footprint human activities are leaving in your focus area for both the current population and future generations. Construct an action plan for how the United Nations are assisting to create a more sustainable future for the area. This should be at least 500 words. Possible keys and hats to use are prediction, disadvantages, BAR, different uses, brick wall, alternative, black and yellow.
	Locate and collate a collage of images to reflect the ethnic, cultural, social and economic diversity of the World region you have selected plus the current crisis being addressed. For each image attach an explanation of each pictures relationship to topic.	Design and create a resource or tool which would improve the living conditions of the people in the World area chosen. Highlight any programs that the United Nations may already be investigating. This should include a written explanation of this ideas impact on the society chosen. (300 words).	Create a crossword including 20 clues which illustrate cultural activities and issues of the World area chosen. Each clue should be in sentence form. Possible keys to use are alphabet, question, brainstorming, invention and white.

(Continued)

	Column 1	Column 3	Column 2
Level 2	Compare some the United Nations bodies and how they contribute to solving current world issues. Possible keys and hats to use are commonality, brick wall, yellow and white.	In what ways are some traditional cultures being challenged to adopt more egalitarian society? Present your findings as a Photostory. Possible keys and hats to use are ridiculous, brainstorming, forced relationships, black and yellow.	Investigate a natural disaster which has occurred in the World that has occurred in recent times. Explain the impact on the people of the region and steps being taken by the United Nations to make improvements in both the immediate and long term future. Possible keys and hats to use are what if, ridiculous and black.
	Construct a bar graph using a table to show the life expectancy for males and females of the region you have selected. Suggest a reason for the variations within this region and the statistics for Australia. Possible keys and hats to use are combination, forced relationships, interpretation and blue.	Make a model which illustrates both the issues requiring resolution by the United Nations and your suggested solutions. Possible keys and hats to use are disadvantages, combination, BAR, variation, picture, invention, brick-wall, construction, black and yellow.	Write a letter to your family at home illustrating your experiences during a visit to a current area where the United nations is working describing the conditions which exist in this area and how the United Nations and Aid agencies are making a contribution to resolving the relevant topics. Possible keys and hats to use are reverse, interpretation, green and red.

(Continued)

	Column 1	*Column 3*	*Column 2*
Level 3	Explain where the bulk of the population of the world lives. Suggest reasons for this pattern of where people live. Present a map and an interpretation as part of your submission.	Describe the work being completed by aid agencies to overcome problems related to water in underdeveloped nations. Possible keys and hats to use are commonality, invention, brick wall, green and white.	Select one of the United Nations millennium goals and predict whether this will be achieved in the time given. Provide reasons in your response. Possible keys and hats to use are prediction, question, brick wall and white.
	Provide a report on the structure and organisation plus the member states of the United Nations. Possible keys and hats to use are variation, brainstorming, forced relationships, white and blue.	On a poster or publisher document present a summary of the key items listed: Markets, traditions, modernisation, literacy levels, education and government structure in one focus country. Possible keys and hats to use are different uses, commonality, and white.	Create a list of key global issues which create hardship for those living in an area. Present your findings as a Wordle which indicates the problems being the most predominant as the largest items. Possible keys and hats to use are alphabet, brainstorming and red.

APPENDIX THREE: PEER ASSESSMENT RUBRIC

Criteria	Excellent	Very Good	Satisfactory	Unsatisfactory
Presentation	Presentation was clearly expressed providing detailed information to the group. Eye contact was made with the audience. Questions were answered with confidence.	Presentation was clearly expressed providing some detail in information to the group. Eye contact was made at times with the audience. Questions were answered showing some knowledge	Presentation provided some information about the project. Some eye contact was made with the audience. Some audience questions were responded to.	Presentation was limited and did not demonstrate knowledge of project. Difficulty answering questions from the audience was evident.
Thinking skills	Student could explain and apply a large range thinking skills in the development of the project.	Student could explain and apply some thinking skills in the development of the project.	Use of a range of thinking strategies for exploring possibilities and responding appropriately to the questions about the United Nations.	Use of a small range of thinking strategies to the questions about the United Nations and AID agencies.
Research material	The final product contains detailed information about the work of the United Nations.	The final product contains good information about the work of the United Nations.	The final product contains some information about the work of the United Nations.	The final product contains limited information and lacks detail about work of the United Nations.

Comments:

Questions asked of presenter:

APPENDIX FOUR: SELF-ASSESSMENT RUBRIC

Criteria	Excellent	Very Good	Satisfactory	Unsatisfactory
Use of class time	I utilised all lessons effectively and located resources, took notes and prepared my project for presentation.	I utilised most lessons effectively and located resources, took notes and prepared my project for presentation	I utilised some lessons effectively and located resources, took notes and prepared project for my presentation.	I utilised minimal lessons effectively. I became distracted from work easily. I did not complete all parts of my project.
Written work/ depth	I presented the content clearly and concisely with a logical progression of ideas and effective supporting evidence.	I presented most of the content with a logical progression of ideas and supporting evidence.	I presented content which failed to maintain a consistent focus, showed minimal organization and effort, and lacked an adequate amount of supporting evidence.	I presented content which was unfocused, poorly organized, showed little thought or effort and lacked supporting evidence.
Sources	I identified highly appropriate sources in a variety of formats, and explained the information gained.	I identified mostly appropriate sources in a variety of formats and the information gained.	I identified a few appropriate sources but made little attempt to explain what information gained.	I identified no appropriate sources in any format or what information was found.
Use of ICT	I was able to use a large variety of ICT tools to locate relevant information and present.	I was able to use some ICT tools to locate relevant information and present.	I was able to use a small variety of ICT tools to locate relevant information and present.	I found it difficult to use ICT tools to locate relevant information and present my project to the group.
Use of thinking skills	During my preparation & presentation of my project I used a wide variety of the thinking skills covered.	During my preparation & presentation of my project I used several of the thinking skills covered.	During my preparation and presentation of my project I used some thinking skills covered.	During my preparation and presentation of my project I used limited or no thinking skills covered.

MARY KEEFFE

11. DEVELOPING STUDENT AGENCY IN A TEACHER ADVISOR PROGRAM

INTRODUCTION

Enacting personalised learning involves developing students' self-reflection on their cognitive, metacognitive and affective attributes as learners (Meyer, Haywood, Sachdev, & Faraday, 2008). In the same way that a personal understanding of selfhood can inform decision-making and problem-solving in a social context, a robust appreciation of the self as learner can inform choices made about curriculum topics, learning processes, engagement and how to become more self-directed/independent in learning.

In many learning contexts, the learner becomes aware of the attributes of problem-solving and critical reflection from learning activities embedded in the curriculum content of various disciplines. Yet, such a subtle acquisition of learner autonomy poses a challenge for many students who need or prefer a more explicit approach to learning skills. In this chapter we argue that a problem-solving approach to learning for young adolescents from low socio-economic backgrounds cannot be separated from the skills required to understand and address complex social contexts and decision making in life. Personal agency is linked in a unique way to understanding the self as a social being and as an autonomous learner, yet this relationship seems undervalued in learning contexts where public credibility for schools lies in success in standardised learning outcomes alone. In this chapter we analyse a Teacher Advisor (TA) program at Ironbark College that connects a personal understanding of self with explicit skills for developing the ability to become an independent learner.

Building Learner Agency

Various theorists have emphasised the importance of agency in learning, particularly in self-directed learning (see for example: Engle, 2006; Lipponen & Kumpulainen, 2011). While Gillespie's (2012) definition of agency as acting independently of an immediate situation may give us some insight into the transfer of skills involved in the cross-over from personal problem-solving to learner problem solving, it is Sugarman and Martin's (2011c) theories of relational agency that provide the framework to interpret the structure and outcomes of the TA program. From their theory on personal agency we gained an understanding of students' developmental, emergent and decisive understandings of self and learning within the student groups and therefore insight as to how the TA curriculum encouraged these capacities. Anne Edwards (Edwards, 2009, 2010, 2011, 2012) theories of relational agency in professional settings provided a framework for understanding the teacher partnerships that are a vital part of the TA program.

Context

Ironbark College had approximately 580 students in 2013. It is classified as a below average SES school with a proportion of 57% of its students in the lowest and only 3% in the highest SES quartile (ACARA, 2014). Before restructure the school experienced a pattern of poor academic performance, low learner resilience, disengagement and high absenteeism (Prain et al., 2014). The authoritative approach of teachers, with an emphasis on behavior management rather than learning, and low expectations of student academic performance, resulted in teacher frustration and a high staff turnover.

The mandate for improved learning and relationships were provisionally linked to a government grant to build new open-plan teaching spaces where a personalised learning approach aimed to address student engagement and performance (see Chapter 1). At Ironbark College, the leadership team recognised that students needed to learn self-awareness and problem-solving skills, and teachers needed to adopt a relational agency approach (see Edwards, 2005, 2007, 2011) to build the strong relationships with students that would underpin the students' journey towards autonomy. In the initial stages of the TA program, the school aimed to change the nature of the relationships between teachers and students to develop an ethos of responsive attitudes and actions so that a platform of personalised learning could be prioritised. Essentially, the school wanted the teachers to care more about the personal lives and unique qualities of each student so they could identify with a meaningful relationship within the school.

In Prain et al., (2014) we analysed the capacity building of teachers and students that changed the nature of the relationships within the school. In particular we discussed the evolution of the TA program at Ironbark College as a structure to build student independence through relational agency. In this chapter, we focus on the TA program as a vital part of Ironbark College's whole school approach to student wellbeing (see Chapter 4) and argue that the program's success depended upon (a) the quality of the relationships among teachers and students in the TA group and (b) the teaching and learning of an explicit curriculum that combined social and emotional learning with the teaching of the generic skills that underpinned academic achievement.

Methodology

Qualitative data were collected in this study through interviews, observations and document analysis over three years of the TA program from 2011 to 2014. A series of interviews with principals (2), neighbourhood leaders (8), TA program co-ordinators (3), beginning and experienced teachers (6 and 17 respectively), and students (15) provided perspectives from all involved in the program. A students-as-researchers project (8 student leaders and four student led focus groups) was conducted in the final year of the study to examine the students' perspectives on their understanding of personal agency as it was developed through the conduct and operation of the TA groups. Data were analysed using a qualitative coding method of recurring themes that were cross-referenced for each year of the study and with each participant.

The study made three important findings:

1. that the program must be strategically positioned to develop a student–centric school culture of responsiveness through relational agency;
2. that an explicit TA program of skilling students in life skills and in learner autonomy must involve a curriculum, learning and advocacy framework;
3. that students who are empowered by their own development in agency regarding life and learning contexts need to be active in learning choices and pathways.

In summary, the study found that a Teacher Advisor program (TA) that is structured to make learning skills explicit must be embedded in strategic goals and structured with developmental activities for relational agency for both teachers and students. In the next section direct quotes from participants in the Ironbark College case study and some themes from the literature are explored to link a whole school approach to changed relationships that promote personal agency and learning.

STRATEGIC SUPPORT FOR A RESPONSIVE SCHOOL CULTURE

Phillippo (2010) argued that an effective TA program must align the school vision with structures of support for TA with the explicit aim that a whole school approach values social and emotional learning and student wellbeing. Part of that school alignment involves a strategic commitment to time and resources where the school encourages changed relationships and where teachers feel supported in their expanded roles. As one teacher claimed:

> It's building relationships and it's the strength of those relationships that needs to be the foundation for everything else we do here. I think there's more opportunity to do that now the way the TA is set up. We have more time now and it's valued more because of the resources that are put into it. We acknowledge as a school that this is so important which is why this new approach came about.

Ironbark College's vision statement, "Challenging educational experiences in a supportive environment" recognised the need to raise students' learning aspirations within a caring environment that connected with students' interests and community. The school had a well-established culture of support for its student cohort through community connections and it achieved this through a focus on respect for self, the school and others while encouraging confidence, courage, persistence and teamwork (see Chapter 4 and Prain et al., 2014). This was also evident in the strong focus on developing an effective TA program to support students personally and academically.

To improve the connection between teachers and students and between peers, the school's strategic support for the TA program included:

- TA groups of 25 students with two TA teachers working in partnership;
- a dedicated 20 minute time for TA activities each day;
- the TA groups stayed together for the four years of junior secondary school;
- the TA teacher taught their students in as many classes as possible;
- a network of support provided referential expertise (counselors and wellbeing officers) for students who experienced more serious problems;
- a neighbourhood leader modeled collaborative conversations with families and students.

Teachers were deliberately paired to complement each other according to gender, skills, interests and experience. For example, innovative approaches from a beginning teacher complemented an experienced teacher's understanding of structure and process. Teachers shared expertise to build skills and broaden the ways in which problems could be resolved (Edwards, 2010). The strategic support offered within the community structure and the support network at the school facilitated a collaborative exchange of skills and perspectives that built confidence in how the teachers accommodated the expectations of their role as Teacher Advisor. At the same time, students valued consistency in the contact and communication they shared with their teachers:

We have her for English as well so we have her four times a week. We really know her and she's relatively influential on us. (Grant, Year 8)

AN EXPLICIT TA CURRICULUM

Curriculum Content

The TA program at Ironbark College was structured to teach personal problem solving, learner resilience and student autonomy in an explicit way. The program planners based developmental progressions on Maslow's Hierarchy of Needs (from Years 7 (age 11–12) to Year 10 (age 15–16) with set learning activities, provocations, and discussions proposed for each topic area. The timely development of learning skills, goal setting, planning and reporting were also included. The teachers worked with the students to explore a topic that provided information relevant to students' lives together with learning activities designed to promote discussion questions and encourage reflection. Supporting resources included: media reports, dvds, advertisements, songs, visiting artists, guests, sports people, Youtube, and a range of influential trends, technologies or fashions. Teachers provided feedback to the TA coordinator as to how effective the provocation activities were in creating a reflective consideration of the issues involved. Eventually, the students were also asked for feedback on the activities and more recently the school began working on student led provocations and TA group activities. Table 11.1 below shows the structured approach to the TA curriculum.

Table 11.1. Extract from teacher advisor curriculum framework

Year 7	Year 8	Year 9	Year 10
Safety	Belonging and Love Needs	Belonging, love and esteem needs	Esteem
Emotions are useful Managing emotions	Being in charge of what makes me tick	Self-awareness How others see me	Self-awareness Self and community
Attitudes to work and effort Beliefs about learning Motivation	Being a confident learner Being a resilient learner	Self-discipline Impact of major stressors	A confident and resilient learner Learner autonomy
Positive participation Working on strengths and weaknesses	Having goals Getting support Supporting others	Asking the right questions Supporting others Integrity	Citizen values
Communicating feelings	How do I see myself in the world?	Postschool possibilities pathways	Postschool connections and pathways
Metacognitive skills Learning how to learn Organisational skills Graphic organisers	Post-school options Team work Group dynamics Self reflection	Open communications	Study skills Self directed learner Implementing your plan Networking
Bullying Drug education Mental health	Different world views Different learning styles Personal learning goals Post school options	Analysing information	Sharing a world view Critical thinking Academic standards required for post school options

The curriculum activities were made compulsory and taught three days a week in the twenty-minute TA sessions. Teachers signed a summary statement to say that they had completed the learning activity and they provided a brief evaluation of the success, or otherwise of the learning activity in engaging the students and its relevance to their lives. The TA coordinator used this teacher and student feedback to refine the program.

The compulsory nature of the program was the focus of criticism from some teachers who would have preferred more freedom to prepare their own group activities. However, it serves to highlight the importance the school placed on building the skills required for personalised learning in the challenges of the Ironbark context. Three days of a structured program and two days for more specific teacher or student led activities provided the required flexibility to suit the teaching styles and individual learning needs of specific groups

The learning activities aimed to build relational agency so that teachers could assist students to develop confidence in their own self-awareness of problem solving and critical thinking. Sugarman and Martin (2011a, 2011b) argued that young people learn about their own agency by reflecting on their understandings of themselves, their actions and their life contexts. While the safe and trusting environment of the TA group provided a sound platform to discuss diverse or contentious points of view, the dynamics of those discussions were not insulated from the worldly influences that shaped the tacit and taken for granted assumptions of developing teenagers. Teachers were challenged when students made reference to life experiences and events that were beyond their own sphere of influence of worldly experiences. One student claimed:

> Our teacher gave us some ridiculous suggestions on how to avoid bullying. Her ideas were just dangerous.

Clearly, the teacher's insight into the interpretation of contentious socio-cultural contexts could not be taken for granted. To address this issue the school combined TA groups so that teacher attributes could complement each other. Teachers and groups were paired according to levels of experience, personality attributes, gender, life interests or outlook.

Learning Skills

Students from low socio-economic school settings may not be well supported by learning rich home environments, time or resources (O'Brien & Johnson, 2002). To address this problem the school in this study aimed to facilitate learner self-awareness through the TA program by making learning skills explicit. A comprehensive appreciation of the importance of developing student self-awareness challenges the limited notion that learner attributes emerge in isolation or that students develop problem solving and critical self-awareness as skills that are somehow separate from their daily lives. The whole school approach for personalised learning implemented at Ironbark College explicitly linked learning skills with daily life decision-making in the TA program. The learning skills component of the TA program had two important priorities:

- that students would come to understand themselves as learners;
- that students actively participated in decision making that related to their learning choices and pathways.

In a comprehensive report on personalised learning Meyer, Haywood, Sachdev, and Faraday (2008) claimed that students should be informed of their own learner attributes in cognitive, metacognitive and affective domains. Student discussions within the TA program related to "How do I learn best?" and "What do I have to do to be a resilient learner?"

In the Year 7 program students began their journey in understanding themselves and their attributes as learners. Angelique (Year 7 student) remembered that "at the start of Year 7 there were a lot of getting to know you activities which we could use in our lives to get to know other people more". Students identified their strengths, interests and abilities in living and in learning and some discussions centred on the processes involved in getting organised for learning. Students were encouraged to understand how they experienced barriers to learning and how these were linked to life choices. Questions such as "What are the consequences for my learning when I stay up all night playing computer games?" were discussed.

The Year 8 TA program linked personal learning goals to potential life pathways. TA groups discussed ambitions and possibilities and explored post-school options and pathways. Year 9 included an investigation of teamwork and how to participate in projects as an effective team member. Year 10 included an analysis of social competencies within a work or community environment. Study skills, planning and learner resilience were recurring themes at all year levels.

The notion of understanding the self as learner developed as students became informed of their achievement levels on national benchmarks or curriculum standards. Many students were initially dismayed to find that their literacy or numeracy skills were two, three or even four years below their age level peers on national benchmarks. The process of negotiating learning goals helped to address the discordance experienced in performance, expectation and achievement. The TA began the conversation and more information was gathered from the teacher in the particular domains such as English, mathematics, science or humanities. Together the teachers and student made informed choices about learning goals that were both realistic and aspirational. The student involvement in this process increased over each year level as students realised how much they could achieve, how barriers impinged on their learning, how organisational and resilience skills influenced commitment and progress, and how their goals connected with their learning and living futures. The students reflected on questions such as. 'What do I want to achieve?', 'How will I do that?' and 'Who can help me achieve my goals?'

The reality check provided by an informed understanding of achievement levels needs cautious consideration from the TA. Encouragement has to be provided with learning structures that are relevant to each student to maintain motivation and a purposeful focus on achievement. Personal support, care, high expectations and encouragement from the TA can only make the learning goals achievable if students maintain a level of ownership over their own learning. For many of the students at Ironbark lack of self-confidence in learning stems from their family background. In families that experience entrenched unemployment, students may have been afforded limited opportunities, and limited access to, or aspiration for, higher education opportunities.

The school aimed to identify and encourage aspirations that could overcome the barriers of low socio-economic backgrounds and empower students to see learning as a tool to achieve personal and ambitious goals for life and learning. Visitors were invited to the school to motivate students to consider a range of possible pathways towards employment and career options. Doctors, nurses, lawyers, musicians, film producers and sound technicians discussed life stories and pathways as school activities merged and complemented the structured TA program.

Students connected in many ways with the local community to experience and model positive learning and engagement practices. For example, they participated in "coaching" lessons at the local primary schools, visited elderly people in their homes, and cared for pets at the local pet rescue. Science students built energy efficient cars to compete in a community competition while music concerts, film productions and art galleries provided realistic and community connected learning activities that motivated students to achieve high levels of participation and encouragement.

The effect of these multiple ways of broadening students' horizons and encouraging their aspirations is reflected in these general comments on his goals by Sam (Year 8 student):

At the start of the semester we do learning goals and stuff like that. My learning goals are generally just to keep improving as much as I can. I want to be an architect when I get older so I want to work towards that. I want to go to uni when I get older. My main goal is just to keep improving as much as I can.

The important role of the TA as learning guide and mentor can be deduced from Sam's comments. Sam displayed enthusiasm and high aspirations but at Year 8 level, would need considerable guidance and encouragement to more specifically work out what he needed to do to reach his goal, to set pathway steps in place, and to work with the people who would help him to realise his dream.

ADVOCACY

Advocacy was a significant part of the TA role. The TA teacher was expected to advocate for the needs of each student in their group in learning, behavior and social contexts. The TAs knew their students well and through the discussions related to learning goals they made expectations explicit. The TA aimed to promote student aspirations, understand their learning strengths and difficulties, become familiar with their out of school interests and activities and, most importantly, to be the first and most reliable contact between the family and the school. In the often complex relationships between the students and home settings the TAs learned from the neighbourhood leaders who modeled problem solving and effective communications with parents in contentious situations.

In broad terms of relationships the teachers were mostly comfortable in their relationships within the TA groups and in their areas of discipline expertise, yet the demands of the problems that characterised their students' lives were an ongoing challenge. The reality of the contentious issues in students' lives was mirrored in the purposeful discussion of contentious topics in the TA learning activities. This made teachers and students feel most vulnerable in the TA structure yet it also gave the TA curriculum relevance and currency. Discussions about contentious life circumstances provided a boundary tension for the teachers and a challenge for the program planners. As experienced teacher, Hilary, reflected:

> It's a teacher/student relationship. It's not over familiar but you get to know them well. You talk to the parents on the phone, you talk to the kids a lot, you know what's going on in their lives. If there is something concerning them it comes out quickly and easily and gets dealt with too. It's a lot more caring and there's a lot more family feel to it.

A Year 10 student described the development of positive, nurturing relationships within the TA program as an acculturation process:

> The Year 7s come in and try to assert themselves with fights and swearing and they think "I've got to prove myself" then they get over it and it gets better. I think that is because in primary school the teachers are the authority figure whereas in high school the teachers are still an authority figure but they are more like your mates or something. They still have to keep you on track but it is more your own responsibility.

Themes of belonging and aspiration recurred in the students-as-researchers (SAR) component of the study. When asked to depict their perspectives on the purpose of the TA group the students proposed:

> TA group makes me feel confident. I can fly like an eagle. I am flying towards the future. I am strong and free.

Figure 11.1. Students' perspectives of the positive outcomes of the TA group

STUDENT AGENCY

The nature of student agency is complex and unclear in most school contexts. On the one hand, students' developing confidence in their own abilities to solve problems in life and learning contexts occurs over time and is mediated through life and school experiences. In the TA program, the students examined information about their own learning attributes. They explored dreams, ambitions and set goals. Networks of friendships and collegial relationships supported their efforts through successes and challenges. On the other hand, however, the agency that students developed through their interactions in the TA group, the school, community and their peers was constrained by factors that, in some cases, were beyond their control. We have already acknowledged the influences that poverty and unemployment have on limiting student choices. We now need to consider the balance between developing student agency and activating a responsive school system where students have a say in determining learning pathways and decision-making processes that suit their own strengths, interests and abilities.

Bland (2006) and others (Keeffe, 2007; Keeffe & Andrews, 2014) claimed that students-as-researchers (SAR) projects could create an empowering voice for students to have a say about their own learning contexts. The SAR project conducted in this study provided a framework for students to critically reflect on the TA program and to provide the researchers with a level of insight into students' perspectives on the purpose, nature and conduct of the TA group. Eight Year 10 students (community leaders) met each week for one semester to develop and implement a research design that would allow them to investigate students' perspectives of the TA program. After a researcher-facilitated discussion about the purpose of research the SAR students determined the following research questions:

- What are the advantages of the TA program?
- What are the barriers to participation?
- How do students experience voice and choice through the TA curriculum?

The SAR group decided on a research design that included four phases:

1. Peer interviews identified the scope and possible issues for investigation. This involved a broad discussion about the strengths and difficulties associated with the TA group.
2. Four focus group interviews with 12 students randomly selected from each of the 4 learning neighbourhoods (48 students). The notion of garnering student perspectives from students who were not fully engaged with school activities was an important consideration for the SAR group.
3. Photo elicitation of the recurring themes in the focus groups. SAR students used their phones and flip cameras to identify photographic symbols of the components of the TA program.
4. An analysis and discussion day at the university. This involved: explaining the symbolic representations in the photos; clustering the photos into themes; and

presenting the summary photographic clusters to the SAR group for discussion. The discussion about positive aspects of the TA group, improvements that could be made, and students understanding of their own sphere of influence through the TA group were summarised and coded by consensual opinion.

The SAR students demonstrated quality leadership and respect during the focus groups. They made the groups feel comfortable and confident that their opinions would be valued. They asked broad questions of the group and specific questions of individuals and pursued topics as students raised different issues. They sought clarification when unsure of the students' perspectives. During the post focus group discussion the SAR students offered interpretations from the insights they had in connection with the broad student experience. Their findings informed the photo elicitation phase of the SAR project.

The SAR group summarised the advantages of the TA program in terms of an embedded level of trust and respect between the teachers and students and between the peers in each group. This resulted in a feeling of safety and an appreciation of the diverse needs, backgrounds, talents, interests and difficulties of everyone in the group. Discussions about contentious topics in the TA group (high risk behaviours, bullying, arguments, friendships) led to the expression of personal beliefs and reflections, but it was in the daily sharing of time, school and personal issues that the students developed an understanding of the complex lives they each shared in some way. One student explained:

> We are all different but we all get on. It is not so much that we like each other like friends but we respect each other. We would pretty much just go nuts if we had to go straight into school.

It seems that this level of respect and support provided the safe environment to help students cope with the challenges of school. The timeliness of the TA session at the beginning of the day provided a social connection that was distinct from difficulties they experienced at home and it also helped to get students organised for learning. As Ben (Year 9) explained, "She (TA) sees if I have a pen or if I have done my homework. Yeah, she sort of gets me ready".

The students suggested that some activities within the TA program needed review. Students requested fewer worksheets, more activity, more challenging and interesting activities that involved sport, music, Youtube or DVDs, and they would have liked more say in the TA process, school decisions and learning pathways. Students at the SAR debrief offered the following overview of student voice:

> I think you have to know that at this school, if a kid has something to say they will say it. You speak your mind. We know that people will listen to us. I don't think the Year 7's know that because they have too much of the cliché stuck in their heads about this school (negative) even though it is nothing like that.

Positive aspects of the TA group included images of: belonging, risk, safety, respect, encouragement, friendships, sharing, future oriented, and decision making. Barriers to participation in the TA group included: boredom, repetition, lack of relevance, not enough time to explore some issues, and the negative influence of a selfish or narrow minded teacher.

Figure 11.2. SAR student summary of TA positives and negatives on university feedback day

CONTENTIONS WITH AUTHENTIC STUDENT VOICE

The SAR feedback provided a strong affirmation of the supportive culture that the TA groups created within the school. Student identified barriers and challenges that were largely operational as students wanted a more relevant, engaging and embodied approach to the learning activities. While the participation of all students in the focus group, interviews and students-as-researchers project was insightful and informed, the unspoken boundaries of student decision making, as argued by Lodge (2005), could still be identified, particularly as they related to links with learning. Students were still locked into set learning pathways that were limited by the difficulties they experienced in core subjects rather than the strengths they had in other subject areas. The systemic problems of encouraging students to know and understand themselves as learners must be fully supported by more flexible approaches to curriculum and study or career pathways. This problem extends beyond the students, the TA group, and the school culture to political possibilities for further education. One student explained:

> I am not real good at school but I do like cooking. I plan all my own menus and cost them out and my teacher challenges me with different tasks just like Master Chef. I would rather do cooking than any other subject at school. I like coming to school on the days I have cooking.

Student voice in decision-making is another area of concern identified in this study. Professional development in recognising levels of student voice (Hart, 1997) was not able to change the practices of a student council that made arbitrary decisions about student involvement. Authentic participation in decision-making with regard to their own learning and school policies that influenced their own destinies was an ongoing developmental task for the school leadership. On the ethics involved with an understanding of authenticity, Taylor (1991) alerts us to three conundrums that can inform our understanding of the success, or otherwise of the TA group experience.

A significant challenge in establishing an authentic student voice can be the pressure within school cultures for conformity to long-established norms. The SARs were able to assert the balance that existed between recognition of their own value and worth alongside the cultural and life-long aims of the TA group and its links with school culture, the community and their futures. The structure of the TA program progressed from a personalised focus on individual identity to a community awareness of roles and responsibilities. Students gradually realised that they had more to gain from belonging to the wider community culture of the school than by trying to argue against its norms. They aspired to belong because they felt safe and respected in such a community. It gave the students a sense of higher purpose. They believed that their friendships were lifelong and the school was a better place because they contributed to its culture. The conformity of consensual identity has many strengths for those students who belonged. Our evidence did not 'find' the opinions of those who struggled to belong to the school culture even when we actively sought those opinions. However, the school needs to be alert to the possibility that some students will find such loyalty confronting and will choose not to belong.

A further challenge to authenticity in student voice and experience is the economic rationale that underpins school policy and design. Perhaps the greatest costs to the school in initiating and progressing the TA program were the changed expectations of the role of the teachers and the time commitment the program demanded in order to make a contribution of strategic importance. Each year the school had to justify continuing the program against a raft of centrist priorities and requirements. It was an annual argument to justify the time and effort required to maintain the program's integrity. Issues that recurred included: induction of new staff; active student participation; local needs; and reflection on feedback. The TA group would not be as effective if the structures of support were not readily available to students who experience a crisis, yet, due to financial constraints, the roles of counselor, nurse and career advisor were constantly rationalised. To address the perceived vulnerability of these services, the school developed a strong network of community interactions to promote shared responsibilities and student engagement. The issue of flexible learning pathways is an ongoing national accreditation problem in which Ironbark College has an active and respected voice.

A final challenge for authenticity in student involvement in their own learning futures involves the political agenda as it relates to poverty, unemployment, abuse and neglect. Our understanding of authentic student voice leads us to believe that students will be empowered to make informed decisions about their own life circumstances and learning futures. The aims of the TA program linked a critical awareness of the students' own life circumstances with choices they could make about study, careers and life-long learning. However, while the TA program at Ironbark College was imbued with admirable intentions, the reality of present and future options for many of their students were not as positive. Unemployment and various contentious issues that the school has minimal control over will remain a recurring theme in the community. It is commendable that the TA group provides an influential life experience in a safe environment but the contention remains: Will the student's self-awareness and learning skills be robust and resilient enough to help them through a lifetime of challenges and opportunities?

REFERENCES

Australian Curriculum and Assessment Reporting Authority (ACARA). (2014). *My school.* Retrieved from http://www.acara.edu.au/reporting/my_school_website_page.html

Bland, D. (2006). *Researching educational disadvantage: Using participatory research to engage marginalised students with education* [PhD Thesis]. Brisbane, Queensland: Queensland University of Technology.

Edwards, A. (2005). Relational agency: Learning to be a resourceful practitioner. *International Journal of Educational Research, 43*, 168–182. doi:10.1016/j.ijer.2006.06.010

Edwards, A. (2007). Relational agency in professional practice: A CHAT analysis. *Actio: An International Journal of Human Activity Theory, 1*, 1–17.

Edwards, A. (2009). Relational agency in collaborations for the well-being of children and young people. *Journal of Children's Services, 4*(1), 34–43. doi:10.1108/17466660200900004

Edwards, A. (2010). *Being an expert professional practitioner.* Dordrecht, The Netherlands: Springer.

Edwards, A. (2011). Building common knowledge at the boundaries between professional practices: Relational agency and relational expertise in systems of distributed expertise. *International Journal of Educational Research, 50*(1), 33–39. doi:10.1016/j.ijer.2011.04.007

Edwards, A. (2012). The role of common knowledge in achieving collaboration across practices. *Learning, Culture and Social Interaction, 1*(1), 22–32. doi: /10.1016/j.lcsi.2012.03.003

Engle, R. (2006). Framing interactions to foster generative learning: A situative explanation of transfer in a community of learners classroom. *The Journal of the Learning Sciences, 15*(4), 451–498. doi:10.1207/s15327809jls1504_2

Gillespie, A. (2012). Position exchange: The social development of agency. *New Ideas in Psychology, 30*(1), 32–46.

Hart, R. (1997). *Children's participation: The theory and practice of involving young citizens in community development and environmental care.* London, UK: Earthscan Publications, UNICEF.

Keeffe, M. (2008). *Students-as-researchers: Perspectives on student leadership.* Paper presented at the International Congress on School Effectiveness and Improvement, January 6–9. Auckland, New Zealand.

Keeffe, M., & Andrews, D. (2014). Towards an adolescent friendly research methodology. *International Journal of Research and Method in Education, 1*(14). doi:http://www.tandfonline.com/action/showCitFormats?doi=10.1080/1743727X.2014.931367

Lipponen, L., & Kumpulainen, K. (2011). Acting as accountable authors: Creating interactional spaces for agency work in teacher education. *Teaching and Teacher Education, 27*(5), 812–819. doi:10.1016/j.tate.2011.01.001

Lodge, C. (2005). From hearing voices to engaging in dialogue: Problematising student participation in school improvement. *Journal of Educational Change, 6*(2), 125–146. doi:10.1007/s10833-005-1299-3

Meyer, B., Haywood, N., Sachdev, D., & Faraday, S. (2008). *Independent learning literature review: Learning and skills network*. London, UK: Department for Children, Schools and Families.

O'Brien, M. L., & Johnson, K. (2002). *School is for me: Student engagement and the fair go project: A focus on engaging pedagogies in primary classrooms in low socio-economic status communities in south-western Sydney*. Paper presented at the Australian Association of Research in Education Conference, Brisbane. Retrieved from http://www.aare.edu.au/data/publications/2002/obr02357.pdf

Phillippo, K. (2010). Teacher-advisors providing social and emotional support: A study of complex role enactment in small high schools. *Teachers College Record, 112*(8), 2258–2293. Retrieved from http://www.tcrecord.org/Content.asp?ContentId=15955

Prain, V., Cox, P., Deed, C., Dorman, J., Edwards, D., Farrelly, C., Keeffe, M., … Yager, Z. (2014). *Adapting to teaching and learning in open-plan schools*. Rotterdam, The Netherlands: Sense Publishers.

Sugarman, J., & Martin, J. (2011a). Persons acting in worldly contexts. In R. Frie & W. Coburn (Eds.), *Persons in context: The challenge of individuality in theory and practice* (pp. 71–88). New York, NY: Taylor & Francis Group.

Sugarman, J., & Martin, J. (2011b). Theorizing relational agency. *Journal of Constructivist Psychology, 24*(4), 283–289. doi:10.1080/10720537.2011.593455

Sugarman, J., & Martin, J. (2011c). Theorizing relational agency: Reactions to comments. *Journal of Constructivist Psychology, 24*(4), 321–323. doi:10.1080/10720537.2011.593472

Taylor, C. (1991). *The ethics of authenticity*. Cambridge, MA: Harvard University Press.

VAUGHAN PRAIN, PETER COX, CRAIG DEED, DEBRA EDWARDS,
CATHLEEN FARRELLY, MARY KEEFFE, VALERIE LOVEJOY,
LUCY MOW, PETER SELLINGS AND BRUCE WALDRIP

12. REMAKING SCHOOLING THROUGH OPEN-PLAN SETTINGS

Some Conclusions and the Future

In assessing a major educational reform of the kind enacted in the BEP, many questions are raised, requiring comprehensive, evidence-based answers. Was the original Plan well-conceptualised and effectively enacted to meet the needs of these twenty-first century learners? What are the short-term and long-term effects of this major reorganisation of schooling? What are the gains and losses (if any) of this approach? To what extent were initial goals achieved, and enacted strategies effective, and why? How sustainable are the emerging signs of positive changes to student academic attainment and wellbeing? What are lessons for like contexts and future schooling? Elsewhere (Prain et al., 2014), we have sought to answer some of these questions around BEP goals, implementation strategies, and outcomes, including key enablers and constraints.

In this book we have focused on how widely acknowledged challenges facing participant and like schools (high concentrations of low SES students, ineffectual curricula, and poor levels of student engagement/attendance/wellbeing), have been addressed in the BEP (up-scaling learning communities and curricular renewal through teacher professional learning and team-teaching). Our account of this solution, (personalising learning in open-plan schools), and its effects, have been elaborated in the preceding chapters through case studies of new teacher and student practices in different subjects. More provocatively, we have viewed personalising learning as a proxy for quality learning processes, while also considering quality across the curriculum as entailing disciplinary propositional, procedural and dispositional knowledge, skills and value perspectives (as enshrined in official curricular policies and only partly measured in national testing regimes). As noted by Muijs, Harris, Chapman, Stoll, and Russ (2004), and many others, making learning personally meaningful for low SES students is fundamental to achieving quality learning as both process and outcome.

In this chapter we draw together these insights about the relationships between altered physical settings, teacher and student change, curricular renewal, and learning quality, and consider key implications for the BEP schools and other schools and systems. We review the effects of the key BEP strategies, including (1) the open-plan settings as a catalyst for curricular change, (2) teacher professional learning, including the formal and informal development of teachers' professional knowledge to enable effective teaching, learning, and student wellbeing in the new settings, and (3) curricular reform leading to a more explicit, differentiated curriculum, replacing a traditional age-based curriculum with a stage-based one. We conclude by considering further questions and implications arising from this research for participant schools as well as for curriculum in education systems more generally.

The Open-Plan Settings as a Catalyst for Curricular Change

Past research on the relationship between physical settings and student learning has tended to be inconclusive about the impact of physical settings on learning gains or teacher practices (Hattie, 2009), or claimed the need for more research (Mahoney, Hextall, & Richardson, 2011). For Hattie (2009) past research on open-plan settings had not established a case for strong learning gains, and Mahoney, Hextall, and Richardson (2011) argued that the complex relationships between school physical settings and possible beneficial academic or wellbeing outcomes remained to be established. Our research into the BEP schools indicates there is a complex reciprocity between the new settings, curricular reform and organisational change, and that this reform/change can lead to improved academic attainment (as noted in Chapter 1) and increased wellbeing (Chapter 4). As indicated in the emergence of new teacher roles and practices (Chapter 2), and the synchronised team-teaching of English (Chapter 6) mathematics (Chapter 7), science (Chapter 8) and studio arts (Chapter 9), the new larger settings enabled teachers to experience and review past traditional curricular practices, note shortfalls or discrepancies across different instances of the same subject in their schools, and work together to envisage a richer vertical curriculum that could be team-taught to address all students' needs. This is not to argue for architectural determinism, where larger spaces ensured change, but rather to argue that the spaces provided an impetus for teachers to imagine and adapt new practices as practicable in these settings.

As we have reported elsewhere (Prain et al., 2014), not all teachers welcomed the increased exposure of their practice, or the new imperative of collegial cooperation. Some teachers left these schools. Others took up the opportunities for new roles and new in situ collegial teaching. For these teachers the new settings catalysed the need for curricular review and necessitated and encouraged reform. For some teachers, like Bob in science, (see Chapter 8) the teaching team affordances of the larger settings aligned with his prior beliefs about how to optimise student learning by enriching the teaching and learning resources and expertise available, whether actual or virtual. Other teachers were persuaded about the virtues of team-teaching and shared space through various influences. These included: dissatisfaction with past approaches, advocacy from colleagues, exposure to workable practices in their own community, or in other like settings and other schools, through informal learning first-hand of the gains of an in situ collegial approach, or through recognising the need for new adaptive practices in these larger settings (see Prain et al., 2014). The case studies presented in earlier chapters in this book reflect, in some cases, two or more years of teacher exposure/adaptation to these settings, and various iterations of curricular and organisational experimentation and refinement.

As noted in Chapter 1, the teachers' initial exposure to the larger settings also foregrounded structural challenges around the organisation of daily life in each learning community. This entailed experimentation with block timetabling, and organising the distribution of staff expertise within and across communities. The larger spaces also dictated the necessity to establish student behaviour protocols for internal traffic, as well as movement in and out of communities. Staff members also had to establish protocols around organisation of furniture during and after lessons, noise levels within communities, and transitions between 'classes' (see Prain et al., 2014). All these challenges compelled a focus on school-wide teacher-imposed structures to enable productive constraint of student focus and activity as a basis for workable daily curricular experiences. In these ways, the larger settings prompted new expectations on daily routines, prompting new teaching and learning practices.

Our research into the BEP schools also supports Gislason's (2009, p. 4) claim that open-plan design fosters a "sense of community among students", depending, according to Gislason, on staff commitment to team-teaching in interdisciplinary subjects and willingness to collaborate in block-timetabled teaching. These strategies enable a productive intensification of curricular focus, resources, and expertise. As noted in Chapters 4, 7, 9, and 11, and in our research elsewhere (Prain et al., 2014), students in the new settings appreciated access to more teachers and students, and to an increased sense of participating as members of a supportive community. However, as noted by Boys (2011) the effective use of open or closed physical space for learning depends entirely on how participants understand their roles and purposes, pointing to the critical role of a quality curriculum as both content and teaching and learning processes in the open-plan settings. As evident in every case study in this book, personalising learning has entailed new challenges and opportunities and altered roles for teachers and students.

Teacher Professional Learning

We have reported elsewhere on the multiple sources for teacher professional learning in these settings, including from external curricular support as well as from colleagues (Prain et al., 2014). Here we synthesise insights from the preceding chapters about the emergence of teacher "common knowledge" (Edwards, 2014, p. 206) about effective professional practice in the open-plan settings. By "common knowledge", Edwards means a shared understanding of "what matters" (p. 206) for all participants, with this understanding then providing a resource through which collaboration and alignment of motives can be mediated, validated, and advanced. As noted in Chapter 2, through extensive experience in the new settings, teachers sought to extend learning experiences from well-tested traditional practices, such as explicit instruction to a conventional 'class' of 25–30 students in a closed space, for example in the Socratic Studio, to more independent technology-mediated individual and group work in larger spaces. We theorise teacher adaptation to the new settings as a complex problem-solving process, characterised by the interplay of past practical knowledge, contextualised experience, experimentation, reflection, and feedback (Chapter 2). Subsequent chapters in our book instantiate some key principles in teachers' practical reasoning about workable approaches to teaching and learning in these settings.

A recurrent theme across our case studies of different subjects is that teachers 'want' a manageable order to the curriculum in terms of their own and their students' roles. Students, for their part, also want predictability and security in daily expectations (see Prain et al., 2014, Chapter 10). Teachers in our case studies aim to provide an enabling structure and focus for student learning but then expect and allow more student initiative in engaging with learning tasks. This expectation of increased freedom of student learning pathway arises, we speculate, partly from the governing educational orthodoxy that teachers should develop independent student learners (Akinsanmi, 2011; Ledward & Hirata, 2011), but also because the larger spaces provide workable enactments for diverse activity. In terms of the "division of labour" (Engestrom, 2000, p. 960) between teacher and student roles in teaching and learning, this "letting go" of tight teacher control of learning processes represents a plausible shift from the traditional tight managerial classroom role for teachers. This shift is evident in teacher expectations of increased student agency and independence as problem-solvers in the games-based learning program in Chapter 3, where students are expected to make full use of available actual and virtual resources. It is evident in the teacher expectation of flexible students' problem-solving strategies and representational diversity in the mathematics programs (Chapter 7) the science case studies (Chapter 8), the English programs (Chapter 6), the studio arts program (Chapter 9), and the social science unit (Chapter 10). It is evident in the expectation that students will monitor, analyse, and self-manage their learning through use of a virtual dashboard in Chapter 5. In each case, the teachers provide or negotiate criteria for task success, offer timely coaching for groups and individuals as needed, and give precise feedback on student performance, but students are given some spatial and strategic freedom to tackle tasks.

This entails a significant shift from the role of teacher as deliverer of a tightly packaged program. As indicated by Edwards (2014, p. 208) in commenting on the BEP, the teacher is now charged with the dual role of creating a cultural environment where learners "move themselves forward", but where teachers also "make demands on learners which ensure that in their sense-making they engage with publicly valued meanings". This formulation nicely captures the balance in personalised learning between student freedom, initiative, and teacher productive constraint. This balance is a key feature of how the sense-making of learning is personalised effectively in the case studies of different subjects reported earlier in our book. As noted in Chapter 5, this dual teacher role also applies to working with students as they make sense of (and act upon) assessment of their work as recorded on the Whirrakee dashboard. Students' private individual sense-making and learning strategies need to feed into discussion/feedback with teachers to develop a shared public understanding (language) about what enables quality reflection and informed action.

Complementing this common knowledge between teachers and students, teachers also build a common knowledge around the strengths of colleagues as contributors to team-teaching, as shown in the English, science and studio arts cases, where teachers aim to complement areas of expertise. Common knowledge also entails distributed expertise, where subject teachers, such as in the mathematics and science case studies, develop multi-level understandings of key underpinning concepts and content appropriate for a wide student ability range. Common knowledge further includes a shared understanding of an individual teacher's sphere of influence with students in relation to both teacher advisor groups and subject areas. Common knowledge also includes shared understandings and contributions to the curriculum in each subject, as demonstrated in the mathematics case study, where the curriculum functions for teachers as a collaborative tool.

Processes for sharing knowledge include planning, enactment and review meetings to monitor constructed boundaries (syllabi, subject choices, team-mixes, community leadership within and across communities) to ensure these structures continue to serve shared long-term goals. While some decisions are appropriately made by staff alone, such as the staffing-profile mix, other decisions can entail student input and negotiation around the design, enactment, and review of teaching and learning goals, methods, processes, and space usage (see Prain et al., 2014).

At Waratah College, where only a few classes were taught in open-plan settings, staff also developed a common knowledge around new practices. Teachers reported that the team processes facilitated shared understanding of what quality teaching and learning could mean and the role of assessment in these processes. It caused the year-level teachers to think more about the qualities of good teaching, how to monitor learning, and how to share ideas and support each other. Teachers felt it was important for students to know that their teachers had a common goal. They now felt that it was important that this shared understanding and knowledge was developed, so that students would take on a positive view of learning processes, and recognise that success was expected of all students. As the year-level coordinator put it, "It is too important not for us to take advantage of the changes to improve student learning". Another teacher noted, "we have focused on building collaborative teams. We analyse data. We collaboratively plan together. We are all active participants. We are trying to build a teach-the-team model. We have come a long way. It becomes a default behavior for students to talk about their own learning".

Curricular Reform Leading to a More Explicit, Differentiated Curriculum

As claimed in Chapter 1, the open-plan settings enable personalised learning and student wellbeing, provided they function as supportive communities where teams of teachers address learners' individual and collective academic and wellbeing needs. Our case studies of academic subjects point to mutual responsibility, the cooperative synchronicity, and the improvised flair and creativity of individual teachers as they worked in teams to enact the curriculum. The primary affordance of shared space, mutual visibility, and flexible, multiple teacher roles enabled secondary affordances, such as (a) increased informal learning, as in skyping and blogs between scientists and Year 8 science students, (b) impromptu/formalised mini-class problem-solving sessions, as in mathematics, science, English and studio arts, (c) space for students to work individually or in groups within or beyond a learning community, or rehearse and refine presentations, as in the English case studies, (d) scope for targeted challenges for the least and most able students, as in the mathematics and English case studies, and (e) changes to assessment processes and student roles, as in the social studies program.

We view the explicit developmental personal curriculum of the teacher advisor program (Chapter 11) as a crucial complementary support to the effectiveness of ongoing staff-student relationships in learning communities and the sustained promotion of student wellbeing. This critical role in building supportive communities for all learners is evident in teacher and student feedback on this curriculum (Prain et al., 2014, Chapter 10), and is particularly needed to engage low SES students.

The case studies of different curricular areas highlight similarities and differences in the challenges of creating effective differentiation of student learning. Our case studies point to the need for a connected sequence of cumulative challenges. However, subjects such as mathematics and science are more tightly sequenced in terms of concept development and connected or chained understandings of the big ideas or processes in each field. This potentially makes it easier to provide a fine-grain approach to monitoring student progress. By contrast, subjects such as English, studio arts, social studies/humanities and the teacher advisors' personal development curriculum are more loosely defined in terms of evaluating precise evidence of student attainment and progress. This points to the need for a robust shared sense of evaluative interpretation by teachers in these fields as well as the need for stimulating rich learning tasks, of the kind evident in the English and social studies/humanities programs. Such tasks are likely to flesh out specific characteristics of different levels of student attainment that can become a collective resource for future assessment practices and also a guide for future students. The nature of the personal development program implies the need for teacher sensitivity and flexibility in dealing with planned and unplanned issues that may not be easily 'sequenced' developmentally across four years of schooling. The result, noted by teachers in disciplinary teams, is that a team-taught vertical curriculum is always evolving via teacher and student input, and should be constantly open to new tasks, and reviewed to check the efficacy and trajectory of learning experiences realised in each domain.

Some Further Questions around Personalisation of the Curriculum

The BEP aimed to replace an age-based curriculum with a stage-based one, but as we noted elsewhere (Prain et al., 2014), this radical change to student learning trajectories has only been partially achieved, with some subjects operating across two age levels, such as Years 7–8 and 9–10. Constraints on more thorough personalisation of student goals and progress include challenges around teacher expertise and resourcing of subject areas in learning communities, and a teacher belief in the socialisation benefits of students having extended schooling experiences with students their own age and at the same general level of social development. At the same time, as noted in the intended changes to the Dashboard at Whirrakee College, some schools are looking at extending the scope for a curriculum that students can customise deeply to suit their developing abilities, goals, and interests. It will be a significant challenge for each school to extend student options in this regard, but the open-plan settings do not block such possibilities.

Curriculum personalisation also raises the question of the evolving role of student voice in the design, enactment, and review of learning goals and experiences in the BEP schools. Again, as noted in the studio arts case study and in various strategies already implemented to include student consultation and empowerment on these matters (see Prain et al., 2014), the schools are shifting from a traditional division of roles on this question. How quickly or slowly this shift will occur remains an open question, but we would suggest that the increased informality created in the open-plan settings is a positive influence on teachers recognising the necessity to incorporate student voice and agency into the curriculum, especially with more senior students who have experienced three years in the learning communities. Where a strong community-building focus has been established in a learning community, then there is considerable scope to expand student agency into all aspects of the community's life.

A further question is whether the new open-plan settings suit all learners. As noted often in this book, the settings presuppose learners who are comfortable in larger communities than classrooms, who can thrive on daily opportunities for access to multiple teachers and many students, and who welcome/take on more self-reliant and self-initiating attributes as learners. The preliminary finding that boys were slightly more positive than girls about these new settings (Chapter 4) needs to be researched further to identify underlying influences on both group's responses, and possible changes to enhance wellbeing for all students. Teachers in all the schools have also been concerned about the potential for distraction and discomfort for some students with particular needs who do not fit the implied assumptions about student capabilities or preferences in these settings. Various strategies have been put in place to address these concerns, including student withdrawal to more traditional enclosed settings, or opportunities for students to work independently from groups in various break-out areas in each school. Again, this remains an open question about the extent to which these schools, like traditional schools, effectively accommodate the needs of all students.

Our study also sheds light on the question of how curriculum differentiation by teachers relates to students experiencing their learning as personalised. As noted in earlier chapters, we argue that teachers can differentiate some or all of the following components of learning to suit individual student needs: curricular goals, learning tasks, resources, learning sequences, and feedback. In this way teachers contribute to students finding curricular experiences more personalised through targeted approaches to their needs and capabilities. However, over time students can also develop increasing independence around topic choices and learning processes and thus personalise their learning further. In this way, curricular differentiation is a teacher-regulated strategy that can provide the foundations for increased student self-regulation of learning, leading to more personalised goals, processes and learning outcomes.

Concluding Remarks

We have learnt much from our research into the BEP about personalising learning. At the risk of offering a reductive analogy, we consider that the teacher's role in these new settings is like being a driving instructor. When teaching young people to drive, you do not spend the majority of time in the driver's seat, making the learners watch and listen (although adequate preparation is required). You sit beside them, leaving them in charge of the car, responsible for changing gears, steering, braking and accelerating. Certainly, you are there to guide and support them. You have expertise and if necessary you will apply the spare set of brakes or grab the steering wheel, but you only take over in an emergency because your ultimate goal is that they will learn to be an independent, competent, considerate, safe, and highly skilled driver. Clearly, quality learning at school entails larger challenges than learning to drive, and includes creative risk-taking, and informed insights into personal preferences, intentions, and strengths and weaknesses, and sustained effort. However, the driving analogy points to key dimensions around trust, guided opportunities, and practical conditions for enacting personalised approaches to student learning.

We consider that the creation of the case-study practices reported in our book represents a major achievement in establishing new and more engaging ways for low SES students to experience school curricula and to connect to schooling. We are fully aware that these successes were hard-won, in the face of many challenges and obstacles. These include initial teacher and parent resistance to new practices, dangers of teacher burnout in the new intensification of teacher work in these settings, and turnover of staff and leadership. Teachers have needed to learn new understandings and practices around being agile educators in these settings, as have students in being co-learners in new up-scaled classrooms. On balance, for all the reasons covered in this book, we consider that the new settings represent important gains over traditional schooling, especially for low SES students, in terms of improved learning and belonging. We fully recognise that in establishing this new form of schooling, teachers initially had greatly increased demands on their time, expertise, creativity, and willpower. However, we argue that these demands decrease as a rich curriculum is built, shared, refined, and elaborated by all participants. While there is extensive rhetoric about how twenty-first century learners need to develop as independent, creative, critical, problem-solving team-players, who excel at communication, our research on the strategies (and effects on participants) of the BEP indicate practicable ways to achieve these outcomes for these students, and other like cohorts.

REFERENCES

Akinsanmi, B. (2011). The optimal learning environment: Learning theories. *Design Share E-Newsletter*. Retrieved from http://www.designshare.com/index.php/articles/the-optimal-learning-environment-learning-theories/

Boys, J. (2011). *Towards creative learning spaces: Rethinking the architecture of post-compulsory education*. Abingdon, England: Routledge.

Engeström, Y. (2000). Activity theory as a framework for analaysing and redesigning work. *Ergonomics, 43*(7), 960–974. doi:10.1080/001401300409143

Gislason, N. (2009). Mapping school design: A qualitative study of the relations among facilities design, curriculum delivery, and school climate. *Journal of Environmental Education, 40*(4), 17–34. doi:10.3200/JOEE.40.4.17-34

Hattie, J. A. C. (2009). *Visible learning: A synthesis of over 800 meta-analyses relating to achievement*. London, UK: Routledge.

Ledward, B. C., & Hirata, D. (2011). *An overview of 21st century skills*. (Summary of 21st century skills for students and teachers). Pacific Policy Research Centre, Honolulu: Kamechamcha Schools-Research & Evaluation. Retrieved from http://www.ksbe.edu/_assets/spi/pdfs/21st_Century_Skills_Brief.pdf

Mahoney, P., Hexstall, I., & Richardson, M. (2011). Building schools for the future: Reflections on a new social architecture. *Journal of Education Policy, 26*(3), 341–360. doi:10.1080/02680939.2010.513741

Muijs, D., Harris, A., Chapman, C., Stoll, L., & Russ, J. (2004). Improving schools in socioeconomically disadvantaged areas – A review of research evidence. *School Effectiveness and School Improvement: An International Journal of Research, Policy and Practice, 15*(2), 149–175. doi:10.1076/sesi.15.2.149.30433

Prain, V., Cox, P., Deed, C., Dorman, J., Edwards, D., Farrelly, C., Keeffe, M., … Yager, Z. (2014). *Adapting to teaching and learning in open-plan schools*. Rotterdam, The Netherlands: Sense Publishers.

ANTHONY EDWARDS

13. SOME REFLECTIONS

I don't intend to draw the strands of the research together in this book to any great extent unless it adds to my own narrative. The authors have done this very ably in both Chapter 1 and Chapter 12. However it is worth commenting on the elements that make up the two books in this series (of which this is the second) and ask whether they can stand on their own or if they are inseparable. Book One is split into four sections which each in their turn set the parameters for the research into the Bendigo Education Plan (BEP), examine the role of leaders and teachers in this context, explore the effects on learners and identify and comment upon any emergent new practices and knowledge. Book Two is divided into two sections, the first of which focuses on a number of broad themes including quality learning, teacher adaptation, student agency, adolescent wellbeing, and digital technologies in open-plan settings. The second section focuses on some of the changes in approach that have occurred in learning and teaching in English, humanities, mathematics and science, problem solving and ends with some conclusions about remodelling schooling resulting from the implementation of the BEP. The trajectory of the research is clear. Whilst the first book generally examines some of the broad themes associated with the Plan the second inclines naturally towards a more visceral investigation into the impact on the day-to-day issues that affect the functioning of any educational institution, regardless of its formation. Once the team had undertaken the first broad theoretical sweep it was inevitable that they would want to look deeper into practice and the two books represent this journey very clearly. Despite the connection between them there is no doubt in my mind that both are independently viable. In addition the transition from a macro to micro focus adds to, rather than detracts from, the value of each as a separate resource. It's very tempting to suggest that this trajectory should be continued as part of the route map for future research. It would indeed be useful to investigate a host of questions associated with initiatives like the BEP such as how do open-plan environments.

- Effect the management of specialist resources.
- Diffuse the boundaries between subjects.
- Lend themselves more readily to learning and teaching in certain subjects.
- Necessitate a redefinition of the curriculum.
- Are heavily reliant on the use of new technologies in order to function effectively.

V. Prain et al. (Eds.), Personalising Learning in Open-Plan Schools, 231–235.
© 2015 Sense Publishers. All rights reserved.

However, simply continuing to examine practice, laudable as it might be, could help to reinforce the false notion that the changes result entirely from some form of architectural determinism, unless it is tempered by looking outwards as well as inwards. It is essential to bear in mind that, no mater how important at the outset, the environment was only one component part of the story. There are at least three universal issues (amongst a multitude) emerging naturally from the project that are, despite their complexity, worthy of much further scrutiny. They are associated with risk taking, and community, and the nature of schools for the future.

The scale and scope of the original Bendigo initiative was so radical that it could not be conceived or implemented without recognising that a certain amount of risk was involved. The risks, which could result in some form of loss or other, were distributed across the entire spectrum of stakeholders. Politicians, policy makers, and parents all had something to loose but it was students and their teachers who shouldered the burden of coping with much of the uncertainty involved in the Plan. Students were immediately exposed to new ways of working and relating to each other, and their teachers to new pedagogies. The story of how the resulting opportunities and threats were coped with has been admirably told in the two books. However, there is a strong case for re-examining what has and is happening using the concept of risk taking as a single focal point. Although risk taking may be associated with uncertain outcomes, it is an essential human behaviour that allows us to adapt and change readily (Trimpop, 1994). As such it is an integral feature of any educational change, no matter how great or small. It is important here to make a distinction between risk and risk taking. The former could result from the vagaries of fortune whilst the latter, with which I suggest the research team should mainly be concerned, involves making deliberate choices.

For the students, risk taking, particularly in relationship to adolescence, can have negative connotations. It sometimes is linked directly to delinquent behaviour (Chapman, Buckley, Sheehan, & Shochet, 2014). Nevertheless there may be very strong connections between the willingness to take risks and creativity in its broadest sense that are worth cultivating. The National Advisory Committee on Creative and Cultural Education (NACCCE, 1999) in the United Kingdom and Csikszentmilhalyi (1996) suggest that there might indeed be a connection between risk taking and creativity. Nickerson (2008) is more forceful stating that risk taking is central to creative activity. This connection may be more evident or more readily fostered in open-plan settings. There may also be gender differences in risk-taking behaviour, clearly exposed in this context, that are worthy of further investigation. Work done by Booth, Cardona-Sosa, and Nolen (2014) with first year university students, has already found that there is a link but it would be useful to test this notion in what are quite a unique set of circumstances.

For the educator there are very specific challenges in relationship to risk-taking. On one hand they are encouraged to be flexible, dynamic, and willing to take risks and yet on the other are "…continually monitored, managed and held individually accountable for every hour of the day". (MacLaren, 2012, p. 161). There is also a further pressure resulting from the teacher's perceived role as a moderator who seeks to reduce risk behaviours amongst those in their care (Chapman et al., 2014) The authors also make the point in their concluding remarks at the end of the book that as a result of exposing teachers to the inevitable risk taking as a result of the BEP tested, amongst other things, their capacity to adapt. It would be useful to explore whether there is a strong correlation between the willingness to take risks and the ability to adapt amongst teachers. To a certain extent some of these tensions have already been explored as underlying themes in a number of chapters, particularly those relating to changes in practice.

Le Fevre (2014) suggests that the costs of risk-taking are not neutral, but lead to positive or negative outcomes. This initiative is rich with opportunities to examine the decision-making process leading to risks being taken. It would be extremely useful to investigate how various stakeholders, particularly politicians and policy makers, view the balance between threats and opportunities. This is important. Ellison (2009, p. 46) contends that it is imperative, given global economic trends "... that policy makers and educators need to find a way to institutionalize experimentation, specialization, and innovation into public schooling". Institutionalised experimentation and innovation are synonymous with risk-taking.

Community is the second overarching theme, which could extend the research activity of the team. Once again this permeates almost every chapter but it is worth highlighting one of the findings from Chapter 4 on whole-school approaches to adolescent wellbeing. The authors of this chapter conclude with the notion that there is a direct link between the

> ... quality of the connections among the multiple groups that contribute to a school community such as students, teachers, families, professionals from community agencies, and other involved local groups and individuals, reflect the degree of social capital in the school environment.

Both the nature and quality of this connectedness are rich with research opportunities but there are three specific aspects of this I would wish to explore further.

For students and their teachers the changes have meant that the way they relate to each other and their practices have been altered. Working effectively in teams and tailoring the learning specifically to the needs of the individual now appear to be paramount in this environment. Does the reshaping of the learning space that has resulted from the Bendigo initiative affect the relationship between the school and the agencies, communities and group. In other words do the effects of the 'experiment' stop at the gates of the school? How has the indigenous community been affected by and been able to affect these changes is of particular importance. Nichol (2011) contends

> ... that the provision of the most appropriate education for indigenous students is extraordinarily complex and presents an enormous challenge to educators ... (xviii)

Additionally it is worth asking if this is a blueprint for helping to reimagine the notion of community for all schools of the future or just a local solution to a local problem.

In considering the way in which opening up the learning spaces by the schools involved in the Plan has affected the broader community it hard to ignore the role of new technologies in also reducing some of the constraining effects of bricks and mortar. In a sense the use of social media and search engines in education has already done much to bring the 'outside world' more readily into the classroom, but it is worth asking if, when combined with the changes resulting from BEP, the formation and reformation of learning communities is more powerful because of the very nature of the Plan itself.

My last grand theme concerns the shape of the environment itself. This Plan is now very well established, with a large number of students who have either been, or are currently involved in, learning in this context. They represent a well-informed community whose insights and understanding are invaluable. It is essential to ask them about how they would shape the future of schools bearing in mind their experiences. Noriega, Heppell, Bonet, and Heppell (2013, p. 144) urge us to trust this generation of learners because they have:

> ... much more information to use and because they are using their tools to develop or nuance their new worlds. Most likely, they are not going to create the elitist places previously imagined, nor fulfill established design criteria. Does this matter? Probably not, the relevant issue is the best possible learning, and typically this embraces collegiality, reflective practice, meta-cognition, and offers no modal switch between playful and serious learning and work.

The authors themselves have specifically identified a number of areas that they consider worthy of further investigation and it is important to highlight them here. As a result of their work on teacher adaptation in open-plan settings (Chapter 2) they concluded that there is a constraining action of institutional routine on teacher agency and whilst wishing to counteract the tendency to regard this as overly pessimistic viewpoints suggest:

> ... that a space does exist for thinking and acting differently, and that this is generated from the expressions and authorisations of the up-scaled open-plan environment.

They contend that there are opportunities to examine more closely the factors that effect the permanence of any change. This potentially has a much wider application than in projects similar to the BEP and it should be undertaken with that in mind. In Chapter 3, which explores the use of gaming to afford teacher and student agency the authors have identified a central tension – how does a learner move from dependence to independence (or co-dependence) as a worthy extension to their research. They suggest that the balance between student's self-management of their own emerging agency and the co-regulation by educators should be further investigated. This is a very broad field and it is good to note that their interest lies in investigating this balance as the complexity of learning tasks and possibly the unpredictable nature of learning activities increases. It is particularly relevant because one of the emergent themes from the whole of the work they have done on the BEP is that teachers seek manageable order to the curriculum in terms of their own and their students' roles and students likewise appear to desire certainty and security.

Finally there is one central question that many in the world of education and beyond, wish to be answered – was it all worth it? The chance to undertake longitudinal studies provides very real opportunities to seek a meaningful answer to this question.

REFERENCES

Booth, A., Cardona-Sosa, L., & Nolen, P. (2014). Gender differences in risk aversion: Do single-sex environments affect their development? *Journal of Economic Behaviour & Organization, 99*(C), 126–154. doi:10.1016/j.jebo.2013.12.017

Chapman, R., Buckley, L., Sheehan, M., & Shochet, I. (2014). Teachers' perceptions of school connectedness and risk-taking in adolescence. *International Journal of Qualitative Studies in Education, 27*(4), 413–431. doi:10.1080/09518398.2013.771225

Csikszentmilhalyi, M. (1996). *Creativity: Flow and the psychology of discovery and invention.* New York, NY: Harper Collins

Ellison, S. (2009). Hard-wired for innovation? Comparing two policy paths toward innovative schooling. *International Education, 39*(1), 30–48.

Le Fevre, D. (2004). Barriers to implementing pedagogical change: The role of teachers' perceptions of risk. *Teaching and Teacher Education, 38*, 56–64. doi:10.1016/j.tate.2013.11.007

MacLaren, I. (2012). The contradictions of policy and practice: Creativity in higher education. *London Review of Education, 10*(2), 159–172.

National Advisory Committee on Creative and Cultural Education (NACCCE). (1999). *All our futures: Creativity, culture and education.* London, UK.

Nichol, R. (2011). *Growing up indigenous.* Rotterdam, The Netherlands: Sense Publishers.

Nickerson, R. S. (2008). Enhancing creativity. In R. J. Sternberg (Ed.), *Handbook of creativity.* New York, NY: Cambridge University Press.

Noriega, F., Heppell, S., Bonet, N., & Heppell, J. (2013). Building better learning and learning better building with learners rather than for learners. *On the Horizon, 21*(2), 138–148.

Trimpop, R. M. (1994). *The psychology of risk-taking behavior.* Amsterdam, The Netherlands: North-Holland.

Whitehouse, D. (2009). Designing learning spaces that work: A case for the importance of history. *History of Education Review, 38*(2), 94–108.

INDEX

A

Achievement,
   academic, 21, 59, 65
   educational, 20
   in mathematics, 122, 128, 138, 139
   in studio arts, 173, 175, 177
   in teacher advisory (TA), 206, 211
   low academic, 18
   personal, 15
   role of learning dashboard in recording, 77, 80, 82
   student reflection on, 14, 31, 51; *see also* national tests (NAPLAN)
Activity theory, 11, 79, 101, 106, 224; *see also* theoretical perspectives
Adaptation,
   model of teacher adaptation, 27, 35, 36
   of students to new practices, 43–53, 97–117
   of teachers to new practices, 27, 34, 43–53
   of teachers to up-scaled learning communities, 27, 34, 37–39, 223, 224, 234
   role of agency in, 35–37
   role of university in teacher adaptation, 39
   The Future is Wild Adaptation unit in science, 145–149; *see also* curriculum, team teaching
Advocacy, 212–214; *see also* teacher advisor
Affordance theory, 79, 101; *see also* theoretical perspectives
Agency,
   in teacher advisory, 205–218
   nested, 16–18
   relational, 16–18
   student, 23, 34, 35, 43–53; *see also* relational agency, theoretical perspectives
   teacher, 36, 37, 43–53
Assessment, 8, 21, 50
   and school ranking in literacy and numeracy, 18, 19, 88, 89, 128
   in English, 100, 107, 113, 115
   in humanities, 181–196
   in mathematics, 123, 124, 126, 138, 139
   in science, 146, 147
   in studio arts, 168, 170, 176
   role of learning dashboards in, 80, 82, 85–87, 90, 91; *see also* AusVELS, Bendigo Education Plan, personalised learning, curriculum, differentiation
Attendance, 4, 9
   and wellbeing, 57–73, 58, 66
   need for policy on, 184
   role of learning dashboards in recording, 79, 81–84; *see also* Bendigo Education Plan
Attitudes to School Survey, 59–61
AusVELS,
   explanation of, 124
   in humanities, 191
   in mathematics, 126, 130, 131, 133–137
   in science, 145, 149
   recording on learning dashboard, 81

B

Bendigo Education Plan,
   context, strategies, rationale including equity and social justice, 3–23

outcomes, 221–229, 231–235
well-being issues, 57–73
Bullying,
    and Bendigo Education plan strategies, 4, 59
    and relationship to student wellbeing, 57, 58, 63, 72
    building resilience in teacher advisory; 209, 215

C

Capacity building, *see* professional learning
Choice,
    in game design, 46, 50–53
    relationship to agency, 37
    student, 13, 18, 32
    teacher, 39, 43; *see also* games-based learning, humanities, mathematics, science, learning; studio arts
Collaboration in open-plan settings, *see* team teaching
Co-regulated learning, *see* learning
Curriculum,
    differentiated, 14–16, 18–21, 164–167, 226
    for student wellbeing, 57, 65, 69, 72, 73
    in English, 97–117
    in games-based learning, 43–53
    in humanities, 181–203
    in mathematics, 121–139
    in science, 143–159
    in studio arts, 163–178
    in teacher advisory, 205–218
    open-plan settings as catalyst for change, 222, 223
    personalising learning through, 8, 13, 164–167
    planning, 3–23, 43–53, 57–73, 97–117, 121–139, 143–159, 163–178, 181–203, 205–218
    quality, 3, 16, 53, 145, 223
    renewal and reform, 3, 221–229; *see also* assessment, personalised learning

D

Dashboard, 9, 77–92, 224
    and power of feedback, 82, 85–91
    building common knowledge, 90–92
Differentiated curriculum, *see* curriculum
Distributed leadership, *see* professional learning
Division of labour, *see* activity theory, teachers, students
Domains, *see* English, humanities, mathematics, science, social studies, studio arts

E

Educational disadvantage, 18
    addressing through curriculum, 121–139, 181–203
    and low SES, 3–5, 9, 13, 15–17; *see also* Bendigo Education Plan
Embodied learning, 70; *see also* theoretical perspectives
Engagement,
    and PLEQ, 47, 48, 186, 187
    and student wellbeing, 58, 59
    in English, 110, 115
    in games-based learning, 45, 51, 53
    in humanities, 181, 182, 195
    in mathematics, 134, 139
    in science, 144, 158, 159
    in studio arts, 175, 177, 178
    student, 3, 4, 13, 19, 27, 72, 212, 217
    student engagement officer, 71; *see also* Bendigo Education Plan, personalised learning, students, teachers

English, 97–117
  affordances of the open-plan learning space, 115, 116
  conceptualising quality teaching and learning in, 97–100
  year 8 film case study, 102–109
  year 7 book trailer case study, 109–117; *see also* higher order thinking, reasoning, Whirrakee College
Epistemic learning, 16; *see also* theoretical perspectives
Epistemological learning, 16, 70, 102, 145; *see also* curriculum quality, domains, personalised learning, theoretical perspectives
Evaluation, 3–23, 221–229; *see also* BEP strategies

F

Feedback, 7, 13, 224–226, 228
  and dashboard, 82, 85–87, 89–91
  in mathematics, 123, 124, 126, 130, 136, 137, 139
  in science, 145, 147, 149, 153
  in teacher advisory, 208, 209, 216, 217; *see also* curriculum, domains, global science forum, professional learning, student, teacher
  peer feedback in humanities, 182–185, 187–189, 191–195
Framework for personalising learning, 3–23; *see also* theoretical perspectives

G

Games-based learning, 43–53; *see also* Grevillea College
Gender, differences in perceptions of well-being, 62
  gender differences in risk-taking behaviour, 232

  pairing of teacher advisors, 208
  responses to mathematics survey, 131, 132
Global science forum, 150–153
Goals,
  Bendigo Education Plan, 3–23, 221–229
  cognitive goals in art, 163
  contested views of, 16
  curricular goals, 104, 105, 108, 147
  intrinsic and extrinsic, 163
  personalising learning goals, 7, 11, 100, 191, 207, 227
  role of dashboard in recording, 77–92
  role of formative assessment in aligning, 195
  student learning goals, 8, 13, 20, 108, 159, 177, 184, 188, 209–212, 214, 227
  student wellbeing goals, 14, 211–214
  teacher role in setting and negotiating, 15–17, 20, 21, 103, 164, 167, 168, 175, 211, 225
Grevillea College,
  context, 9, 10
  engaging boys through technology, 43–53
  games-based learning at, 48–51
  NAPLAN literacy and numeracy scores compared with similar schools, 18, 19, 128, 129
  organisation, 10
  PLEQ, 47, 48
  practitioner inquiry into optimal use of learning spaces, 30–35
  student perceptions of relationships and wellbeing, 61; *see also* attitudes to school, games-based learning, learning communities, learning environment

239

H

Higher order thinking,
   in English, 99, 100, 102–109, 117
   in games-based learning, 49, 51, 53
   in humanities, 187, 191, 192; *see also* Bendigo Education Plan, learning, reasoning

Humanities, 181–203
   development of thinking skills in, 191, 192
   personalising learning in, 183–185
   PLEQ student responses, 186
   preparatory professional learning, 185–187
   student perceptions of peer-and self-assessment process, 194
   student voice in learning and assessment, 181–183
   teacher perceptions of peer-and self-assessment process, 192–194
   value of peer-and self-assessment, 194–196
   year 8 case study, 187–192

I

Identity,
   and community, 45
   and self-assessment, 185
   formation, 14, 15, 20, 58
   in mathematics, 121, 122, 138
   in science, 144
   in teacher advisory, 217
   stronger sense of in older students, 64; *see also* domains, wellbeing

Informal learning,
   and social networking in game design, 45; *see also* open-plan settings
   encouraged by school design and structures, 5, 6, 22, 69, 222, 226

Information Communication Technologies; *see* dashboard, English, games-based learning, multi-modal texts, virtual learning

Ironbark College,
   curriculum, teaching and learning, 69, 70
   learning communities, 60, 63
   mathematics program, 124–126
   NAPLAN ranking among similar schools, numeracy and literacy, 18, 19, 128, 129
   organisation, 10
   partnerships and services, 70–72
   profile, 9, 10
   school ethos and environment, 66–69
   student perceptions of relationships and wellbeing, 61, 62
   student perspectives on mathematics program, 134–137
   teacher advisor program, 206–218; *see also* attitudes to school survey, learning communities, mathematics, teacher advisor

Inquiry, *see* pragmatism

K

Knowledge,
   common, 17, 20, 43, 90–92, 223, 225, *see also* pragmatism, theoretical perspectives, adaptation, teacher, epistemic; epistemological directions

L

Leadership,
   distributed, 7, 20
   school leadership contributing to personalising learning, 16, 138, 184
   student, 81
   students-as-researchers, 215–217

Learning,
   and student agency, 205
   co-regulated, 18, 181
   developing self-directed learning in teacher advisory, self-regulated, 14, 44, 134, 159, 178; *see also* Bendigo Education Plan, curriculum, domains, personalised learning, professional learning
   quality learning, 16, 97–100
   self-directed, student perceptions of ability to self-direct learning in PLEQ, 48, 187
   use of dashboard to encourage self-directed learning, 84
Learning communities,
   addressing individual student needs in, 20
   affording quality learning in English, 98–100
   challenges of, 6, 7, 22, 106, 227
   design of, 5, 6
   need for continuous participant review of, 22
   organisation of, 5–11, 60
   positive effect on student wellbeing, 63
   protocols in, 67
   teacher adaptation to, 27–39
   teacher perceptions of affordances of, 12, 22, 23
   team-teaching in, 8; *see also* domains, relationships in open-plan settings, teacher advisor
Learning environment, 3–23, 221–229; *see also* open-plan settings, well-being
Literacy,
   BEP concerns, 4
   BEP strategies to address, 7–9
   development of critical literacy in English, 104
   English case study, 97–117
   health literacy, 69
   NAPLAN ranking against similar schools in, 18
   need for multi-literacy in 21st century, 99
   recording on dashboard, 81, 83; *see also* dashboard, multi-modal texts, National Assessment Program-Literacy and Numeracy

M
Mathematics,
   mathematics case studies, 121–139; *see also* Bendigo Education Plan
   student achievement levels, 3–23, 77–92, 121–139
Melaleuca College,
   academic attainment, 3–23, 77–92, 121–139
   mathematics, 121–139
   school structure, 10, 11
   science, 143–159
   studio arts case study, 163–178
Multi-modal texts,
   in game-based design, 43–53
   in personalising learning, 3–23
   in reasoning in English, 97–117
   in science, 143–159
   in social studies, 197
Multi-theoretic perspectives, *see* theoretical perspectives

N
National Assessment Program in Literacy and Numeracy (NAPLAN),
   NAPLAN data, 3–23, 77–92, 121–139; *see also* mathematics, literacy

O
Open-Plan Settings,
   affordances of, 3–23

INDEX

effects on student learning, 97–117, 121–139, 143–159, 221–229
effects on student well-being, 57–73, 221–229
increased visibility in, 221–229
student perceptions of, 57–73, 97–117, 163–178
teacher adaptation to open-plan settings, 3–23, 43–53, 77–92, 121–139, 143–159, 163–178, 221–229
varying gender effects, 57–73
Outcomes of BEP,
student academic outcomes, 3–23
teaching outcomes, 221–229

P

Pedagogy,
BEP prescriptions, 7
teacher adaptation, 27–39, 43–53, 166
Peer relationships, see teachers, students, relationships in open-plan settings, relational agency
Personalised learning,
definitions of, 3–23
driving instructor metaphor, 228
enactment of, see literacy, mathematics, studio arts, games-based learning; assessment of, 3–23
personalised learning experience questionnaire results, 47, 62, 186, 187
principles that support personalised learning, 19–22, see assessment
rationale for, 3–23
Pragmatism, 3–23; see theoretical perspectives
Professional learning, 6, 7, 20, 21, 27–39, 57–73, 77–92, 221–229

Q

Qualitative research methods, see 12, 55, 57, 75, 79, 123, 124, 133–138, 140, 141, 206, 207
Quality learning,
definition, 12–16
in English, 97–100
in mathematics, 121, 122, 138
in science, 143–145
in social studies, 181, 221, 223, 225, 228
in studio arts, 178
relation to agency, 50, 53
teacher perceptions of, 31, 32, 39
Quantitative research methods, 57, 78, 79, 88, 123, 128, 134, 138, 223

R

Relational agency, 16–18, 24, 25, 43, 46, 51, 54, 58, 67, 71, 74, 79, 167, 174, 205, 210, 218, 219; see also theoretical perspectives
Relationships in open-plan settings, 5, 8, 20, 35, 46, 52, 57–73, 165, 174, 176, 177, 186, 187, 200, 201, 206, 207, 212–214, 221, 222, 226
Reasoning,
about dashboard, 85, 86
in science, 143, 144, 153, 158–160
student reasoning and wellbeing, 69, 70
student reasoning in English, 98–102, 104–119, 121–139
teacher reasoning, 29, 32, 37–39, 44, 53, 224
Research methods, see quantitative and qualitative research
Resilience, 9, 59, 75, 163, 167, 175, 206, 208, 211

INDEX

S
Science, 143–159
Self-efficacy,
   of students, 18, 47, 48, 53, 59, 61, 138, 140, 186
Self-regulated learning, *see* learning
Shared space, *see* open-plan, learning communities, learning environment
Social Studies, *see* humanities
Sphere of influence, 7, 12, 17, 22, 23, 43, 44, 71, 98, 101, 106, 116, 210, 215, 225
Statistical analyses, *see* personalised learning
Students,
   academic performance, 18, 19
   agency, 34, 43–55
   in English, 97–117
   in mathematics, 121–139
   in science, 143–159
   in social studies, 181–203
   in studio arts, 163–178
   perceptions of learning, 84
   profile in BEP, 3–6, 8–11
   student voice, 181–203, 205–218;
   wellbeing, 57–73, 227. *See also* agency; co–regulated learning; self–regulated learning; gender, academic attainment, attitudes to school
Student as researcher, 205–218
Student voice,
   challenges, 57–73
   future directions, 227
   in the teacher advisor program, 205–218
   rationale, 3–23
   use of in Social Science, 181–203
Studio Arts,
   personalising learning in, 163–178
   team–teaching in, 163–178

T
Teacher advisor program, 67–70, 205–218
   curriculum, 209
   rationale, 205, 206
Teachers,
   adaptation, 27–39, 43–53, 221–229; *see* common knowledge
   BEP professional learning, 7, 8
   enacting personalised learning, 16–18
Team teaching, 3–23
   see teacher adaptation, 27–39
   case studies in English, 97–117
   mathematics, 121–139
   science, 143–159
   studio arts, 163–178
Technology, see ICT
   dashboard, 77–92
   games-based learning, 43–53
   science, 143–159
Theoretical perspectives,
   activity theory, 11, 24, 74, 118
   affordance theory, 12, 22, 23, 34, 50, 52, 77, 93, 98, 101–103, 115–118, 226
   embodied learning, 109, 114, 216; *see also* adaptation, sphere of influence, epistemic learning, epistemological learning
   nested agency, 3–23
   personal agency, *see* agency
   pragmatism, 3–23
   relational agency, 3–23, 43–53, 77–92, 121–139, 163–178, 181–203, 205–218

U
Up-scaled learning communities, 6, 12, 23, 79, 98, 106, 117, 228, 234

V

Virtual learning,
   in science, 143–159
   use of dashboard, 57–73
   use of digital technologies, 77–92

Visibility,
   effects on teachers, 12, 23, 226
   on students, 63, 133

Voice, see student voice

W

Waratah College, case study, 143–159
Wattle College, case study, 181–203

Wellbeing,
   programs for improved well-being, 57–73
   student experiences in BEP schools, 57–73, 97–117, 205–218
   teacher understandings of, 57–73
   theory, 57–73
   threats to wellbeing, 58

Whirrakee College,
   dashboard case study, 77–92
   English case studies, 97–117
   mathematics case study, 121–139
   profile, 8–10